ORGANIZING YOUR HOME

KNACK™

ORGANIZING YOUR HOME

Decluttering Solutions and Storage Ideas

EMILY WILSKA

Guilford, Connecticut
An imprint of The Globe Pequot Press

Copyright © 2009 by Morris Book Publishing, LLC

Front cover photos (left to right) courtesy of Elfa, courtesy of Calypso Chris-
tiane Celle, courtesy of Stacks and Stacks, courtesy of Ikea
Back cover photo courtesy of Elfa
Photo research by Anna Adesanya
Additional photo research by Lisa Wilder
Text design by Paul Beatrice

Library of Congress Cataloging-in-Publication Data.
Wilska, Emily.
   Knack organizing your home : decluttering solutions and storage ideas /
Emily Wilska.
      p. cm.
   Includes index.
   ISBN 978-1-59921-387-3
   1. Storage in the home. 2. Orderliness. I. Title.
   TX309.W5675 2009
   648'.8--dc22
                                2008032474

Printed in China

10 9 8 7 6 5 4 3 2 1

To Poppa, who would be so proud.

CONTENTS

Introduction viii

Chapter 1: Basics
Clearing Clutter. xiv
Developing Systems. 2
Maintaining Organization. 4

Chapter 2: Kitchen
Kitchen. 6
Countertops. 8
Countertops (Continued) 10
Cabinets. 12
Drawers 14
Under the Sink. 16

Chapter 3: Food Storage
Food 18
Pantry 20
Fridge 22
Freezer 24
Cookbooks and Recipes 26
Tabletops and Mealtimes 28

Chapter 4: Bathroom
Bathrooms Great and Small 30
Medicine Cabinet. 32
Under the Sink. 34
Towel Racks 36
Tub. 38
Shower. 40

Chapter 5: Linen Closet
Linen Closet 42
Storing Towels. 44
Storing Bed Linens. 46
Paper Goods. 48
Utility Supplies 50
Personal Supplies. 52

Chapter 6: Bedroom
Bedroom 54
Bedside Table. 56
Under-Bed Storage 58
The Remains of the Day. 60
Dresser Top and Vanity. 62
Accessories. 64

Chapter 7: Bedroom Closet
Bedroom Closet 66
Weeding Clothes 68
Closet Organizing 70
Closet Organizing (Continued). 72
Dresser Organizing 74
Shoes 76

Chapter 8: Entryway
Entryway 78
Foyer 80
Small Entryway 82
In-and-Out Center 84
Hall Closet: Coats and Jackets. 86
Hall Closet: Everything Else 88

Chapter 9: Utility Area
Mudroom and Laundry Room 90
Wet Areas and Pet Care 92
Recycling. 94
Cleaning Supplies 96
Laundry: Washing 98
Laundry: Drying, Folding, Ironing 100

Chapter 10: Living Room
Living Room. 102
Photos and Memorabilia. 104
Collectibles. 106
Entertaining Supplies. 108
Reading Material 110
Music, Movies, and Video Games. 112

Chapter 11: Dining Room
Dining Room 114
Dishes and China 116
Glassware 118
Linens 120
Serving Ware 122
Special Occasion Items 124

Chapter 12: Home Office
Home Office. 126
Paper: Sorting and Weeding 128
Paper: Filing 130
Desk. 132
Office Supply Closet 134
Family Schedule 136

Chapter 13: Home Technology
Home Technology 138
Software, Games, and Manuals. 140
Cord and Cable Management. 142
E-mail: Sorting and Weeding. 144
E-mail: Organizing 146
Electronic Files 148

Chapter 14: Child's Room
Young Child's Room 150
Baby Gear 152
Toys: Sorting and Weeding. 154
Toys: Organizing 156
Organizing Clothes .158
Memorabilia and Artwork. 160

Chapter 15: Older Child's Room
Older Child's Room .162
Toys: Sorting and Weeding. 164
Toys: Organizing 166
Organizing Clothes .168
Memorabilia. 170
Schoolwork and Papers. 172

Chapter 16: Attic
Attic. 174
Sorting and Weeding 176

Organizing Holiday Gear. 178
Seasonal Clothes 180
Organizing Luggage 182
Organizing Archived Papers. 184

Chapter 17: Basement
Basement 186
Sorting and Weeding 188
Pantry and Household Supplies. 190
Exercise Equipment. 192
Workbench. 194
Paints and Chemical Products. 196

Chapter 18: Garage
Garage 198
Bulk Goods 200
Sporting Goods 202
Tools 204
Yard and Garden Supplies 206
Car 208

Chapter 19: Craft Room
Craft Room 210
Sewing Supplies. 212
Quilting Supplies 214
Scrapbooking Supplies 216
Kids' Crafts 218
Other Crafts 220

Chapter 20: Small Spaces
Apartments and Small Spaces 222
Space Planning: Studios 224
Space Planning: Small Homes. 226
Multifunction Furniture 228
Using Vertical Storage 230

Resources
Organizing Calendar. 232
Resources 234
Photo Credits. 237
Index. 239

INTRODUCTION
Five steps to a more organized, less cluttered home

Images of organization are everywhere: in newspapers, books, and magazines, on TV shows, in catalogs, and on-line. When you see a photo of a perfectly neat room in which everything is arranged just so, it's easy to think that you're looking at the very definition of organization.

But don't be fooled: There's no single organizing ideal. What's perfect for one person might be utterly wrong for someone else. Being organized doesn't mean having to give away things you love or keep a home that's staid and spotless. Rather, it means having systems and habits that give you easy access to the stuff you need, use, love, and find beautiful and that help you create a home that's comfortable.

Because the specific definition of organization is different for each person, the first steps in the organizing process are figuring out what your frustrations are, identifying what's not working, and setting your own organizing goals.

If you're like most people, you probably want to jump right in and start sorting, weeding, and moving things around so you can see visual signs of progress. You can put that enthusiasm to smart, efficient use—and can increase your chances of success over the long term—by taking the opportunity to create an organizing plan that will help you get from where you are to where you want to be. That plan will incorporate the organizing sugges-

tions throughout this book and will stem from your answers to five questions:

- Dream: What do you want your space to be like?
- Get real: What is the space like now?
- List your frustrations: What bugs you?
- Get specific: What's not working well?
- Set some goals: What do you want to achieve?

These questions represent five steps in the process of organizing your home. Considering them will help you define your own vision of successful organization.

1. Dream: What Do You Want Your Space to Be Like?

Getting organized gives you the chance to create a home that looks, feels, and functions like you want it to. The first step in this process, then, is to brainstorm what you want each space in your home to be like. (If you're focusing on organizing particular areas in your house, devote your envisioning to those rooms.)

If you were my client, one of the first things I'd ask you in each room, as we walked through your house, is, "What do you want this space to be like?" Many people have ideas, even clear visions, in mind. They want the place to be soothing: "A calming retreat at the end of the day." They want an active and highly functional space: "I'd love the kitchen to be a place where the whole family can gather and make dinner together." Or they just want relief from the mess: "I wish the front hall didn't have piles of bags and shoes on the floor and that terrifying stack of mail on the table."

But you might be like some of my clients who struggle with this question. "But that's why I bought this book—so I can get ideas about what this room should look like and what stuff I need here!" Sure, this book will give you plenty of ideas about useful supplies for organizing and great ideas for storing things. But first, two reminders.

One: Organizing isn't the same as decorating. When I ask what you want your space to be like, I don't really mean picking a color scheme or decorating style, or even deciding where specifically things should go within a room. Yes, the pictures in this book offer many ideas about both. But my underlying message is about helping you figure out how you want each the area to feel and function.

Two: You're getting organized for your own benefit (and maybe for your family members', too), so other than those with whom you share your home, it doesn't matter much what anyone else thinks each space should be like. I can offer advice, direction, and assistance to help you figure out your own definition of organization. And the pictures in this book suggest a wide variety of styles and ideas. You pick and choose the ones that work for you.

So get ready to dream. Think about each room in the house, and ask yourself:

- What would the space be like if it truly felt organized?

- What tasks and activities would you be able to do there?
- How would the room feel?
- If other people in the house also use the space, how would they answer these questions?

Write your replies on a pad or in a notebook, and keep it handy because you'll be using it again.

Remember, you don't need to specify details like what furniture should be in the room, how it should be arranged, what color the walls should be, or where things should be stored—but, of course, you can add those details if you want. Be as specific or as general as you'd like.

After you've finished dreaming, it's time to move on to the next question.

2. Get Real: What Is the Space Like Now?

Before you can create an accurate plan for getting to where you want to be organizationally, you need to know where you are. The beginning of the organizing process is a great time to look at each room with clear eyes and get a fuller sense of how you're currently using the space and what's in it.

To answer this question (and the two that follow), get real. Take a tour of your home, with your notebook and pen in hand, and perhaps a friend or family member in tow. Start either in the most commonly used room in the house or in the one that causes you the most frustration.

Take a close look at the room (this includes opening closets, cupboards, and drawers). In your notebook, describe what the space is like. Is it clean and functional, or does it feel messy and disorganized? List what you (or other members of your family) do there. Detail what sorts of things are in the room. List who uses the room.

Again, your replies can be either general or highly detailed, but be sure to include at least some basic information—what happens in the room, what stuff is there, and how it feels—about each space in the house.

3. List Your Frustrations: What Bugs You?

The motivation to get organized often stems from specific frustrations. Perhaps you're fed up with the towering pile of mail that greets you from a hall table each time you open the front door. Maybe it feels like there's too much stuff everywhere in the house, or that something is always in the way no matter where you are or what you're doing. You might be tired of constantly having to look for things you're sure you have but just can't find.

As you tour your home, make a list of what bothers you—the things about the current state of each room and the house in general that

- annoy you,
- tire you,
- make you angry, or
- make you sad.

Your list can be as general (too much stuff everywhere!) or as specific (overcrowded hall closet) as you'd like. If you find that you're able to jot down a long list of frustrations for certain rooms, there's a good chance those rooms will be good spots in which to start your organizing work.

4. Get Specific: What's Not Working Well?

After you've made a list of organizing frustrations, highlight those about the specific areas, systems, or habits in your home that aren't working. Use a highlighter pen, or simply add to your list. For example, take that terrifying stack of mail. Highlight it in your list, and think about why it happens. Perhaps there's not a convenient or logical spot for incoming mail, so it ends up in a stack on a table. If one of your frustrations is that cooking, cleaning, and putting dishes away are chores, maybe your kitchen cabinets and drawers are so stuffed that it's hard to get anything into or out of them. If there's a mountain of shoes in your bedroom closet, perhaps that's because there's no space for a shoe rack on the floor.

Describe each problem in as much detail as possible: Knowing specifically what doesn't work well will make it easier to find effective solutions. You don't have to write down solutions to the problems you identify now; you just need to know what those problems are. The rest of this book is designed to help you create effective solutions.

5. Set Some Goals: What Do You Want to Achieve?

After you've toured your home and answered the four questions above, spend some time thinking about your organizing goals. How do you want your home to look, feel, and function? What do you want to be able to do there that you can't do now? What tasks will be easier or more pleasant when each space is well organized?

To help identify specific goals, try to fill in the blanks after these statements:

- I want my home to feel more _____.
- I want to spend less time looking for _____.
- I want _____ (task or activity) to be easier and more pleasant.
- I want a space where I can do _____ (task or activity).

Write your goals in your notebook, and keep this list in a safe, prominent spot (with your purse or briefcase, perhaps, or tucked into this book) as you work through your organizing project. Use your goals lists, as well as your answers to the four questions above, to identify the organizing solutions in this book that will be most useful to you, to motivate yourself, and, most importantly, to mark and celebrate your progress as you get organized.

What's Stopping You?

- "I'm such a slob."
- "I don't know why I can't just do this. I must be really lazy."
- "What's my problem? My friend has three kids and keeps a perfectly organized house. I have only one child, but my space is constantly a mess."

- "When I try to get rid of any of my mother's things, I get paralyzed, even though I don't really want them and know they're taking up a lot of space."

Do any of these sound familiar? If you've struggled with disorganization, chances are you've had thoughts like these before. Perhaps others have said similar things to you or have criticized you for not being as organized as they think you should be. Maybe you've seen organizing shows on TV, or have read books and magazine articles on the subject and are discouraged because the big transformations presented seem out of reach to you.

The truth is that while the component tasks of organizing—sorting and weeding, categorizing, putting things in containers, labeling—might not be extremely complex on their own, the entire process of getting organized often feels overwhelming, especially if you don't know where to start or how to work through a project in an effective way. Why?

Emotions. Organizing—sorting and weeding in particular—can be emotionally draining. Many of the things in your home, the very things you'll be dealing with during the weeding process, can have far deeper meanings than are obvious from the surface. They might be reminders of pleasant experiences that you won't get to enjoy again, or of people who have passed away or otherwise left your life. They might represent things you once were or did, or things you wanted to be or do but may not have had the chance to. They might give you a sense of control in a life that otherwise feels out of control.

My advice? Go ahead and acknowledge these feelings as you go through your belongings. Joy, regret, sadness, anger, longing: Be prepared to experience them all. Deal with the emotions that come up for you, perhaps by sharing with a sympathetic friend or family member what an item means to you, by taking photos of meaningful stuff you're ready to let go of and writing down why these things were special to you, or by making it a point to pass things along to people you know will use and appreciate them.

Make it a goal not to brush aside or ignore any strong emotions that come up for you as you organize. Ignoring these feelings can make you feel overwhelmed and can bring the process to a halt. Remember, letting go of things that don't make you happy or support your life as you're living it now can keep you mired in the past. Organizing can help you focus more on the present.

Time. Sometimes it can seem impossible to find the time to get organized, whether you work inside or outside the home, whether you have a large family or live on your own, and regardless of how many or few activities you or other members of your household might be involved with. When it seems like you have to choose between doing organizing tasks and getting dinner on the table, dinner will probably (and understandably) win.

If you're pinched for time, break organizing tasks down into small chunks that are easy to tackle. For example, rather than trying to sort and weed every item in your kitchen at once, start with one drawer, then move on to other drawers and cabinets when you're finished. Setting aside twenty to thirty minutes each day to work through the organizing process can help you make progress without having to add another overwhelming item on your To Do list.

Having to do it alone. Not being able to go through the organizing process on your own because you don't have the time, emotional energy, or motivation to tackle it without assistance does not mean you're a failure or that there's something wrong with you. It simply means that it would be a good idea to bring in some help. You might enlist a friend, family member, or neighbor to lend a hand. Bribe a buddy by offering a few free beers. Entice your sister with promises of cast-off jewelry or clothes. Get a neighbor involved by offering to lend a hand on a project she's tackling. Look for someone who can be gentle or give you a nudge when needed and, most important, who's able to be supportive and nonjudgmental. This last point is crucial: The last thing you want is an assistant who will criticize you, reinforce any negative beliefs you might have about yourself because of the disorganization in your life, or judge you for the decisions you make.

Weeding out your closet, for example, with a friend who can help walk you through the decision-making process about what to keep and what to toss by asking constructive questions ("Do you like those pants? Are they comfortable? Do they make you feel confident when you're wearing them? When is the last time you wore them?") is likely to be effective and may even be fun. On the other hand, enlisting someone who'll be critical or cruel ("That looks terrible on you. That fabric looks cheap. How much did you pay for that shirt, anyway?" or, if you were sorting a closet full of gadgets, "You still have every cell phone you've ever owned? You actually bought that tool advertised on late-night TV?") will leave you feeling exhausted and beaten down and can keep the organizing process from moving forward.

Needing professional advice. If you need a boost or don't know where to start, consider hiring a professional organizer. A pro can help guide you through the organizing process, lend support when you reach sticky spots, come up with systems, and help keep you moving forward. Professional organizers come from many different backgrounds, have a variety of working styles, and focus on numerous types of clients, from seniors to students to homemakers to the chronically disorganized. You'll find more information about working with a professional organizer at the end of this book.

Needing a guide. Sometimes you can tackle the organizing process on your own as long as you have something to get you started and guide you along the way, so

let this volume help! I have a particular take on organizing, and throughout this book I use words like "simple," "easy," and "basic" to describe organizing tasks, systems, and habits. That's because I honestly believe that the tasks, systems, and habits themselves aren't terribly complex, and I present them here in a way that's designed to make organizing a straightforward and manageable process.

Keep in mind, though, that even simple tasks like sorting and weeding can be challenging, especially when emotions are involved or when you have to do them during times when you'd rather be doing other things. If you find yourself struggling with something I describe as easy, or if you find that basic habits feel like anything but, don't beat yourself up, and don't abandon the progress you've made. Take a breath, enlist help, and give yourself time to get back on track.

How you go about getting organized (on your own, with a friend, with a professional), how long it takes you, and whether the process is a fun and exciting one or a challenging and emotional one will vary from person to person. What matters is that you find the organizing process, systems, and habits that will help you reach your goals, create the home you want, and live your life as you want to live it. This book is designed to be your guide.

CLEARING CLUTTER
Remove things you don't want, use, or need to clear clutter and create space

A common misconception about getting organized is that it requires getting rid of things you really want to keep. Let this idea be the first thing you let go of. The purpose of sorting and weeding is to clear out excess stuff so that it's easier to store, find, and use the things you want, need, and love.

Without a doubt, weeding takes time, thought, and effort. Choosing what to keep and what to get rid of requires many decisions, and it can be the most challenging, difficult, and tiring part of getting organized. But letting go of unwanted stuff gives you a powerful sense of accomplishment, not to mention a less cluttered home.

Getting Ready

- Before weeding, set up bags, boxes, or bins for the things you decide to let go of and those you want to keep.

- Label the containers Keep Here, Donate, Move Elsewhere, and Clean/Repair; keep trash and recycling bins handy, too.

- Decide on a charity to which you'd like to bring the items you're letting go of to lessen the chances of these things hanging around your house indefinitely.

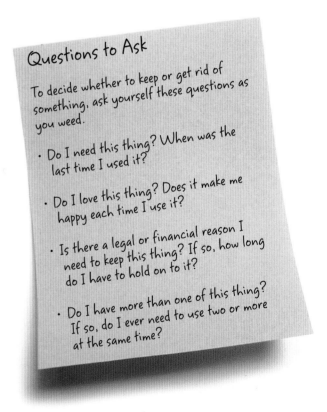

Questions to Ask

To decide whether to keep or get rid of something, ask yourself these questions as you weed.

- Do I need this thing? When was the last time I used it?

- Do I love this thing? Does it make me happy each time I use it?

- Is there a legal or financial reason I need to keep this thing? If so, how long do I have to hold on to it?

- Do I have more than one of this thing? If so, do I ever need to use two or more at the same time?

Make this process easier by creating some guidelines up front to help direct you as you weed and to keep you from having to make many of the same decisions over and over again. For example, you might decide that you'll get rid of any clothes that don't fit, don't make you feel confident, have been tucked in the back of the closet for years, or are out of style. Keep these guidelines in mind (or on paper) as you approach your closet and dresser.

Having a list of general questions to ask yourself, such as the sample lists below, is another useful practice. As you sort and weed, you might have other additions to my list. It can also be helpful to have someone else around as you go through the clutter-clearing process to lend an ear, to add things to your donation pile as you decide what to let go of, and to support you as you work through challenging decisions.

In the end, aim to keep only stuff you truly need, use on a regular basis, love having, or find beautiful. Things that don't fall into at least one of those categories are likely to end up as clutter.

More Questions to Ask

- Is this thing in good repair, or is it broken, stained, or damaged? If it's not in good shape, is it worth my time and effort to fix it?

- Am I keeping this thing only because someone gave it to me or I paid good money for it?

- Am I keeping this thing because I think I might need it someday? If I did need it someday, could I get it again at that point?

- Is this thing worth the space, time, and effort it takes me to store it and keep it clean?

Cleaning Up

- Unless you're working in a space that you can close off until your next weeding session, aim to clean up when you're done sorting for the day.

- Set aside the contents of your Keep Here box. Return things in the Move Elsewhere box to their rightful homes.

- If possible, arrange to drop off the contents of your Donate box to the charity you've chosen.

- Bring the things in the Clean/Repair box to the spot where you'll work on them (or put them near the door if you'll bring them to someone else, such as a dry cleaner).

DEVELOPING SYSTEMS

Find homes for the things you want to keep and create systems that work for you

One of the most important parts of getting organized—and making it easy to stay that way—is creating systems that fix what's not working and help you meet your organizing goals. These systems include not only where you store stuff but also how you store it and how you access it. A system can be as simple as a recipe box or as complex as a totally new storage plan for your kitchen cabinets and drawers.

Creating systems doesn't require blueprints, complicated calculations, or advanced space-planning skills. All you need to know is what you want to store, how to store it, and what tools and techniques to use so that things are easy to access and put away.

What to Store

- What you store in each room in the house—and in each area within that room—depends largely on what you do there.

- A rule of thumb is to store things as close as possible to where you use them—pots and pans near the stove, for example, and bags and umbrellas near the door.

- Think of the space in each room as real estate. Aim to devote the most valuable real estate, or the most accessible spots, to storing the things you use most frequently.

How to Store

- Look for ways to keep like things together (shoes with shoes, for example) and to make things easy to get out and put away.

- Think creatively about containers (racks, shelves, boxes, bins, drawers, hangers), and don't be afraid to use nontraditional ones.

- Choose containers that hold what you need them to hold and fit the space, and that you enjoy. A functional container you hate is a container you won't want to use.

It's important to remember that organizing systems need to be flexible. When you create a new system, you're essentially making an educated guess; it's impossible to know for sure whether the system will work perfectly. Once you set up a system, use it regularly for a few weeks, and if you find that it's not quite working, feel free to change it. Make it simpler if it seems too complex, or more detailed if it's too basic. Move things around, try new storage containers, do another round of weeding—make whatever small changes you think will help. (Avoid completely overhauling the system unless it's a true disaster.)

Also give yourself the flexibility to modify your systems over time, especially as your life changes. A system that works well now won't necessarily be effective five years from now, just as one that worked in the past might not do what you need it to do today. Revisit your systems over time and revise them as needed to be sure they support your life as you're currently living it.

Labeling

• Labeling helps make organizing systems clearer and more functional, especially when more than one person uses them. Labels also make it easier to stay organized over the long term.

• Use labels wherever you need to clarify the contents (oregano, sugar, bills to pay) or ownership (Hannah's, Jonathan's, Mom's) of something.

• Be sure the labels make sense to everyone who uses the organizing systems.

• Labels can be handwritten, printed from a computer, or created on a label maker.

Updating Systems

• To update systems that no longer work, start with small changes: Clear out any clutter that has accumulated, reconsider where you've stored things, use different containers, and modify labels.

• A system is too complex if it doesn't make sense to one or more of the people who use it, if it requires more than a few steps to use, or if you find yourself avoiding it because of the effort it requires.

• A system is too basic if it doesn't solve the organizing problem or, worse, causes problems that weren't there before.

3

MAINTAINING ORGANIZATION

Develop simple (but important) habits and routines to maintain progress and stay organized

You've cleared your home of clutter, planned how you want to use each room, created organizing systems to keep things contained and accessible, and labeled things so that it's easy to find what you need. You've reached your organizing goals, and your home finally feels like it's a truly comfortable, welcoming, pleasant place to be.

Now all you have to do is keep it that way.

It's easy to forget that getting things organized once doesn't mean they'll stay organized forever—just as mopping a floor or making a bed one time doesn't mean an end to those tasks. Maintaining the progress you've made requires developing a few new habits.

Less-Than-a-Minute Habits

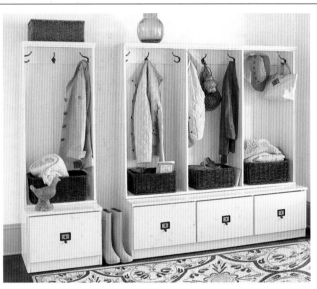

- Put things back where they belong when you're done with them. Ask other family members to do the same.

- Toss any junk mail in the recycling bin or shred pile as soon as it comes into the house.

- Hang up coats, jackets, and bags as soon as you take them off.

- Put your keys, glasses, and wallet in the same place each time you come home.

Daily Habits

- Walk through the house to pick up and put away anything that's migrated away from the place it belongs.

- Wash dishes or load them into the dishwasher after each meal.

- When getting undressed at the end of the day, put dirty clothes in the hamper and hang or fold clean ones and put them away—and have your kids do the same.

- Get bags, clothes, and papers for the next day ready the night before to avoid a morning rush.

Less-than-a-Minute Habits are tasks you can do in under a minute to keep things in order and save time in the long run. Even though they take little more than a few seconds, they can have a big impact.

Daily Habits should be planned so that they're easy to fit in and require minimal time commitments for day-to-day maintenance. The thought of adding anything complicated to your daily To Do list can be overwhelming, so focus instead on small, simple tasks. They're one key to staying organized.

Weekly Habits are a bit more involved than Daily Habits,

but they make daily maintenance easier. To make scheduling these habits easier, try pegging them to activities you already have planned: You might use the time after taking the kids to sports practice to pay your bills, for example.

Monthly and Seasonal Habits need to happen only a few times a year—and in some cases only once a year. Aim to do these organizing activities at the same time you take care of other seasonal tasks, such as spring cleaning or hanging storm windows.

Weekly Habits

- Schedule time once a week to open and process the mail you've gathered in your mail sorter.

- Go through the papers your kids have brought home from school (with your children's help if they're old enough). Recycle anything they don't need, add activi-ties to the family calendar, and store any papers the kids need or want to keep.

- At the start of each week, plan your meals, create a grocery shopping list, and update your family's sched-ule for the coming week.

Monthly and Seasonal Habits

- Do an intensive clutter-clearing session a few times a year. Scheduling these sessions before gift-giving holidays is a good way to clear out the old to make room for the new.

- Rotate your clothes each time the season changes. Weed out clothes you no longer want, that don't fit, or that are damaged beyond repair.

- When putting away holiday decorations, take the time to organize them to keep them safe and make the next year's holidays easier to plan for.

KITCHEN
Identify your kitchen personality and discover the best ways to make this room work for you

No two kitchens are the same, and no two people use their kitchens in exactly the same way, so it follows that one set of organizing tips won't fit everyone. For ideas and recommendations specific to the way you use your kitchen, find the kitchen personality here that best describes you, and then check out the tips for that personality below the photo.

Gourmet Chef

I love cooking, and do it almost daily. For me, the more elaborate the recipe, the greater the challenge. I need plenty of counter space to spread out while I'm cooking. My pots and pans need to be neatly organized and easy to grab. My kitchen needs enough storage for everything I use.

If You're a Gourmet Chef . . .

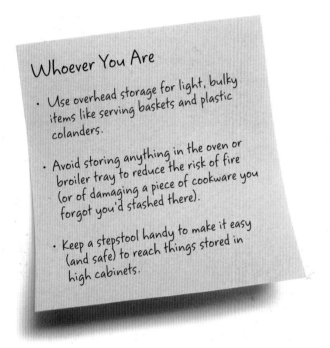

Whoever You Are

- Use overhead storage for light, bulky items like serving baskets and plastic colanders.

- Avoid storing anything in the oven or broiler tray to reduce the risk of fire (or of damaging a piece of cookware you forgot you'd stashed there).

- Keep a stepstool handy to make it easy (and safe) to reach things stored in high cabinets.

- Invest in a hanging rack so that you can keep all of your pots and pans in one place and easily find the ones you need.

- Use a rolling kitchen cart to give yourself extra counter space while you're cooking. As a bonus, most carts have shelves or cabinets underneath.

- If you don't have enough drawer space for all of your cooking gadgets, store them in crocks or canisters on the counter or stashed in a cabinet.

Simple Everyday Cook

I cook a lot—mostly straightforward meals on weekdays, with fancier dishes on special occasions and some weekends. My ideal kitchen has counters that are uncluttered so I can cook or my kids can do homework while I work. I need simple storage in cabinets and drawers for my basic supplies and gadgets. There are certain cooking tools I use all the time, and I want to be able to grab them with my eyes closed or with a kid hanging on my leg.

Occasional Cook

My idea of an ideal kitchen is one in which someone else does the cooking. On the rare occasions when I make more than toast, I need quick and easy access to my basic cooking gear. I want my kitchen supplies consolidated so I don't have to open more than one drawer and one cabinet to find them. I'd love to be able to use the storage in my kitchen for other things. (I never do seem to have enough space for books.)

If You're a Simple Everyday Cook . . .

- Designate an area of the counter or the kitchen table as the kid food-prep zone, where children can help with basic tasks like mixing and measuring.

- Store your everyday cookware—the pots, pans, bowls, baking dishes, and colanders you use all the time—in one spot, such as the cabinet closest to the stove.

- Set aside one cabinet as the storage spot for the supplies your kids need to do homework in the kitchen.

If You're an Occasional Cook . . .

- Get rid of any cookware or gadgets you don't (and are unlikely to) use, such as cake pans and waffle irons.

- Rather than spreading things out, designate one for pots, pans, bowls, and other cookware; one cabinet for plates and glasses; and one for utensils and gadgets.

- If you have extra storage space after you've stored your kitchen supplies, use it for other things such as books, papers, or electronics; just be sure to keep these items separate from your cookware and pantry items.

COUNTERTOPS
Clear off the clutter and find the space you need for everyday essentials

In a perfect world, kitchen counters would be clean and clear all the time, standing at the ready to be used for food preparation. Unless you have an especially large kitchen, though, or don't have much by way of appliances, gadgets, and cooking supplies, chances are your countertops tend to attract clutter.

While it might not be realistic to aim for always-clear counters, organizing your space so that your countertops store only things you use regularly—leaving room for chopping, mixing, and other cooking-related tasks—will make your kitchen more functional, and the work you do there more efficient.

Before you decide what should go where on your counters,

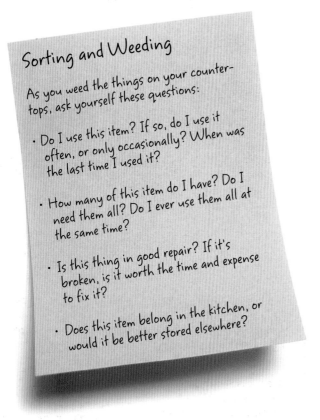

Sorting and Weeding

As you weed the things on your countertops, ask yourself these questions:

• Do I use this item? If so, do I use it often, or only occasionally? When was the last time I used it?

• How many of this item do I have? Do I need them all? Do I ever use them all at the same time?

• Is this thing in good repair? If it's broken, is it worth the time and expense to fix it?

• Does this item belong in the kitchen, or would it be better stored elsewhere?

The Food-Prep Zone

• The main zone in most kitchens is the food-prep zone, where tasks like chopping, measuring, and mixing happen. Put the zone close to the stove so that it's easy to switch between food prep and cooking.

• Keep this space free of appliances and gadgets you don't use on a regular basis. However, the appliances you turn to every day—a coffeemaker, a toaster, a blender—deserve homes here.

• Also keep knives, cutting boards, and mixing bowls here.

8

take the time to clear off the clutter: gadgets, loose papers, cooking supplies you don't often use, and anything that belongs either elsewhere in the kitchen or in another room. This is a great time to reconsider whether you truly need these things; if you don't use them, don't like them, or never seem to have space for them, it's time to let them go.

After you've weeded, take a look at what you're keeping, decide how you want to be able to use your counters, and start thinking about zones: different areas of the kitchen where you do different tasks.

GREEN ● LIGHT

If your kitchen is small and counter space is at a premium, consider expanding it with things like a cart with a butcher-block top, a chopping board that fits over the sink, or a pull-out cutting board that fits under the counter and that can be tucked away when it's not in use. Freestanding shelves, which increase storage space, are another great option.

The Cooking Zone

- The cooking zone is where boiling, sautéing, baking, and roasting happen. Situate this zone next to the stove, near the food-prep zone.

- Keep the counters near the stove uncluttered to make room for cooking supplies, including spoons, spatulas, basic spices, and potholders.

- If you have limited storage space, use the walls and ceilings to hang items. Racks can hold pots and pans, and simple wall hooks can store potholders and colanders.

Food-Prep and Cooking-Zone Safety

- Wipe down your food-prep and cooking areas when you're done using them to help prevent food-borne illnesses.

- Keep your cooking zone clear; any type of clutter here can be a safety hazard.

- Use color-coded cutting boards for different types of foods to prevent cross-contamination: red for meats, for example, and green for vegetables.

- Stash a small fire extinguisher, a box of baking soda, or another form of fire retardant near the stove in case of flare-ups.

COUNTERTOPS (CONTINUED)
Create space for easy cleanups and keeping track of household goings-on

A cluttered sink area can give an otherwise orderly kitchen a veneer of disarray—and, worse, can be a breeding ground for mold and germs. Keeping your cleaning zone clear of unneeded things and preventing dirty dishes from piling up will make the washing-up process quicker and more efficient.

Because it tends to gather water, food particles, and dirt, the counter area around your sink can be a challenge to keep clean. Make the process easier by decluttering this zone and stocking it with only the supplies you need for the tasks you do there.

Another common kitchen headache is the tendency for things like papers, keys, toys, and mail to wind up on the

The Cleaning Zone

- Store here supplies such as sponges, scrubbers, dish detergent, a drain stopper, and a dish drainer.

- Wash dishes (or load them into the dishwasher) as you prepare meals rather than waiting to clean up everything at the end. This initial cleanup can save time.

- After each meal, finish loading the dishwasher, and run it as soon as it's full. If you wash by hand, get this task out of the way right after the meal.

Think Vertical

- Put the vertical space in and around your sink to good use. Suction holders stick to most surfaces and keep sponges, scrubbers, and cleaning brushes at the ready.

- Invest in a sturdy, spacious dish drainer, which will let you clean up in large

batches without having to hand-dry dishes. Wall-mounted dish drainers are great for small spaces.

- A wall-mounted shelf can hold soaps, sponges, and brushes, leaving your counters open.

10

counters, taking up valuable space and causing clutter. Creating a household management zone lets you keep the information and supplies you need close at hand without having to sacrifice food-prep or cooking space.

This zone is a place to collect and use the things that come into the kitchen but aren't related to cooking or eating, as well as supplies you use for paying bills, scheduling, and other management tasks. Creating a designated spot for these things keeps them accessible and keeps counters clutter-free.

The Household Management Zone

- This zone should have a spot for incoming mail, a place for important papers from school or work, and storage for small electronics like cell phones and PDAs.

- Set up an inbox for each family member to collect mail, schoolwork, and other papers. A simple cup or basket can hold basic office supplies. Use another basket or a recharging station for electronics.

- If you have the space, use a small desk in an out-of-the-way spot for this zone.

A Wall-Based Management Zone

- For smaller areas, create a household management zone on a wall. Upright file holders are great for inboxes. Other accessories include key hooks, pen holders, and small shelves.

- A family calendar and a bulletin board are useful additions. The calendar allows each family member to track important events, and the bulletin board is a handy spot to stick things like invitations and appointment reminders.

- An electronics recharging station can be an elegant way of corralling and charging small electronics.

CABINETS

Increase your kitchen's efficiency and practicality by reconsidering how you use your cabinets

Overstuffed, hard-to-use cabinets are a common sight in many kitchens. Cabinets are generally the main storage space, but they're often not used efficiently, which can make finding what you need a challenging prospect; in addition, cluttered cabinets increase the chances of unpleasant surprises—such as avalanches of stuff—when you open the doors.

Spend some time clearing out your cabinets. Get rid of cookware you don't use, as well as anything that's warped, missing handles, or otherwise damaged beyond repair. Move anything that should be stored elsewhere—that is, whatever you don't use in the kitchen but is taking up space in the cabinets, such as toys, laundry supplies, and papers.

Pots, Pans, and Lids

- Keep pots and pans in a low cabinet close to the stove to make them easy to grab.

- Store flat cookware like frying pans vertically in an upright rack.

- Install a slide-out tray in the cabinet for easy access to pots and pans.

- Use a wooden peg rack or a rack mounted to the inside of a cabinet door to store lids.

- Place a layer of coffee filters or soft paper towels between nested pots and pans to prevent scuffs.

Everyday Dishes and Glasses

- The lower shelves of above-counter cabinets are a good choice for everyday dishes and glasses. Use shelf expanders to maximize space.

- When storing cups and glasses, line them up in rows, back to front.

- If the shelves in your cabinets are tall enough, install mug hooks and wineglass racks to the undersides to expand the space.

- To help protect dishes and glassware, use shelf liners, which are easy to measure, cut, and install.

Assign cabinet space based on how you use the surrounding areas. For example, store glasses near the sink and dishes near your food-prep zone. Another option is to store things together that you'll use together—stash everyday cups with everyday plates and bowls, for example, so that setting the table at mealtime is a snap. Wherever you store them, make sure the things you use most frequently are the easiest to access.

MAKE IT EASY

Ceiling- or wall-mounted pot and pan racks are an easy way to make the most of the space in your kitchen. Look for a rack that won't get in your way, that's large enough to store all of your cookware, and that's sturdy enough to keep heavy pans safely stored.

Lightweight and Infrequently Used Items

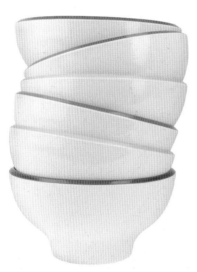

- Use higher cabinets to store items you use less frequently, such as extra dishes and specialty gadgets. Shelf expanders can help increase storage space and keep things orderly.

- Higher shelves aren't ideal for storing things you need on a daily basis or for heavy items, which could fall and injure someone or break.

- Keep tabs on the things you stash up high by creating a list of what you have and where it's stored. Post this inventory in an accessible spot, such as the inside of a cabinet door.

Odd and Out-of-the-Way Cabinets

- Earmark cabinets built into odd and hard-to-reach spots, such as above the fridge, for things you rarely need, like special occasion gadgets and holiday cookware.

- If you store small things in these cabinets, corral them into clear, sturdy plastic bins.

- Don't use the cabinets above the fridge or stove to store things that are heat-sensitive, such as wine and spices; keep these in cooler spots.

- List anything you put in these cabinets on your storage inventory.

DRAWERS
Declutter, divide, and contain to regain control over your drawers

Kitchen drawers are the most headache-inducing spots in the room, crammed with utensils, gadgets, and unknown clutter. Disorganized drawers aren't just annoying, though; they can also be dangerous (think knives on the loose) and can make everything you do in the kitchen less efficient.

To bring your drawers under control, start by emptying them out completely and getting rid of the things you no longer need or use. After you've purged, decide what goes back into each drawer based on what it's near (the stove, the sink) and what you do there. Group things together by size, task, and/or frequency of use—all small gadgets together, for example, or all baking supplies.

Finally, use drawer dividers to contain things to keep them from scattering each time you open the drawer. (This works

The Basic Utensil Sorter

- Use a utensil organizer to hold your everyday silverware in a drawer that's easily accessible.

- Store special occasion flatware in a separate drawer near its coordinating china and serving ware. If your silver came in a padded box, keep it there to reduce wear and tarnishing.

- Most utensil organizers have small cubbies on the ends that are great for items that might otherwise roam free in your drawers, such as bottle stoppers, corkscrews, and church key can openers.

Custom Dividers

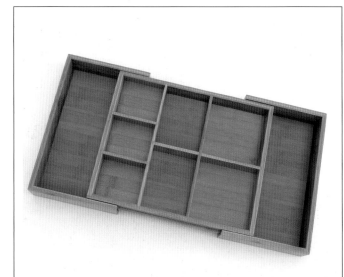

- Another option for non-silverware utensils is custom dividers. These consist of strips of hard plastic and mounts that adhere to the front, back, or sides of the drawer.

- Measure the strips to the lengths you want, score them with a utility knife, and snap them apart. Then slide them into the mounts to keep them in place.

- Use strips of varying sizes within the same drawer to create larger or smaller compartments by simply changing the positions of the mounts.

particularly well for utensils.) Drawer dividers come in a variety of sizes and materials, including plastic, metal, and bamboo; many are adjustable, so you can use them in oddly sized drawers. Be sure to measure your drawers carefully before choosing organizers, and check to see that the ones you select have enough compartments for the things you want to store in them.

Modular Dividers

- Another drawer option is to use modular dividers, which are separate small containers that can be mixed and matched to fit different spaces and hold various things.

- These dividers come in a variety of materials, including metal, plastic, and wood; some have rims that allow them to snap together.

- Once you have your modular organizers in place within the drawer, keep them there by sticking double-sided tape, museum wax, or Velcro on the bottom.

In-Drawer Racks

- In-drawer spice racks are like "stadium seating" for your jars and tins, making it easy for you to see your spices. Choose a drawer that's close to your stove but not directly next to it, as high temperatures can cause spices to lose flavor.

- In-drawer knife blocks help keep knives stored safely and also help keep them sharp.

- Measure your drawers before buying a knife block to take into account the sizes of the knives you need to store.

15

UNDER THE SINK
Smart ways to keep this area organized and clutter-free, with space to stash essentials

The space under the kitchen sink can be a great area for storing cleaning supplies, trash and recycling, and other utilitarian things you need to keep your kitchen running smoothly. All too often, though, this area becomes a jumble of boxes, bottles, and forgotten gadgets. A cluttered under-sink space can cause wasted time (when you have to search for what you need) and money (when you find yourself buying multiples of things you know you have but can't locate). It can also be a breeding ground for mold, mildew, and pests.

To avoid chaos under the sink, start by weeding the things you currently store there. Get rid of anything that doesn't belong, that you have in excess (such as half-empty bottles of

ORGANIZING YOUR HOME

Cleaning Supplies

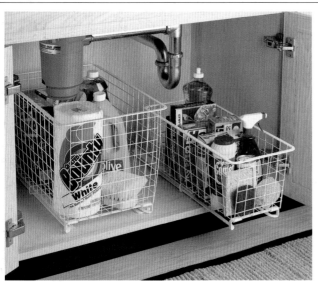

- The under-sink area is a good spot to store cleaning supplies such as spray cleaners, dishwashing soap, and extra sponges.

- A bucket with a handle, a plastic caddy with separate compartments, or a slide-out shelf is a good choice for holding supplies.

- Look for simple water- and rust-proof bins for fewer supplies.

- If you have pets or young children, install safety locks or latches on any cabinets you use to store cleaning supplies and other potentially hazardous materials.

Pullout Trash Cans

- Keeping the trash under the sink makes your kitchen look neater and also helps prevent pests.

- Look for a bin that fits well under the sink and is large enough to hold the amount of garbage your household generates.

- If you keep recycling and compost under the sink, choose bins that fit well side by side.

- For easy access, consider a pullout can, which has gliders that attach to the bottom of the cabinet and a bin that snaps into the frame.

cleaning supplies, which can be combined with their mates), or that's past its prime (like rusted scrubber pads).

After you've weeded, decide what you want to store under the sink and what should go elsewhere; then corral supplies and other small items in simple containers. This will make them easier to take out and put away and will also keep them from migrating to the back of the cabinet.

Finally, get in the habit of keeping this area clean: Empty trash and recycling bins as soon as they're full, return supplies to their containers, and deal with spills and leaks quickly to

avoid mold and other unpleasant surprises. Keeping the cabinets under your sink organized will make kitchen cleaning tasks less of a chore and will keep you and your family safer.

Freestanding Trash Cans

- If you keep your trash bin out in the open, look for a can that's sturdy and has a lid to keep pests out and odors contained.

- Consider a model that's stylish and works well with the decor of your kitchen.

- Another option is a traditional step can, which features a foot-operated lever that will open the lid when you press it—especially useful in the kitchen, where your hands are likely to be in contact with food.

Door-Mounted Storage

- Racks that mount onto the insides of cabinet doors keep supplies like foil, food wrap, and spray bottles organized and accessible.

- Before choosing a rack, think about the supplies you want to store in it, and then measure your cabinet door. Install the rack with

enough room for the supplies to stand upright without preventing the door from closing.

- Under-sink cabinet doors are also a good spot for plastic grocery bag storage units, which keep bags contained and neat.

FOOD

Identify your cooking personality to find the most effective food organizing techniques

The way you cook has an impact on the types (and amount) of food you need to store, as well as the best ways to store it. To create food organizing systems that work like you need them to, start by identifying your cooking personality. Choose the description that best describes you, and then read the tips for your personality type below the photo.

Whoever You Are

• Clean out your fridge and freezer before a major holiday, such as Thanksgiving, to create room for the food and drinks you'll need for the celebration.

• Be sure boxes and bags are tightly sealed before you store them in your pantry for maximum freshness. Better yet, transfer foods from open bags to airtight storage containers.

• Before you buy a new cookbook, test-drive it by borrowing it from the library to ensure you don't waste valuable space or money on an unused book.

Gourmet Chef

I have lots of jars, bottles, and boxes to store, and I want to find them easily. My cookbook collection needs to be stored neatly and in a way that makes it easy for me to find the recipes I need. I want an easy way to remember what I have in the fridge, freezer, and pantry so that I don't buy more than I need.

If You're a Gourmet Chef . . .

• Use expandable shelf racks in your pantry for easy storage of small things and to see everything at a glance.

• Keep a lazy Susan on the counter (but away from the heat of the stove) for basic oils, vinegars, and seasonings.

• If you buy the same foods regularly, create a grocery checklist template on your computer. Print it out before you shop, check off what you need, and write in any additions on the bottom of the list.

Simple Everyday Cook

I need super-efficient pantry storage for the staples I use all the time, as well as for the unusual spices and specialty foods I turn to occasionally. My freezer needs to be well organized so that I have space for the meals I make in advance. I want easy access to my favorite cookbooks and recipes, as well as a way to keep track of new ones I come across.

Occasional Cook

I want pantry space for canned foods, dry goods, and the basic supplies I use when I decide to cook. My fridge is rarely full, but it needs to be organized so that I don't forget about the things I have there. Above all, I want easy access to my favorite take-out menus.

If You're a Simple Everyday Cook . . .

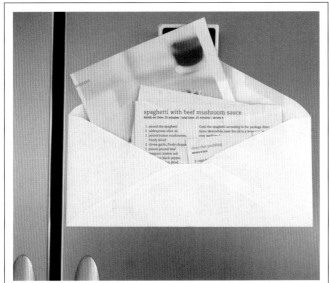

- Divide your pantry into zones based on how often you use the things stored there. Keep your daily necessities on easily accessible shelves, and reserve the upper and lower shelves for special occasion foods.

- Do the same in your fridge: Keep everyday supplies front and center and stash specialty items out of the way.

- Tack an envelope to a bulletin board or on the front of the fridge to collect recipes you've clipped. When it gets full, transfer the recipes to books or cards.

If You're an Occasional Cook . . .

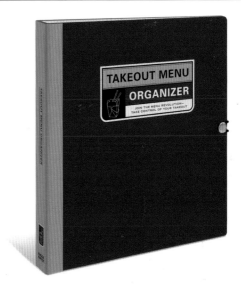

- Keep a list on the outside of your fridge detailing what's inside, when you bought it, and when it should be eaten or tossed.

- Store pantry items in sealable bags or containers to keep them fresh longer.

- Use a three-ring binder with sheet protectors to store take-out menus. Create sections with tabbed dividers, and store the binder near your phone.

PANTRY

Create simple, effective storage systems to keep food fresh and make prep efficient

Pantries, whether dedicated cabinets, separate rooms, or space in standard kitchen cabinets, can often attract chaos and clutter. A disorganized pantry results in wasted time, effort, and money and can be a gathering spot for food-loving insects who are attracted to open containers and spills. If you take the time to get your pantry in order, you'll not only keep food fresh longer, but also save time when you cook.

Before you create a storage plan for your pantry, consider the space you're working with. If you don't have a separate pantry room or cabinet, choose a cabinet or two in the kitchen to dedicate to food storage. Short on cabinet space? Consider

Glass and Ceramic Jars

- Use glass and ceramic storage jars to hold bulk foods like flour, sugar, dried beans, and pasta.

- Look for jars that have a ring of plastic or rubber under the lid so that it seals tightly. This makes the jars safer to move around (as there's less chance of the lid falling off) and keeps the food fresher.

- Because these jars can be heavy, they're best stored on shelves that are at or below eye level, or on counters.

Plastic Snap-Lid Containers

- Plastic containers with snap-shut lids are great for snacks, noodles, rice, and cereal.

- These containers come in a variety of shapes and sizes and are easy to label, clean, and stack. In addition, they're available with convenient flip-up lids so that you can pour out foods like rice or cereal without removing the lid.

- Label each container with its contents to make it easy to see at a glance what's inside.

freestanding shelves, which are an easy, inexpensive way of increasing storage in the kitchen.

When you're ready to get organized, start by emptying your pantry out completely. Toss anything that's stale, past its expiration date, or otherwise gone bad, as well as foods that have been hanging around uneaten for months.

After you've weeded, it's time to contain. Transferring dry foods like flour, noodles, cereal, pretzels, and cookies to airtight containers will eliminate bulky, odd-shaped, hard-to-stack packages and will help keep things fresh. Gather small jars together in a sturdy plastic bin or on small shelves within the pantry cabinet.

When you're ready to restock the pantry, store like with like—breakfast foods, baking supplies, and so on. Store snacks on easily reachable shelves so that your family members don't have to dig through other things to find the treats.

To maintain order in your pantry, take stock of what you have before going to the grocery store and get in the habit of transferring foods to the proper containers when you bring them home. Adding these small steps will keep your pantry in top shape.

Can Dispensers

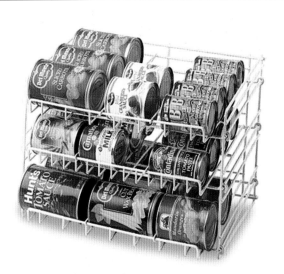

- Keep canned goods and soft drinks under control with can dispensers. These let you store multiple cans front to back and work with gravity. When you remove the front can, the one behind it rolls forward.

- Look for a can dispenser with dividers so that you can store cans of different sizes together easily.

- Soft drink can dispensers are sized for soda cans and can be used in the pantry or in the fridge.

Lazy Susans

- Use a lazy Susan—a circular tray that spins—to hold bottles of things like oils and vinegars so that you don't have to dig into the back of the cabinet to find what you're looking for.

- Look for a lazy Susan that turns easily and has a base that's about the same size as the tray; this increases stability and helps prevent bottles from falling.

- You can also store spice containers and condiment jars here to keep them neat and easily accessible.

FRIDGE

Give unwanted food the boot and organize this space for efficient food storage

When it comes to what's in the fridge, all too often out of sight really is out of mind. It's easy to forget what you have on hand behind that closed door, which can lead to spoiled food and money wasted on buying duplicates of things you already have. In addition, forgotten and poorly stored foods in the fridge are breeding grounds for mold.

An organized fridge makes it easier to remember what you have, find what you need, and keep foods fresh and safe. The first step in the process is to perform a full fridge clear-out.

Before you start, gather together a few supplies to make the job easier. Have a strong garbage bag on hand, one that won't leak. If there are recycling and composting programs in

What to Store Where

- Many fridges are designed with food storage zones, where the temperature and moisture levels are calibrated for specific types of food (such as crisper drawers for fruits and vegetables).

- Avoid storing eggs, dairy,

and other highly perishable foods on the door, which tends to be the warmest spot in the fridge (it's exposed to air each time the door is opened).

- Put kid-friendly snacks on lower shelves so that children can help themselves.

How Long to Keep Foods

Safe storage guidelines

Bell peppers: 1 week

Carrots: 1-2 weeks

Chicken: 1-2 days

Eggs: 1 week

Ground beef: 1-2 days

Yogurt: 7-10 days

- Avoid wasting food and money by labeling packages and storage containers with dates to remind yourself how old they are. For produce and perishables, make a list of use-by dates and check it regularly.

- When restocking, put the new items toward the back, and use up open packages first.

- For a detailed list of recommendations on how long to keep foods in the fridge and the best ways to store them, see the Resources section at the end of the book.

your area, keep bins for recyclable and biodegradable materials handy. Set up a cooler nearby to keep perishable foods cold as you work.

Begin by taking everything out of the fridge and tossing anything that's spoiled, that's past its prime, or that you haven't used for six months or more. While the fridge is empty, take a few minutes to wipe down the shelves and walls, and remove any bins that can be cleaned in the sink.

When you're ready, start moving food back in, remembering to keep like things together (all condiments on a door shelf, for example) and to make the most commonly used items the easiest to grab. Transfer foods like leftovers and cut produce to airtight containers to keep them fresh and safe.

Finally, get in the habit of doing a weekly review of your fridge's contents, tossing anything that's gone bad, cleaning up any drips or spills, and adding to your grocery list anything that needs to be replaced. An inventory list hung on the front of the fridge can help you keep tabs on what's inside, making it easier to find and use the food you have and to buy more of what you need.

Organizing Small Items

- Keep the fridge from becoming a circus of little jars, bottles, and packages by using sturdy, clear bins to hold small items such as condiments and jams.

- Use labels to make it easy to know at a glance what's in each bin: condiments, baking supplies, and snacks.

- If you have the shelf space, consider using a lazy Susan to hold small jars and bottles so that they stay together and easily accessible.

Food Storage Containers

- Sturdy, stackable food storage containers let you use the space in your fridge efficiently. Opt for clear containers so that you can easily see what's inside.

- Get rid of any containers that are warped, cracked, or otherwise damaged; that don't have lids that fit; or that are stained or have odors.

- Glass storage containers are especially convenient because they can be used in the fridge, freezer, oven, and microwave and can be put in the dishwasher.

FREEZER

Optimize this space by purging, creating zones, and keeping tabs on what you have

Freezers can sometimes be places where food gets lost or forgotten about. When something winds up at the back or bottom of the freezer, there's a good chance it won't resurface until it's all but inedible. The good news is that by weeding out what you don't need, planning how to use the space, and bringing in some smart storage solutions, you can make your freezer a well-organized and efficient spot.

Clearing out the old, freezer-burned, forgotten food from your freezer is the first step toward getting things in order. Start by taking everything out and putting back only those things you're sure you will eat; toss everything else. If you have an abundance of one kind of food (several bags of fro-

What to Store Where

- Make the foods you use most frequently the easiest to grab by storing them on the door or at the front of the freezer.

- Keep foods you're storing long-term solidly frozen (and out of the way) by storing them at the back or bottom of the freezer.

- Freezer door shelves tend to be warmer than the rest of the space, so don't use this space for storing dairy-based products or other foods that can melt or spoil easily.

Smart Storage Containers

- Sturdy, stackable food storage containers help keep foods fresh and make the most of freezer space.

- Choose containers that withstand temperature extremes and seal tightly. Tempered plastic or glass containers are ideal.

- If you freeze foods in plastic zipper bags, choose heavy-duty ones. Write the contents and date on the label strip.

zen peas, for example), consolidate them to save space and avoid clutter. After you've weeded, put things back, storing like items together and locating things in the freezer based on how often you use them.

Some simple habits, such as keeping a freezer inventory, and a few basic accessories, including sturdy food storage containers and shelf expanders, can help you keep track of what you have, maximize space, and keep your newly clean freezer neat and organized.

FOOD STORAGE

Space Expanders

- Use shelf expanders to increase storage space. Choose coated metal versions, which can withstand the cold without cracking.

- Freezer baskets corral small and odd-shaped items, such as bags of frozen vegetables.

- Use baskets in conjunction with shelf expanders (one basket below the expander and one on top of it) to maximize space and order.

Create a Freezer Inventory

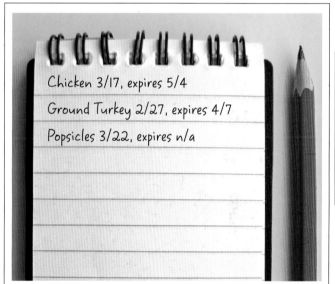

Chicken 3/17, expires 5/4

Ground Turkey 2/27, expires 4/7

Popsicles 3/22, expires n/a

- Make a list of what's in your freezer (especially anything stored at the back or bottom) to remember what you have.

- On your list, note the date when you put each item in the freezer, as well as the expiration date.

- Post your list in a visible spot like the front of the freezer door or a kitchen bulletin board.

- Once a month, use your inventory to clear out old and unwanted food from the freezer.

COOKBOOKS AND RECIPES

Regain control over your recipes and cookbooks to make planning and preparing meals easier

Chances are you have recipes and cookbooks floating around the kitchen. Collecting these in one spot and getting them organized will help clear clutter and make it easier to plan meals, regardless of how classic or adventurous your culinary style.

Step one is to get all of your cookbooks and recipes (whether loose or in books) in one place. This might involve checking drawers and bookcases not only in the kitchen but possibly elsewhere in the house, too. When you have everything together, start weeding. Get rid of recipes for anything you're unlikely to cook or have made in the past but didn't like. Be honest with yourself as you do this: If you tend to make simple meals, what are the chances you'll whip up that twenty-ingredient dish?

Storing Loose Recipes

- A common way to store loose recipes is in a box. You can use one specifically designed to hold recipes, a photo box, or an index card box.

- You can rewrite recipes onto cards, use tape or glue to attach them to cards, or just slip folded recipes into protective plastic sleeves.

- Three-ring binders are another good option. Attach recipes to hole-punched sheets of paper or slip them loose into sleeve protectors. Use tabbed dividers to create categories.

Small Cookbook Collections

- If you own just a few cookbooks and have the space, store the books on your counter, where they'll be easy to access.

- Keep the books upright with bookends, ideally in a style that matches your kitchen decor.

- You can also create kitchen-themed bookends with heavy pantry supplies, such as jumbo cans of stewed tomatoes or sturdy jars of dried beans.

- Stacking books on their sides works well for very small collections and helps save counter space.

Take the same approach with cookbooks. If you've had a book for more than a year but haven't made more than a few things from it, or if the recipes are too complex (or too basic), let it go.

When you've decided what to keep, consider how best to store your books and recipes. If you have a large collection of cookbooks, they'll probably need their own shelf; a smaller number might work well on a countertop or in a cabinet. Loose recipes can be stored in a binder, a box, or an electronic recipe program. Set aside a few hours once or twice a year to sort through recipes and cookbooks, add new ones to your collection, and pass along or get rid of any that no longer fit your cooking style.

Large Cookbook Collections

- Give larger cookbook collections their own storage space in a wide cabinet or on a separate shelf.

- If you have extra space in your pantry, use it for books. A small set of freestanding bookshelves can provide handy book storage space if your built-ins are full.

- Arrange your books in a way that makes it easy to find what you're looking for: by author, by title, by type of food, or by complexity.

Electronic Recipe Organizers

- Electronic recipe organizers are useful for storing and accessing recipes if you're technologically inclined and have access to a computer in or near your kitchen.

- You can use a program designed specifically for recipes or can create your own using a word processing program or database tool. See the Resources section in this book for a few options.

- With your recipes stored electronically, you'll be able to search them easily and won't have to worry about them creating clutter in your kitchen.

TABLETOP AND MEALTIMES
Make mealtimes more pleasant before, during, and after with simple planning tools and routines

In the midst of a busy day, it can be a challenge to answer the "What's for dinner?" question, and even more of a challenge to actually get dinner on the table—especially if the table is buried under papers, car keys, and boxes. With a bit of advance planning and a few easy organizing systems, though, you can avoid mealtime stress.

Perhaps the most important steps in gaining control over dinner (and any other meals you normally prepare and eat at home) are thinking ahead about what you'll cook and making sure you have the supplies you'll need on hand. Planning your meals for the week saves time and effort and can lessen the chances that you'll have to go the take-out route instead,

Meal-Planning Chart

Sunday: Chicken Parmesan

Ingredients Needed: Chicken

Monday: Beef Tacos & Rice

Ingredients Needed: Have everything

Tuesday: Baked Ziti

Ingredients Needed: Mozzarella Cheese

- When planning your meals, use a preprinted weekly chart or create one on your own.

- Leave space to list your courses as well as the ingredients you'll need throughout the week.

- To get into a routine, fill in your chart at the same time each week, ideally at the start of the week or before your regular shopping day.

- Store past charts in a three-ring binder to keep tabs on what meals worked and didn't work.

Table-Setting Basket

- Make table setting easier by storing the things you need (dishes, glasses, silverware, napkins) in a sturdy basket or tray with handles and deep sides.

- Keep the basket on or near the table so the person responsible for getting the table set won't need to bother the cook to gather supplies.

- At the end of each meal, bring the tray to the kitchen, refill it, and return it to the table so that it'll be ready for the next day.

thereby saving you money as well. When you know what to cook, you'll also know what groceries to get, which can make shopping easier and more efficient.

Another mealtime chore that benefits from organized habits and systems is setting the table. Cut down on the time and effort this task requires by creating designated spots for the things that go on the table at each meal, as well as the things that need to come off the table before dinner can be served.

Table Linens

- If you regularly use table linens (such as tablecloths and napkins), store them near your regular dining spot.

- A wide drawer near the kitchen table and a hutch in the dining room are storage options. You can also use a decorative bin or basket to keep linens out but contained.

- If you store linens for more than one table, or for different occasions, together in the same spot, sort them by size, material, and/or occasion.

Multipurpose Table

- If the table you use for dining does double duty—as a sorting spot for mail, for example—set up a system to hold what you clear off before mealtime.

- Use a set of baskets or bins—one for each family member—on a shelf near the table, or use wall-mounted paper sorters.

- Before the meal, put each person's items and papers into his or her box; at the end of the meal, have family members clear their boxes.

BATHROOMS GREAT AND SMALL

Find the description that best matches your bathroom for customized organizing tips

The best way to organize your bathroom depends a lot on whether the space is shared or separate, who uses it, and what you need to store there. Read the following descriptions of different types of bathrooms, choose the one that most closely matches yours, and then read the tips for your bathroom type below the photo.

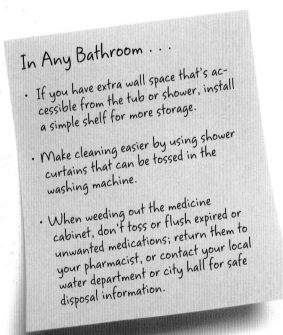

In Any Bathroom . . .

- If you have extra wall space that's accessible from the tub or shower, install a simple shelf for more storage.

- Make cleaning easier by using shower curtains that can be tossed in the washing machine.

- When weeding out the medicine cabinet, don't toss or flush expired or unwanted medications; return them to your pharmacist, or contact your local water department or city hall for safe disposal information.

Small, Shared Space

There's one full bathroom in my house, and I share it with my partner/housemate. I need efficient storage for essentials like towels and toiletries. I also want to be able to keep my stuff separate from my mate's and would love an easy way to distinguish whose stuff is whose.

In a Small, Shared Space . . .

- Put your bathroom's vertical space to use with a shelf unit that fits above the toilet and a rack on the back of the door.

- Assign each person his or her own towel rack, storage shelf, and spot for toiletries in the shower.

- If you buy toiletries in bulk, store only the amount you'll use over a few weeks in the bathroom; keep the original bottles or packages in a nearby closet for easy refills.

Family Zone

My kids share a bathroom, and the adults in the house sometimes use it as well. I want to stop fights about which towel belongs to which kid and about who owns the three bottles of shampoo cluttering up the shower floor. Bath time is enough of a zoo as is. I don't want it to be any crazier, so I'd love easy storage for bath-time essentials.

Spacious Retreat

I have a large bathroom with lots of toiletries and supplies, but I need a more organized way to store them. I'd like to keep surfaces clear so that the room looks neater and is easier to clean. There never seems to be enough space to hang towels and robes.

In a Family Zone . . .

- When it comes to basic toiletries (such as soap), choose items the whole family can use to cut down on tub and shower clutter.

- If there's not enough space in the bathroom for everyone's toiletries, have kids stash their products in portable containers they can carry back and forth to their rooms.

- Consider a multitiered, heated towel rack to hold the whole family's towels, help them dry more quickly, and keep them warm at bath or shower time.

In a Spacious Retreat . . .

- Splurge on built-in drawer dividers to create organized storage space in vanity drawers.

- Install sturdy hooks on the wall or the back of the bathroom door to hold large towels and heavy robes.

- Use decorative pumps and containers on the vanity and in the shower to keep these spaces looking neat, cohesive, and uncluttered.

MEDICINE CABINET

Clear the clutter and reorganize to make this bathroom staple a smart storage spot

ORGANIZING YOUR HOME

The medicine cabinet is meant to hold the lotions and potions that keep us healthy and looking good. Often, though, this space becomes cluttered with half-empty, out-of-date bottles and tubes amidst a jumble of cotton swabs, hair bands, and toothbrushes, making it hard to find anything. You can help your medicine cabinet reach its potential by doing some weeding, containing, and reorganizing.

Start by emptying the contents of the cabinet and tossing anything that's old, expired, potentially dangerous, or unusable. Resist the temptation to hold on to things you haven't used just because you paid good money for them, such as

What to Store

Toothpaste

Face cream

Toner

Cotton swabs

Tweezers

Bandages

Antibacterial cream

- Because it's subject to heat and moisture, the medicine cabinet isn't an ideal place to store prescription medications, which can be affected by high temperatures. Keep these in a cool, dry place out of the reach of children. (See page 52 for tips on storing medications.)

- Heat and moisture also damage makeup, changing the consistency and encouraging bacteria growth.

- The medicine cabinet is fine for most toiletries, basic first aid supplies, and dry goods like cotton balls and swabs.

Smart Containers

- Small containers that fit on your medicine cabinet shelves can corral items that tend to get scattered and messy, such as cotton swabs and small ointment tubes. Apothecary jars and rectangular pharmacist's boxes are two good options.

- Choose containers that are clear so that you can easily identify what's inside.

- Go for glass or sturdy plastic, both of which can stand up to heat and moisture while keeping their contents protected.

an expensive bottle of face cream, or because you might need them someday (such as multiple half-used tubes of first aid ointments). Reserve the space in the medicine cabinet exclusively for things you need and use on a regular basis.

After weeding, give the cabinet a quick cleaning, and then refill it. If your medicine cabinet has adjustable shelves, try moving them around to optimize the space for the things you're storing.

Keep things like cotton balls and hair accessories together in containers that fit on the shelves. These containers·can be useful for holding small portions of things you buy in bulk, such as cotton swabs: Fill a jar with enough swabs to last a few weeks, and store the rest of the box under the sink or in a closet for easy refills.

Take time every few months to purge the medicine cabinet of anything you no longer need to ensure that what is there is safe, useful, and easily accessible.

Creating Extra Storage

- If you don't have a built-in medicine cabinet, or if you need extra storage space, use shelves or drawers near the sink.

- Follow the same steps you would to organize a cabinet: Collect small items in containers, group things in logical categories, and label shelves or drawers so that everyone knows what's where.

- Drawer dividers can help bring an extra measure of order, especially in deep drawers; they can also prevent things from falling over when you open the drawer.

Easy Organizing Systems: Dividing the Space

- Group things in the medicine cabinet by categories that make sense to you: size (all tall bottles together), type of product (all first aid supplies together), owner (all of one family member's items together), or how you use the products (all morning-routine supplies on one shelf).

- If you share the cabinet with others, label the shelves so that everyone knows what should go where.

- Keep shared and kid-friendly items together on an easily accessible shelf.

UNDER THE SINK

Use this space for supplies and bring an extra measure of calm to the room

The area underneath the bathroom sink often winds up as a holding zone for things that don't fit or belong in other bathroom storage spots, such as extra toilet paper, cleaning supplies, and bulk toiletries. While this can be a smart place to stash these items, it can also become a dumping ground if you don't have a plan for what goes where.

The first step in figuring out how to make the best use of this space is deciding what should go there. Perhaps the area under the sink is a great spot for the big bottles of shampoo that take up too much space in your shower, for example, or for the cleaning supplies you use in the bathroom each week.

Pedestal Sinks

- If your sink isn't mounted in a vanity, rely on separate shelves or cabinets to provide storage space.

- Another option is a sink skirt, which attaches to the edge of the sink and drapes to the floor, hiding whatever is stored underneath.

- Make the most of the space by using bins that fit neatly in the space and hold the things you want to store. Plastic bins with lids are a good bet because they seal tightly and repel water.

Open Shelving

- Decorative baskets and containers are good options for storing things in a visually pleasing way on open shelves under the sink.

- Use large open baskets for rolled or folded towels and washcloths. Containers with lids can hold extra toilet paper and tissue boxes, cleaning supplies, and bulk items like bags of cotton balls and large bottles of shampoo.

- Glass apothecary jars are a clean, uncluttered way of containing bars of soap, bath salts, and other dry toiletries.

With your ideal storage plan in mind, go through the items currently under the sink. Get rid of any trash or unwanted, un-needed things, and relocate anything that you want to keep but that should go elsewhere (such as toys or makeup).

Post-purge, bring in the items you want to stash there. The best way to store things will depend largely on what kind of sink you have and whether there's built-in storage under it. You'll have more leeway if your sink is in a vanity that has cabinets and drawers, but you can easily put the space under and around a pedestal or wall-mounted sink to use with a sink skirt that hides what's stored underneath or with free-standing units.

Once it's organized to your satisfaction, keep this area neat by making it a regular habit to sort through and clear out the things that accumulate to avoid clutter.

Working around Pipes

- One of the challenges of using the area under your sink for storage is working around pipes, which can eat up space and make it hard to fit small shelves and bins here.

- You can work around this obstacle by using an adjust-able shelf unit with a cut-out section for the sink's drainpipe.

- Because these units are cus-tomizable, you can snap to-gether as many sections as you need to fit your space.

Pullout Baskets

- Bring some order to the cabinets under your sink and make it easy to get at everything easily by install-ing pullout baskets. These baskets snap onto gliders that attach to the bottom of the cabinet.

- Pullouts are especially useful if your cabinets are deep, or for anyone who has difficulty bending down to reach what's in the cabinet.

- Look for a basket with a solid base or a liner; small items can easily slip through open-grid baskets.

TOWEL RACKS

Choose the best rack to keep towels at the ready and to increase your overall storage space

If you've ever stepped out of the shower, reached for a towel, and found none—or a damp one that's already done its drying work for the day—you know the frustration of ineffective towel storage. This is especially common in shared bathrooms, where it can be nearly impossible to know whose towel is whose and where towels sometimes seem to disappear without a trace. Choosing a rack that keeps towels in order is an important step in conquering towel chaos.

First and foremost, the rack you select should provide enough space for everyone's towels. In busy bathrooms, a collection of smaller bars or hooks is a better option than a few large racks, because each person will have a designated spot

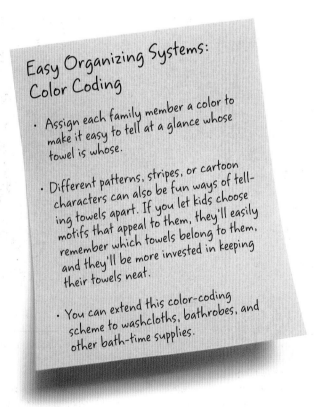

Easy Organizing Systems: Color Coding

- Assign each family member a color to make it easy to tell at a glance whose towel is whose.

- Different patterns, stripes, or cartoon characters can also be fun ways of telling towels apart. If you let kids choose motifs that appeal to them, they'll easily remember which towels belong to them, and they'll be more invested in keeping their towels neat.

- You can extend this color-coding scheme to washcloths, bathrobes, and other bath-time supplies.

Maximizing Wall Space

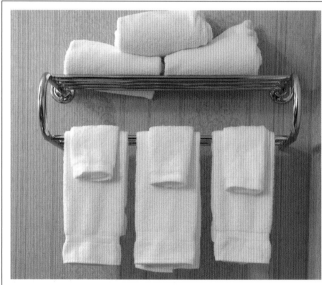

- To make the most of your wall space, hang towel racks or hooks vertically at varying heights, rather than side by side.

- Racks hung high are great for longer towels. Low racks are easy for children to reach; be sure to mount the rack high enough that towels don't drag on the floor.

- If you don't have much wall space, look for a towel rack that hangs over or on the back of the door.

and there will be less potential for confusion and swapped towels. Longer bars work well in bathrooms used by only one or two people.

(If family members dry off in the bathroom and then wear towels back to their bedrooms, install a towel bar or hook on the back of each bedroom door; this will help prevent towels from winding up in a heap on beds and floors.)

The towel storage you choose should also blend with your bathroom decor to present a unified look, which helps make the room seem more open and less cluttered.

Finally, if you're pinched for storage space elsewhere in the bathroom, consider a towel rack that can do double duty, such as one with a shelf above for holding bins or baskets of supplies.

Multifunctional Racks

- For an extra dose of storage space, look for towel racks with shelves above the bars.

- Use these shelves to hold folded towels, baskets of extra toiletries, and kids' bath toys and supplies.

- If your bathroom is very small, use a towel hook to hold a hanging travel Dopp kit, or grooming kit, which can serve as a portable medicine cabinet, corralling toiletries and other personal-care supplies.

Keeping Towels in Place

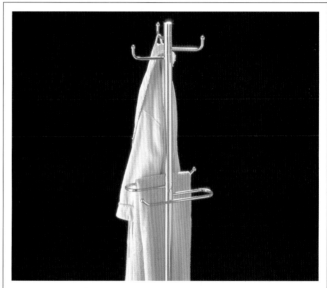

- Keep towels from slipping off their racks by attaching a thin strip of plastic shelf liner to the top of the towel bar. (Make sure the textured side of the liner faces up.) This provides enough friction to keep the towel in place.

- If you use hooks, sew simple fabric loops onto the edges of your towels, and hang the towels from these loops.

- Heavy-duty clips (such as large binder clips) also keep slipping towels in place.

BATHROOM

TUB

Create a safe, clutter-free tub area with bath essentials close at hand

A relaxing bath is often interrupted by kids, pets, and other distractions, not to mention a cluttered tub. Luckily, there are inexpensive, effective organizing systems that keep chaos at bay and keep the bath supplies you need within easy reach.

An organized tub starts with a decluttering session. Gather together everything on, in, and near the tub, including toiletries and tub toys; toss anything that's damaged or has outlived its usefulness, and consolidate toiletries if you have partial bottles of the same thing.

After you've weeded, plan your storage. The systems you choose will depend on what sort of tub you have (one with or without ledges, for example), how many things you need

Using Ledges

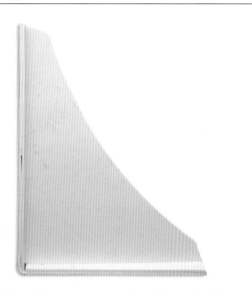

- Most built-in tubs have flat ledges that offer some storage space for bottles of toiletries and small bath toys.

- Prevent things from falling off the ledges on the outer side of the tub with edge shelves, simple wedges of plastic that attach to the tub and the wall with suction cups or adhesive.

- Because ledges don't drain well on their own, be sure to wipe them down regularly, and don't use them to store highly absorbent things like washcloths and sponges.

Vertical Storage

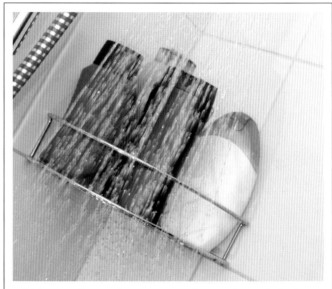

- Make use of vertical storage space with small suction racks that attach to the sides of the tub or the surrounding walls.

- Suction racks tend to drain quickly, making them useful for soap and sponges.

- These racks aren't the best option for heavy toiletry bottles.

- Hang suction racks high enough on the tub sides so that they're not submerged when the tub is full, but low enough so that they're easy to reach when you're sitting in the tub.

to store, and whether there are items that need to be kept within (or out of) children's reach.

Because the tub area gets wet often, it's important to choose storage that allows for easy drainage and drying; items sitting in pools of water can grow mold, especially if they're made of cloth or natural materials (like sponges).

To keep clutter to a minimum in the bath area, avoid storing bulk-size bottles of toiletries like shampoo and conditioner here. If you do buy in bulk, transfer your toiletries to smaller bottles to keep in the tub, and stash the large bottles under the sink or in another out-of-the-way place.

Finally, include putting away toys and supplies as part of any bath-time routine. Getting kids involved with this helps them take responsibility for their own stuff and cuts down on the amount of cleanup work parents have to do.

Over-Tub Racks

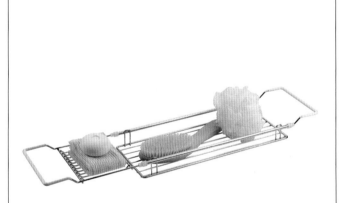

- To keep things easily accessible when you're in the tub, and as general storage in a freestanding tub, use a rack that sits over the tub.

- These racks tend to be expandable, so they fit tubs of different widths.

- Use the rack for your bath supplies (such as toiletries and a book or toys). Between baths, slide the rack out of the way and use it to stash and drain supplies.

Wall-Mounted Organizers

- Keep the tub clear and make the most of the area around it by using a wall-mounted organizer.

- These systems include a base (such as pegboard) and storage units that attach to the base. Look for a system that's customizable to your space.

- Wall-mounted systems aren't ideal for shower-over-tub units, because the wetness and moisture from showers can affect both the items stored in the system and the adhesive used to attach the system to the wall.

39

SHOWER

Make your daily routine more efficient by using uncluttered shower storage

All too often, showers become a complex tangle of bottles, tubes, bars, and gadgets, making the process of washing up more crowded and stressful than it should be. In a well-organized shower, there's sufficient, easily accessible, un-cluttered space to store the things you need.

Before deciding what to stash in your shower and how to store it, take some time to go through what's there and weed out what you don't need. Get rid of empty bottles, toiletries you no longer use, and things like razors and bars of soap that are past their prime. Combine partially full bottles of shampoo, conditioner, and bath gel.

When you've cleared out the shower, choose the best

Showerhead Storage

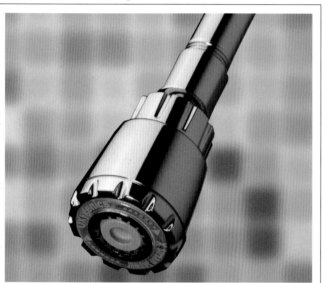

- If your showerhead is firmly attached to the wall, consider a storage rack that hangs from it.

- These racks are especially useful in stall showers, where there may not be any ledges for storing toiletries.

- Choose a rack made of sturdy plastic or coated metal. Look for one that has enough shelves to hold your supplies, and make sure these shelves have high sides to keep bottles and bars from falling off.

Floor Storage

- Another option for stall showers is to store toiletries in a waterproof basket on the floor.

- Choose a basket that is large enough to hold all of your supplies and is made of a sturdy, easy-to-clean material (like plastic or coated metal).

- Having all of your toiletries together in a basket, rather than loose on the floor, makes cleaning the shower easier. Take out the basket when you're ready to clean the stall, and return it when you're done.

way to store the things that remain. Your storage options will depend on what sort of shower you have (one with a showerhead attached to the wall, for example) and on how much you need to keep there. Storage options include over-showerhead racks, waterproof baskets, tension rod racks, and wall-mounted units.

Once it's organized, keep your shower neat by making it a habit to limit open bottles of toiletries to one per type, getting rid of bottles as soon as they're empty, and wiping down walls and shelves regularly.

Tension Rod Racks

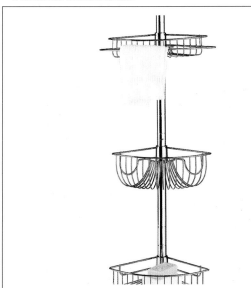

- Increase your corner storage space with a tension rod rack, which has a telescoping rod that can be adjusted to fit showers of various heights.

- Look for a rack with sturdy shelves that have sides high enough to keep bottles and tubes from falling off.

- Also make sure the rod tightens securely to prevent the rack from collapsing when you put things on it.

Neat Toiletries

- To bring an extra measure of neatness to your shower, transfer toiletries from their original bottles to clear plastic bottles.

- Standardizing the size of toiletry bottles can also help even out weight distribution on racks, keeping the racks sturdier and making things less likely to fall.

- Prevent mix-ups by labeling bottles with their contents, using either label tape or an indelible marker.

BATHROOM

LINEN CLOSET

Identify the type of linen closet you have for organizing tips specific to your space

The best way to get your linen closet in great organizational shape depends a lot on what, exactly, your linen closet is: a sliver of space in the hallway, a full closet with room to spare, or a few boxes tucked in various places throughout the house. Take a look at the following descriptions of different linen closets. Choose the one that most accurately matches your space, and then read the specific tips below the photo.

Small but Functional Space

I have a small linen closet with enough space for basic storage, and I want to be sure I'm using it as efficiently as I can. I want to make it easy for other members of the family to find things in

In a Small but Functional Space . . .

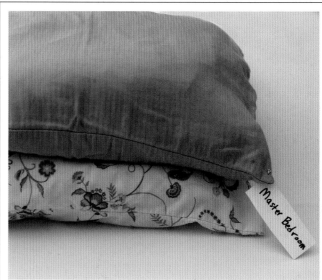

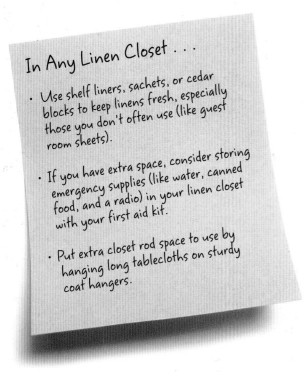

In Any Linen Closet . . .

• Use shelf liners, sachets, or cedar blocks to keep linens fresh, especially those you don't often use (like guest room sheets).

• If you have extra space, consider storing emergency supplies (like water, canned food, and a radio) in your linen closet with your first aid kit.

• Put extra closet rod space to use by hanging long tablecloths on sturdy coat hangers.

• Store sheet sets together in pillowcases, and separate them by bed size or room.

• Use shelf expanders to create extra space if you need it. Store flat and fitted sheets on top of the expander and pillowcases under it.

• Use sturdy plastic bins on the floor or on a high shelf to store utility basics and extra toiletries.

• Keep kids' sheets and towels on low shelves for easy access.

here. If I can find room, I'd love to be able to store a few other things, like some extra toilet paper and a few spare lightbulbs.

Full Closet

I have a full linen closet, but it's not always well organized. I want to keep different linens separate; sometimes they all seem to wind up on the same shelf. There's enough space here to store other things, but I'm not sure how best to use it. I want an easy way to remember where things go so that they get put away in the right places.

No Closet to Speak of

My linen storage isn't in a separate space; it's part of another closet . . . and sometimes under beds . . . and in the bathroom. Sheet and towel sets often get separated because they're stored in so many different spots. I wish I had space to stash toiletries and first aid supplies somewhere I'd remember.

In a Full Closet . . .

- Label shelves with what belongs on each one, or create a storage map—a diagram of what goes where—and post it inside the closet door.

- If linens don't take up the full space of a shelf, install shelf dividers and use the extra space to store other things.

- Use baskets or bins to keep similar linens together— one basket for twin-size flat sheets, one for twin-size fitted sheets, and so on.

In No Closet to Speak Of . . .

- Use plastic or cloth sweater bins to store sheets and towels on bedroom closet shelves or under beds.

- If you have a closet with extra rod space, clip towel sets to pants or skirt hangers and hang them up.

- A freestanding cabinet in a bedroom or hallway can provide contained, unobtrusive storage for linens and extra toiletries.

STORING TOWELS

Keep towels neat, clean, and ready for use with simple, realistic storage solutions

If you've ever experienced an avalanche of towels upon opening a linen closet, you know how challenging it can be to keep control over these piles of terrycloth. Towels can sometimes seem to multiply, unfold themselves, get mixed in with other linens, and generally cause closet chaos, all without any help from humans. It's time to take control.

One of the most common issues with towels is that there are too many of them, which is why step one is gathering all of them together (including any in use) and doing a towel audit. If you come across any that are wearing thin, fraying around the edges, or otherwise showing signs of overuse, get rid of them. The towels that deserve space in your linen

ORGANIZING YOUR HOME

Closet Space for Towels

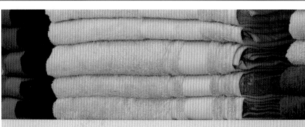

- A linen closet is a great place to store towels, because they won't be affected by bathroom humidity there.

- Designate a specific shelf for towels, rather than storing them together with sheets or other linens. If you

need to share shelf space, use a divider and keep towels on one side, linens on the other.

- Store towels together based on how you use them: by size, by set, or by color.

Basket Storage

- If you don't have a linen closet, or simply prefer to have extra towels handy in the bathroom, consider using a large basket to stash rolled towels.

- Rolled towels are easier to grab from a basket than folded ones, and you won't have to worry about rotating towels from the bottom of the basket.

- Baskets add both extra storage space and a nice decorative touch to bathrooms.

closet or bathroom are those that are soft, absorbent, and comfortable.

Next, choose the best spot for storing your whittled-down towel collection. If you have a separate linen closet, designate a shelf (or part of one) for towels. Otherwise, consider a basket of towels on a shelf or in a stand-alone cabinet in the bathroom.

Finally, fold or roll towels neatly to maximize storage space, make them easy to grab, and keep chaos at bay.

········· GREEN ● LIGHT ············

Make good use of towels that are no longer bathroom-worthy by cutting them into scraps for use as kitchen rags, car-washing cloths, or craft cleanup towels, Or donate them to your local animal shelter, which can use them as bedding for the cats and dogs in its care.

Additional Shelves and Cabinets

- Freestanding shelves or cabinets can provide space for stashing towels if you don't have enough built-in storage.

- Look for a storage unit that has enough space to hold your towels comfortably.

- Don't store towels below anything that could spill or leak on them, such as toiletry bottles.

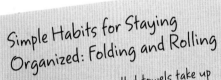

Simple Habits for Staying Organized: Folding and Rolling

- Neatly folded or rolled towels take up less storage space and are easier to organize.

- To fold a bath towel, hold it in front of you with the edge seam facing away. Fold a third of the towel toward the middle, then fold the opposite side over it. Fold the towel in half lengthwise, then in half again.

- To roll a towel, fold it in half or thirds, and then roll it up lengthwise.

LINEN CLOSET

STORING BED LINENS

Make changing sheets easy and efficient with neat, smart, and simple storage

Mixing and matching sheet sets is fine if you do it on purpose—to add an extra jolt of color or pattern to an otherwise staid bed, for example. If you're forced to do it because you can't find a sheet's mates in a chaotic linen closet, though, that's another story. Organized sheet storage makes changing bed linens easier and helps prevent unplanned sheet combinations.

Start by taking stock of the sheets, pillowcases, and other bed linens you have. Thin, worn linens; patterned sheets that have no mates (and that don't match with any of the solid sheets you have); stretched-out fitted sheets; and decorative linens (such as shams and bed skirts) you don't use don't deserve storage space. Cut them into rags or put them in a

Storing Sets

- Make it easy to grab a bed set—flat sheet, fitted sheet, pillowcases—by storing sheet sets together in stacks.

- When you're ready to make a bed, grab the stack you need.

- To make sure parts of a set don't get lost, store the entire set in a pillowcase.

- If there are components of the set you don't change frequently, such as pillow shams or bed skirts, store them behind or under the sheets on the same shelf.

Storing Sheets by Room

Master Bedroom

- If each family member has specific sheets that go on his or her bed, store sheets together by room.

- In a linen closet, label shelves with everyone's name so that it's easy to grab sheets for each person.

- You might choose to store sheets in each bedroom to make changing the bed a snap. Use a drawer or closed basket under the bed, or stash sheet sets on a shelf in the closet.

donation bin (if they're still in good shape).

Next, decide where and how to best store the sheets you want to keep: in a linen closet, in the bedrooms where the sheets are used, or in shelves or a cabinet elsewhere in the house. Where you store your sheets will help determine how to store them: by size, in sets, or by room or family member.

Finally, keep sheets clean and fresh by making sure they're completely dry before you put them away.

Storing Sheets by Size

- If your sheets are interchangeable between beds, store them together by size.

- Keep solid sheets that can be mixed or matched in stacks by type: fitted sheets in one stack, flat sheets in another, and pillowcases in a third.

- If you store sheets somewhere other than a linen closet, keep them in baskets so that they don't get mixed in with other things.

Storing Bulky Items

- Bedding like pillows, blankets, and comforters can take up significant storage space. For these items, consider using compressed storage bags.

- These bags look like large zip-top bags; some have a valve on the side that allows you to extract air with a vacuum cleaner for extra compression.

- Once you've filled them, store compression bags in an out-of-the-way spot like a high shelf in your linen closet.

LINEN CLOSET

PAPER GOODS

Establish a designated storage spot to keep extra paper goods organized and easily accessible

Buying paper goods like toilet paper, tissues, and paper towels in bulk can be a significant savings over purchasing smaller packages. The downside, of course, is finding space to store these items. Even if you're not a bulk shopper, you probably have more paper goods on hand than you're currently using. A smart solution is to keep some reserves easily available in the bathroom and to stash the rest in a linen or utility closet.

Before you plot out space for bulk paper goods, though, think seriously about whether you have room to store them. If you have a small bathroom, no linen closet, and little by way of utility storage, the space and effort it takes to stash

Storage Baskets

- Use baskets or bins to keep paper goods together and organized.

- Decorative baskets (perhaps with lids to hide the products) are a good option if your storage isn't behind closed doors.

- Transferring paper goods from their original packaging to baskets or bins makes it easier to keep track of when your supplies are running low and prevents plastic wrappers from taking over cabinets and closets. It also adds a neat look to your storage space.

Closet Storage

- If you have a linen closet, earmark space in it for storing paper goods.

- A full shelf is ideal (especially for bulk packages), but even a smaller strip of shelf space can be useful.

- On shared shelves, use shelf dividers to keep paper goods and other items separate. Shelf dividers attach directly to shelves and stand upright, making it easy to create distinct stacks.

ORGANIZING YOUR HOME

extra boxes of tissues probably aren't worth the few dollars you'll save by buying in bulk. On the other hand, if you have extra storage available, bulk purchases make sense.

To plan your storage, first determine how much of each type of paper good you can (and need to) store in the bathroom—perhaps three rolls of toilet paper, a box of tissues, and a roll of paper towels. Then, plan how to best store the remainders in your linen closet.

Bathroom Storage

- Whether or not you have storage elsewhere, it's smart to keep a few extra paper goods in the bathroom for quick and easy access.

- Stick some rolls of toilet paper and a box of tissues in a drawer, on a shelf, or in a cabinet. Replenish this supply as needed.

- If you don't have room in a drawer or cabinet, consider a toilet paper roll holder—a cylindrical container that lets you stash three or four rolls.

Cabinet Storage

- When storing paper goods in a bathroom cabinet, use drawers, bins, or other dividers to keep them separate from other supplies.

- Ideally, opt for a drawer large enough to hold both toilet paper and tissues.

- If you use an under-sink cabinet, choose solid drawers or waterproof, covered bins to keep paper goods dry.

UTILITY SUPPLIES

Create convenient storage for basic first aid, home safety, and maintenance supplies

Many homes have storage areas that hold basic household supplies like lightbulbs, batteries, tools, and first aid kits. But if you're on the second floor of your home and your utility closet is on the first, retrieving the supplies you need requires extra effort. It makes sense, then, to keep some essential home care and maintenance supplies in your linen closet so that they're easy to grab when you need them.

These items shouldn't take up too much space in your linen closet—it's meant primarily for linens, after all, and chances are you have additional storage for household supplies elsewhere. To organize your utility supplies, decide what stuff you really need to store here. In most homes, a few flashlights, a

Choose the Right Bins

- Use clear, sturdy plastic bins to store utility supplies. Keep heavy supplies like tools in separate bins from fragile items (such as lightbulbs).

- Look for bins that are easy to stack.

- Label each bin with its general contents (tools, batteries, and so on).

- Keep the supplies you use most often in the top bins so that they're easy to grab quickly.

First Aid Kit

FIRST AID KIT

- Keep a stocked first aid kit with the utility supplies in your linen closet (or in your bathroom if you don't have a linen closet).

- You can purchase a pre-packed first aid kit or create your own.

- Be sure your kit includes these basics: adhesive bandages, sterile wound dressings, burn ointment, antibiotic ointment, cleanser, antibiotic towelettes, emergency prescription medications (such as insulin and asthma inhalers), and latex or other sterile gloves.

pack of batteries, a package of lightbulbs, some simple tools, and a good first aid kit should do the trick. Tuck a small step-stool under the closet's bottom shelf or along the wall if you have room.

Store your supplies together in sturdy plastic bins. If you're pinched for space in your linen closet, you can stack other things on top of the utility bins; make sure, though, to keep a flashlight and the first aid kit out so that you don't have to dig for them in an emergency.

Tools and Repair Supplies

- Make simple repairs quick and easy by keeping basic tools and supplies in your linen closet.

- Include a few standard tools and pieces of hardware (nails and screws), duct and/or painter's tape, a tape measure, batteries, and lightbulbs.

- Another option is a pre-stocked tool kit, which you can find at your local hardware or department store.

- If you have young children, store your utility supplies on a shelf they won't be able to reach.

Keep Tabs on Supplies

AA batteries—use by Jan. 2012
Aspirin—use by end of year
Ken's extra asthma inhaler—use by November
Bandages—check supply at end of month
Sunblock—use by end of next summer

- Create an inventory of your utility supplies, and post it near your supply bins or inside the door of your linen closet. Include expiration dates for medications and other perishables.

- Every few months, check supply levels and replenish them as needed. Also check to be sure that flashlights work and batteries are still fresh.

- When taking inventory of your first aid kit, check the expiration dates on ointments and medications. Replace them if they're past their prime. (Outdated supplies lose potency and efficacy.)

51

PERSONAL SUPPLIES

Use extra linen closet space as storage for extra toiletries, medications, and personal supplies

The linen closet can hold more than linens. If you have additional space there after storing towels and bedding, use it for things you might otherwise have to cram into bathroom cabinets or put elsewhere in the house: extra toiletries, medications, and personal supplies. Keeping these items away from the heat and moisture of the bathroom will help preserve them, and you'll be able to devote bathroom storage space to the things you use every day.

To decide how much room you need for your extra supplies, gather them together in one spot from wherever they're currently stored. This will give you a clear sense of what you have. It will also let you see what you have multiples of: Consolidate

ORGANIZING YOUR HOME

Extra Toiletries

- Keep extra toiletries and personal supplies ready for use by lining them up in an easy-to-access spot in the closet.

- A simple tray, bin, or basket will let you group toiletries together by type (shampoos with conditioners, and so on.)

- If you have toiletry multiples, put the oldest bottle, tube, or package in front and the newest in back to keep your stock fresh and to make it easy to use up the oldest supplies first.

Medications

- Because many medications (both prescription and over-the-counter) lose potency when stored in a warm, damp bathroom, the linen closet is a good alternative spot.

- Gather medications in a bin—preferably one that's clear (so that it's easy to identify what's inside) and has a lid to keep everything contained.

- Store medications on a shelf that kids and pets can't reach.

these if they're not in full containers, and make a note not to buy more until you've worked through your existing stash.

Based on what you have to store, choose a convenient spot on a shelf, in a drawer, or on the floor. Aim to keep all of these supplies grouped together in one area, rather than spreading them throughout the closet. If you have several items, gather them in a container to keep them neat and to prevent them from getting lost.

Storage by Person

- If family members have specific toiletries and medications, use personalized bins or baskets in the linen closet.

- Give each person the responsibility for refilling his or her basket after a shopping trip and for shuttling supplies between the closet and the bathroom.

- Short on tub or shower storage space? Have family members keep all of their toiletries and supplies in portable bins. Store them in the linen closet and bring them to the bathroom as needed.

Keeping a Supply Inventory

- Make sure you always have the supplies you need on hand by creating an inventory sheet and posting it in the closet.

- List the items you normally store here: specific toiletries, personal supplies, paper goods.

- Leave space on the inventory sheet to make a note when it's time to restock a supply.

- Before shopping trips, check this inventory to see what you need to buy.

LINEN CLOSET

53

BEDROOM

Discover your bedroom type and find organizing tips to help make the most of the space

What kind of space do you want your bedroom to be: a clear, simple room? a place to escape from the world? a spot for cuddling up with your kids and your significant other? Discovering what room you want will help you determine the best way to organize it. Choose the bedroom description that most appeals to you, and then read the specific tips for your room type.

In Any Bedroom . . .

- If possible, avoid using your bedroom as an office space. If you must set up a desk here, choose one that closes (such as an armoire), and don't let it serve as a clutter collector.

- Move baby supplies and furniture—such as a crib and changing table—out of the master bedroom as soon as your child is old enough to sleep in a nursery.

- Include a bedroom-decluttering session in your spring cleaning task list.

Simple Space

I like to keep my bedroom as clean and clear as possible, with most of my stuff tucked away. I need accessible storage for everyday things, but I don't want them to be out and visible. My ideal room would have a modern, spare aesthetic but wouldn't feel cold or unwelcoming.

In a Simple Space . . .

- Use a bedside table with drawers or a cabinet to store things you want handy but not out in the open.

- Closed containers under your bed offer more out-of-the-way storage space.

- Choose simple, unembellished furniture and solid bedding to make your bedroom look as uncluttered as possible.

Calming Retreat

I want my bedroom to have few signs or reminders of the outside world. I need to be able to put stuff away quickly and easily at the end of the day so that my space doesn't get cluttered. My ideal room would have a warm, comfortable, inviting aesthetic.

Family Spot

My kids spend time in my bedroom for stories, games, and the occasional overnight, so I want the room to be comfortable and kid-friendly. I want a place to store things like books and toys so that they're easy to take out when the kids are around and just as easy to put away. I need to keep small and valuable stuff out of the kids' reach.

In a Calming Retreat . . .

- Avoid having a TV set in your bedroom. Instead, stock the space with reading material and relaxing CDs.

- Look for furniture, bedding, and paint in soothing tones. Avoid very bright or very dark colors.

- Create storage spots for accessories and everyday essentials on top of your dresser or right inside the closet for easy drop-offs at the end of the day.

In a Family Spot . . .

- Create designated spots for storing books or toys in bedside tables or in the closet, and keep only a few of each on hand at any one time. Most of your kids' stuff should be stored in their rooms.

- Stash coins, jewelry, and other items that aren't kid-friendly in containers on your dresser top.

- Keep valuable or breakable decorative items (such as vases) up high, or use them in other rooms.

BEDSIDE TABLE

Clear the clutter and store what you need to create a calm, peaceful area for sleep

The bedside table is an ideal spot for keeping the things you use for nighttime and morning routines, such as reading material, an alarm clock, and a small lamp. Too often, though, these tables become repositories for clutter, making it difficult to relax. Don't let an overcrowded bedside table be the last thing you see at night and the first thing you see in the morning. With a few easy steps, you can reclaim this space as one for simple storage for essentials.

Start by sorting through the things in and around your bedside table. Throw away any trash, put away or recycle books and magazines you've read, and get rid of anything you don't want, use, or need. Remember that the main purpose of your

ORGANIZING YOUR HOME

Table with a Drawer

- A bedside table with one or two drawers lets you store small items while keeping the tabletop clear and uncluttered.

- You can also use the drawers in a bedside table to stash pajamas, socks, and other clothes you wear to bed.

- If you choose a table with a drawer and a shelf, use the shelf to hold decorative bins or baskets, which you can use to store reading material or other bedside necessities.

Table with a Cabinet

- Choose a bedside table with a cabinet if you want more closed storage space than a drawer can offer.

- A unit that also has a drawer or an open shelf above provides convenient space for stowing smaller things (like earplugs or an eye mask).

- Be sure the table you choose has a cabinet door that opens away from the bed, not toward it.

bedside table is to hold the things you use before and after sleep; if things that belong elsewhere in the bedroom—or somewhere else entirely—have migrated here, return them to their rightful homes.

After you've cleared the space, take a look at your table. Does it provide enough storage for the things you want to keep here? Does it fit the space it's in? Do you like looking at it? If you can't answer yes to all three of those questions, it might be time for a new bedside table.

The table you choose should fit comfortably next to your bed and work with the rest of your bedroom decor. Look for a model that's no more than a foot higher than your mattress to avoid the feeling of being boxed in when you're lying down. Opt for a table with drawers, shelves, or a cabinet if you have several things to store here; if you need only a lamp, a clock, and a box of tissues, consider a simpler table.

Basic Table

- A basic bedside table is a good option if you don't need to store much near your bed. Any flat, stable surface, such as a low stool or a decorative basket, can serve as a bedside table.

- Choose a table that can comfortably fit your essentials: a lamp, an alarm clock, a book, a box of tissues.

- Keep things like earplugs or medication from getting lost by storing them in a small box or basket with a lid.

Guest Room Table

- In a guest bedroom, provide space for simple things like a lamp, a magazine, and a glass of water with a basic bedside table.

- Keep guest room bedside tables relatively clear so that your guests can use them without having to move things around.

- Give guests a warm welcome by leaving water glasses, a few pieces of reading material, and perhaps a small vase of flowers on their bedside tables.

UNDER-BED STORAGE
Create a clutter-free, convenient storage space for bedding, clothes, and other essentials

What's lurking under your bed? If you don't know, it's time to reacquaint yourself with the things you've stashed there. If there's nothing below your mattress, you might be missing out on valuable storage. This space can be a great spot for extra storage.

Before you can make the most of this space, though, it's worth taking the time to clear it. Pull out everything that's currently under your bed and sort through it; toss whatever you don't want, need, or use, as well as anything that's trash. If you come across things that belong elsewhere, return them to their proper homes. You might also want to take this opportunity to sweep or vacuum under the bed.

Built-in Drawers

- If you're in the market for a new bed frame, consider one with built-in drawers underneath.

- Beds with built-in drawers let you significantly increase storage space and bring a clean, uncluttered look to the room.

- Be sure to situate this type of bed so that it's easy to open each drawer all the way in order to make full use of the space.

Separate Drawers

- If your bed frame doesn't have drawers built in, look for separate storage drawers you can use in this space.

- Drawers on wheels or sliders allow for easy access.

- Maintain visual harmony by choosing an under-bed drawer unit that blends with the color and material of your bed frame.

- Measure the space around your bed to be sure there's room to pull drawers out far enough to make full use of them.

Once you've weeded, look at what remains and decide what truly belongs under the bed. (If you start from scratch, think about things you'd like to store in the bedroom that are currently somewhere else.) Good candidates for this space are extra bedding and bulky or out-of-season clothes.

Based on what you need to store and what type of bed you have, choose drawers or boxes that will hold your things, keep them free of dust, and make them easy to access. If you don't want to see what's under the bed, add a dust ruffle or a long comforter to keep the space camouflaged.

ZOOM

According to *feng shui,* the ancient Chinese art of placement, the space under your bed should be kept clear to prevent stuck *chi,* or energy. If you do store things here, keep the space clean, avoid cramming it with too much stuff, and use containers to keep things neat and organized.

Bins and Baskets

- If you don't want or don't have space for a full drawer, sturdy bins and boxes are good options for under-bed storage.

- Look for containers that will fit easily under the bed (even when full), that blend with the room's decor, and that are large enough to hold what you'd like to store.

- Choose containers with lids if you plan to store things you want to keep free of dust, such as bedding or clothes.

Storage Chests

- If you have a low bed frame or prefer to keep the space under your bed clear, consider using a storage chest at the foot of the bed.

- Chests are great options for large or bulky items like blankets and pillows.

- If you'll be using a chest to store bedding or clothes, look for one made of (or lined with) cedar for an extra measure of protection against pests.

59

THE REMAINS OF THE DAY

Create designated spots for things you shed at the end of the day to avoid clutter

ORGANIZING YOUR HOME

A few coins, a business card or two, and a tube of lip balm don't seem like they could do much damage. Over time, though, these things—the small items emptied out of pockets, purses, and briefcases at the end of the day—tend to gain a critical mass and wind up as frustrating piles of clutter on dressers and bedside tables. Add to the mix the clothes

you take off before bed and you have the recipe for a mess. Creating a designated spot for these odds and ends keeps them from overtaking your bedroom.

To design the most effective organizing system for these things, you first need to know what tends to accumulate and how much space you'll need to corral them. Start by collect-

Choosing Containers

- Use decorative containers on the surfaces that tend to collect end-of-day clutter—usually dressers and bedside tables—to store coins, cards, and other items.

- Choose containers that coordinate with your bedroom decor so that they don't look out of place and are more pleasant to use.

- Opt for the smallest container you need to hold a week's worth of stuff, and empty it regularly.

Clothes Hampers

- Keeping a hamper handy in your bedroom makes it easy to toss in dirty clothes as soon as you take them off.

- If you have room, consider a divided hamper so that you can separate whites, colors, and delicates, which will save you time come laundry day.

- You can also use one of the compartments to collect dry cleaning and other items that can't be machine-washed.

ing the coins, cards, keys, and other items that have gathered on any flat surfaces in your bedroom. Toss anything that's trash (gum wrappers, old receipts), as well as anything you no longer want or need. Put dirty clothes in a hamper and hang or fold any that are clean.

Then take a look at what's left and separate things into categories. Those categories will help you determine what storage containers you need; if you find you've collected a lot of coins, for example, you'll want to set up a change jar. Look for containers that won't look cluttered on your dresser and that are large enough to store the things you accumulate over the week.

If you find that the clothes you remove at night tend to pile up on a chair or the edge of the bed, set up a convenient hamper and valet to make it easy to put clothes away.

Valet Hooks

- Hang a valet hook on your closet or bedroom door to create a spot for clothes you might be able to wear again before washing.

- When you take off an item of clothing that doesn't seem dirty, put it on a hanger in the valet rack. Check it the next morning:

If it seems clean enough, return it to the closet; if it's dirty, put it in the hamper.

- Look for a valet hook that folds down when not in use to make it easier to open and close the door.

Simple Habits for Staying Organized: Clutter-Free Habits

- Once your systems are in place, get in the habit of using them nightly. Put things in their containers, hang possibly clean clothes, and toss dirty items in the hamper.

- Set a small wastebasket next to your dresser or bedside table, and use it for wrappers, paper scraps, and other unneeded things you empty out each evening.

- Take time at the end of each week to empty your containers and deal with laundry.

DRESSER TOP AND VANITY

Keep essentials like toiletries and hair care supplies organized, neatly stashed, and easily accessible

When the finer points of morning and evening routines—such as grooming hair and applying or removing makeup—happen in the bedroom, the supplies for those tasks can overrun dressers and vanities, but it can still be hard to find the things you need when you need them. Getting your dresser top or vanity organized can help save valuable time in the morning and remove stress at the end of the day.

Start the organizing process by clearing everything from the surface you're working on and then sorting through things one at a time. Get rid of empty bottles and tubes, toiletries that have gone bad (or that you haven't used in recent memory), and anything that's damaged beyond use or re-

Dresser-Top Essentials

- Storing toiletries like deodorant, perfume, and lip balm on your dresser top makes it easy to access them as you get dressed in the morning.

- Prevent these things from taking over by gathering them on a tray or in a container. Choose one that has enough space for your essentials and looks good on your dresser.

- A nice box or bin with a lid can hold things you'd prefer not to have out in the open.

Dresser-Top Valet

- If your dresser tends to gather more gadgets than toiletries, consider a valet tray to corral them.

- These trays can hold small personal-care products (floss, mints, toothpicks) as well as things you keep in your pockets during the day.

- If you have space in a dresser or bedside table drawer, stash your valet tray there to help keep flat surfaces clear.

pair. Return items that belong elsewhere in the house to their rightful homes, including any toiletries that would be better stored in the bathroom or the linen closet.

As you work, look for ways you might simplify your routines and reduce the number of things you need to keep on hand. For example, if you use multiple creams and powders when applying makeup in the morning, consider combination products (such as tinted facial moisturizers) that can help save time and cut down on clutter.

After you weed, think about the best way to store what's left. Your organizing system should provide enough space for the things you have, make it easy to access them, and allow you to store them close to where you use them. If you use multiple containers, look for those that coordinate both with each other and with the decor of the room.

Once your system is in place, keep surfaces organized and clean by getting in the habit of putting things back after you use them, immediately discarding empty toiletry bottles and tubes, and cleaning out your storage containers if things spill or leak in them.

Makeup Storage

- Keep your makeup supplies and brushes clean and orderly by storing them in divided organizers, rather than thrown together in one box or bag.

- Look for an organizer that has space to hold the types of products you use (lipstick tubes, powder compacts, and so on), as well as brushes and tools.

- Clear plastic or glass organizers are sturdy and easy to clean, and it's easy to see at a glance what's stored in them.

Portable Vanities

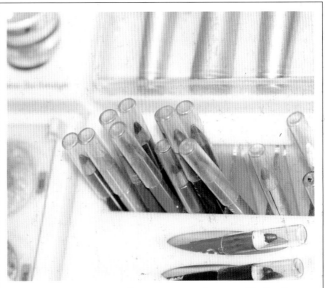

- If your bedroom is small or you prefer to keep toiletries and makeup tucked away, consider a portable vanity: a small table or cart that you can roll or tuck under a table or into a closet.

- Use a tablecloth or a table skirt to hide a vanity cart underneath a table.

- Use the same kinds of containers and organizers to store things on a portable vanity that you'd use on a fixed model.

ACCESSORIES
Add polish to outfits in a snap by keeping accessories organized and accessible

Jewelry, scarves, ties, and handbags can make outfits feel more pulled together and complete. When you have to dig through a tangle of necklaces to find the one you want, though, it can be tempting to simply go without. Getting these finishing touches organized makes it easier to see what you have, choose what you want, and get out the door on

time. As a bonus, organized accessories are less likely to suffer damage while they're waiting to be worn.

Reacquaint yourself with the accessories you have and weed out those you no longer want, like, or wear. If you have a large collection, work category by category—jewelry, belts, handbags, and so on—rather than trying to sort through ev-

Jewelry

- Necklaces stored loose in a drawer or jewelry box are almost certain to get tangled up. Instead, use a padded, wall-mounted board with hooks or a necklace tree, both of which keep necklaces separated.

- Keep fine rings in padded boxes. A small decorative tray or a ceramic hand works well for costume jewelry and casual pieces.

- Earring racks, which you can store in a drawer or hang on the wall, keep pairs together and prevent damage and lost backs.

Scarves

- Corral scarves in over-door shoe pockets. Clear vinyl pockets make it easy to identify folded scarves.

- Store large scarves folded in a drawer or on a closet shelf.

- Keep old or fragile scarves safe by folding them neatly and storing them flat, ideally in acid-free tissue paper to help preserve them.

- If you have only a few scarves, fold them over a padded pants hanger in the closet.

erything at once. Accessories worth keeping are those that fit you well, make you feel good when you wear them, flatter you, and are in good repair. Sell or give away anything that doesn't meet those criteria.

Post-purge, divide your accessories into categories (if you haven't already) to get a sense of what you have. Your goal will be to choose storage containers or systems that keep your things organized, accessible, and undamaged. Be sure the supplies you pick have enough space to hold all the ac-

cessories you have in each category so that, for example, you don't have to store half of your scarves in one place and the other half elsewhere.

Once your accessories are organized, keep them that way by taking a few minutes at the end of each day to put away the things you wore and by regularly weeding your collections to be sure they include only pieces you actually wear. The more things you have, the more difficult it is to store them all and to find the ones you truly love.

Ties and Belts

- Use a wall-mounted rack to keep ties organized in the closet. Look for a rack with grips on the prongs to keep ties from slipping off.

- If you have a small belt collection, a belt hanger (essentially a loop with an opening at the top) on a

closet rod is a good option. For a larger collection, consider mounting a hook unit on the wall.

- Another choice is a drawer divider unit; roll your belts and ties and store them one per compartment.

Purses and Handbags

- Keep purses and fine bags from getting crushed by storing them on pegs or a rack. A short, sturdy coat rack is a good option.

- Another possibility is a series of pegs on the wall of a closet. Hang rows of pegs at different heights to maximize space and create

storage for handbags of different lengths.

- If you have extra shelf space in your closet, use it to store handbags. Line them up and store them upright.

BEDROOM CLOSET

Choose your clothes storage personality for customized tips on organizing your closet and dresser

Depending on your clothing needs, you'll need to use different storage techniques. Do you tend to wear the same basics each day? Or do you thrive on creating new and different outfits whenever you get the chance? From the three following options, choose the clothes personality that best describes you, and read the tips for your type below the photo.

Basic Dresser

I'm a no-frills dresser during the week; I tend to wear the same type of outfit each day. I need simple, super-convenient clothes storage so that I can get dressed in two minutes flat. Folded clothes are a big part of my wardrobe, so I need neat drawer space for them.

If You're a Basic Dresser . . .

Whoever You Are

• Do a quick inventory of your closet before going shopping so that you're less likely to buy things you don't need.

• If you have more space on rods than shelves in your closet, hang as many clothes as you can (even if they could also be folded); if you have more shelf space, fold as many clothes as you can.

• Give closets a deep cleaning at least once a year; this is also a perfect opportunity to weed out unwanted clothes.

• Buy multiples of the clothes you wear all the time so that you can create your favorite outfits even when one piece is in the laundry.

• Install a light in your closet to allow you to see what you're grabbing.

• Dedicate an easily accessible drawer or two in your dresser to the folded clothes you wear each day. Keep less frequently worn items in lower drawers.

Cramped Clotheshorse

I love clothes and have lots of them—but unfortunately not a lot of closet space. I need to be able to keep my clothes neat and pressed so that they're ready to wear when I want them. It's important that I'm able to easily see the clothes I have.

Walk-in Wonder

I have a spacious closet with lots of storage (and quite a few clothes), but sometimes I still find it hard to get my hands on the things I'm looking for. My clothes tend to be stored in mixed categories in my closet, which can make it a challenge to find the shirt I'm looking for or the pants I want. I keep my shoes in their boxes to protect them, but then I can't identify which pair is which. My closet needs to make it easy to see what I have so that I can quickly decide what to wear.

If You're a Cramped Clotheshorse . . .

- Install a double-hung rod to increase the hanging space in your closet.

- If you have space in another room, use a portable clothes rack with a cover to store off-season and special occasion clothes.

- To save closet rod space, look for multipart hangers that let you store several different pieces of clothes on the same hanger, such as a skirt and its matching jacket.

If You're a Walk-in Wonder

- Create designated closet sections for shirts, pants, jackets, shoes and so on.

- Label the sections in your closet to remind yourself (and anyone else who might put away your clothes) what goes where.

- If you want to keep your shoes in their original boxes, tape a photo of each pair to the front of the box for easy identification.

WEEDING CLOTHES

Prep for an organized, efficient closet by clearing out ill-fitting and outdated clothes

Sorting and weeding clothes can be more emotional, difficult, and draining than doing the same with almost anything else in the house. Often, your clothes express who you are and remind you of who you once were. In addition, your wardrobe represents a big financial investment; it can be especially hard to let go of expensive clothes.

That said, there are several benefits of weeding out clothes that you don't like or wear or that don't fit you well: You'll clear out clutter, let go of pieces that make you feel bad about yourself, and gain room for the things you actually feel good wearing. The purging process takes time and effort, but it pays off in the end.

Getting Ready

- Prevent clothes from taking over your bedroom as you work by setting up a portable clothes rack to hold clothing you decide to keep.

- Hang things that will eventually go back in the closet to keep them neat and free of wrinkles.

- If you come across an item you want to keep that's not on a hanger (but should be), put it on one. Simple metal hangers (like the ones you get from the dry cleaner) are fine at this point.

Sorting Bins

- Before you begin, set up three boxes. Label one Clean/Repair, the second Donate, and the third Store Elsewhere.

- As you sort, put things that won't go back into the closet in these boxes.

- Put clothes that need to be dry-cleaned, repaired, or altered into the first box; items to give away (whether to charity or to a friend or neighbor) in the second box; and out-of-season or special occasion clothes you want to keep in the third box.

Take some time to think about the types of clothes you definitely want to keep and those you want to get rid of. Hold onto things that fit you now, that make you feel good when you wear them, and that are in good repair (that is, not torn, worn, or faded). Unflattering, poorly fitting, uncomfortable clothes are good candidates for the giveaway pile.

As you weed, remember to focus on your end goal: clearing unwanted clothing (and negative feelings) from your closet to make room for the things you wear and enjoy now.

MAKE IT EASY

It's best to tackle sorting and weeding your clothes in small chunks, rather than taking everything out of your closet at once. Start with a specific type of clothing (such as shirts or pants), and move on from there.

Categorizing Clothes

- Categorizing clothes by type gives you a narrow area of focus, which makes weeding less overwhelming.

- Choose a category to start with (dress shirts, for example), and take every item in that category out of your closet. This also gives you a realistic sense of how many pieces of clothing in that category you own.

- Remember that ultimately you want to devote the most room in your closet to the categories of clothes you wear most frequently.

Clutter Clearing: Making Decisions

As you weed, you'll find that decisions on some pieces of clothes are very easy to make, while others are much harder. Keep these questions in mind while you're sorting:

- Does this piece fit me well now? (Try it on if you're not sure.)

- Does it flatter me?

- Do I feel good when I wear it?

- When was the last time I wore this?

- Do I have multiples of this item?

- Am I keeping this only because I paid a lot for it?

CLOSET ORGANIZING
Arrange the clothes in your closet into an organizing system that will last

After you weed out the clothes you no longer like or need, you're ready to start rearranging and organizing your closet. How you choose to store your clothes—by category, by color, by how often you wear them, or by outfit—will depend on your closet space, how many clothes you have, and how you usually get dressed in the morning.

There are two important things to keep in mind as you work on arranging your closet. First, the main goal here is to create a clothes storage system that works well for you. It doesn't matter if a friend or a magazine article or an organizing expert recommends setting up a closet in one specific way; what matters is how you want to be able to use your closet.

Hanging Clothes by Category

- Arranging your clothes by category (pants, shirts, jackets, and so on) helps simplify the process of creating outfits and makes it easy to put clothes away.

- Put all clothes in one category on the same type of hanger (dress shirts on wooden hangers, for example) to help visually define the category within the closet.

- Also, put hangers on the closet rod all facing the same way so that you can quickly sort through them.

Shelving Clothes by Category

- You can also apply categories to clothes you store on shelves in your closet, such as sweaters.

- Create categorized stacks of clothes. Because it can be harder to identify what things are when they're folded than when they're hung, consider adding labels to the shelves (such as Dressy Sweaters and Casual Sweaters).

- Use shelf dividers to keep clothes in different categories separate.

Second, remember that if you try arranging your closet one way and decide it really doesn't work well for you, you can always change it, so don't spend too much time worrying about whether you've made the right choice up front. Pick a system that appeals to you, give it a try, and make changes to it as needed.

Two of the most common ways of organizing clothes are by category and by color. In closets arranged by category, all clothes of one type—all dress shirts, all slacks, all skirts, all pants—are stored close to one another. This is helpful if you like to be able to see your options in each category before deciding what to wear.

Another option is to arrange clothes by color: red items together, blue items together, and so on. If you enjoy creating outfits from clothes of different hues, or if you want to know at a glance how many items in one shade you have, this could be a good system for you.

Arranging Clothes by Color

- Dividing clothes by color lets you quickly see the different hues you have and makes it easy to put clothes away.

- When you've separated your clothes by color, hang them in a sequence that makes sense to you: light to dark, frequently worn colors in the middle, and so on.

- Choose whether you'll hang patterned clothes with items of similar colors, or whether you'll give them their own section.

Colors and Categories

- Once you've arranged your clothes by color, you can refine the system by sorting each color into categories (such as shirts with shirts).

- After categorizing, try arranging those categories by length. Within your green clothes section, for example, you might have short-sleeved shirts, long-sleeved shirts, skirts, pants, and dresses.

- When you take an item from the closet, leave its empty hanger in place so that you know at a glance where to return it.

CLOSET ORGANIZING (CONTINUED)

Create easy access to your favorite clothes to make getting dressed a snap

ORGANIZING YOUR HOME

The goal of organizing your closet is to make it quick and easy to find the clothes you want to wear. To achieve that goal, choose a storage system that works with your closet space and supports the way you store and look for clothes. Four general options for arranging your clothes are by category, by color, by how often you wear them, and by outfit.

You'll find information on organizing by frequency of use and by outfit below.

If you find yourself turning to the same few clothes day after day and only occasionally need to wear other things, consider arranging your clothes by how often you wear them. This setup can be especially useful if you tend to wear one kind of

Frequently Worn Clothes

- Arranging your clothes by how often you wear them lets you quickly and easily get to your everyday items without having to wade through other things.

- Hang the clothes you wear most often in the easiest-to-access spot in your closet.

- For an extra dose of organization, sort and hang your everyday clothes by category, such as shirts and pants.

Weekend and Formal Wear

- Make room front and center for your everyday clothes by moving the things you wear less frequently to the back or sides of the closet.

- If you have limited closet space, store things you rarely wear elsewhere in the house (such as a guest room closet).

- Keep everyday clothes folded on closet shelves at eye level or lower, or in a dresser; use higher shelves for less frequently worn items.

clothes during the week and another on the weekend (such as business attire Monday through Friday and casual wear on Saturday and Sunday).

If you're most comfortable sticking with a few tried-and-true clothing combos, or if you like to be able to see at a glance how certain items look together, arranging your closet by outfit is a good option. Store a top and bottom together, pull out one hanger, and you'll be ready to go.

ZOOM

Reorganizing your closet is a great reason to upgrade your hangers. Toss the metal ones you get from your dry cleaner and any that are cracked or broken. Replace them with sturdy hangers designed for the clothes they'll be holding (skirts, pants, shirts). Good hangers keep clothes from getting wrinkled and keep fabrics in better shape.

Arranging by Outfit

- Arranging your closet by outfit means you won't have to spend time in the morning deciding what pieces go together.

- Hang outfits together on suit hangers, which have space for both tops and bottoms, or on separate hangers next to each other in the closet.

- If you wear particular accessories (such as scarves, ties, or belts) with certain outfits, hang them with those outfits.

Creating an Outfit Directory

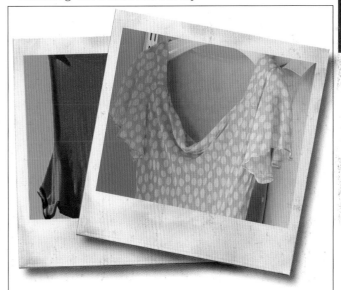

- Take a tip from professional image consultants and keep a record of your favorite outfits by creating a visual directory.

- Lay the outfit on a bed and take a digital photo of it. Print the photo and store it in a notebook or binder in your closet.

- Use the edges of your photos to make notes about accessories to wear, alternate options for coordinated pieces, or other information about the outfits you create.

DRESSER ORGANIZING

Weed out overstuffed dresser drawers to create a more effective clothes storage system

Dressers are meant to be convenient places for storing clothes. Sometimes, though, they seem to become lurking piles of clutter contained within a few pieces of wood. Stop doing battle with your dresser—and wearing the same few things over and over because you can't locate anything else—by clearing out the chaos and reorganizing the clothes you actually want to keep.

The first step in bringing your dresser under control is reacquainting yourself with what's stored there and getting rid of what doesn't fit or flatter you. Approach weeding your dresser the same way you would weeding your closet: Establish some guidelines for what gets to stay and what

Organizing by Category

Top-to-Bottom Organizing

- One of the easiest ways of organizing the clothes in your dresser is by category: undergarments together, T-shirts together, and so on.

- Organizing by category makes it easy to find what you need and to put clothes away; it also lets you take inventory of the number of items within a particular category.

- If one category of clothes doesn't take up an entire drawer, use the remaining space for a similar category.

- Another option is to organize your dresser based on how you get dressed.

- The clothes you put on first (such as underwear and socks) go in the top drawer, the next layer (T-shirts, for example) in the second drawer, and on down to the final layer in the bottom drawer.

- If you do well with routines and sequences, this system could work well for you.

74

doesn't, take it a drawer at a time, and have bins ready to hold clothes you're sorting.

When you finish purging, decide how you want to organize what remains: by category, by how you get dressed, or by owner (if you share the dresser). Choose a system that's logical to you and that will make it easy to find what you need and put it away when you're done with it.

Once you pick a way to organize your drawers, consider using dividers and drawer liners to keep your clothes protected and neat.

YELLOW ● LIGHT

If your dresser is rickety, too small, or has absorbed odors, no amount of organization will make it a piece of furniture you enjoy using. While you're in the midst of bringing order to your dresser, consider replacing it if it doesn't provide the clean, sturdy storage you need.

Organizing by Owner

- If you share your dresser with a partner, it can make sense to divide and organize the drawers by owner.

- Allocate drawers based on how many clothes each partner needs to store; also take into account whether one partner is significantly larger or smaller than the other and would thus need more or less storage space.

- Framed nameplates on the front of each drawer can be gentle visual reminders.

Dividers and Liners

- Drawer dividers help keep clothes separated and neat and can be useful for delineating categories within drawers.

- Dividers are available either as boxes or as expandable strips that can be fit inside a drawer.

- Drawer liners, which are available both scented and unscented, can add a nice touch and are especially useful in drawers used to store sweaters, lingerie, and other delicate clothing.

SHOES
Dig out your unwanted pairs and create convenient storage for your favorite footwear

Disorganized shoes are a big frustration, whether they're lurking in the middle of the floor (no doubt waiting to trip you) or piled in a heap at the back of the closet. Without a good storage system, it's hard to find what you need, and shoes run the risk of being damaged. Organize your footwear to keep it neat, accessible, and in good shape.

Get things under way by gathering all of your shoes (even those stored in other parts of the house) in one place. Go through your collection a pair at a time and ask yourself which are worth keeping. Hint: Anything you've had for more than six months and haven't worn, anything that makes your feet ache for days after wearing, anything with irreparable

Shoe Drawers

- Create a modular storage system with clear shoe drawers, which stack securely.

- Shoe drawers are an especially good option for delicate, lighter-weight shoes, such as heels and sandals.

- Put drawers used to store large, heavy shoes like sneakers and men's dress shoes on the bottom of a stack.

- Be sure shoes are clean and dry before storing them in the drawers.

Shoe Cubbies

- A good option for storing multiple pairs of shoes in a small space is a shoe cubby unit, which has solid sides and a series of open-front slots.

- Generally, you'll be able to fit one pair of small, flexible shoes per slot. Larger shoes, or those made of stiff materials, will need one slot per shoe.

- Store shoe cubbies on your closet floor. As a bonus, the top of each cubby can serve as additional shelf space.

damage, and anything that's too small or too large probably don't merit storage space. Let those pairs go.

Once you have a newly refined collection, take a look at the number of pairs you have, as well as the storage space available to you in your closet and in nearby areas. The storage system you choose should fit comfortably in your closet, provide enough room for all of your shoes, should be easy to access, and, ideally, should keep your shoes tucked away rather than out in the open.

Also be sure to take into account the types of shoes you need to store: Those made of delicate materials (such as suede or satin) require different care than those made of canvas or sturdy leather. If you have several different kinds of footwear, consider blending elements of a few shoe storage systems to create one that works well for you.

Floor Racks

- Expandable floor racks are handy for smaller closets, or in spaces with long hanging clothes above.

- These racks come in different heights and can be expanded or contracted to fit various spaces. Many models are also stackable.

- Floor racks allow shoes to breathe, which can help prevent mold and mildew growth.

- Flat shoes with smooth soles may slip off these racks, so those pairs are best stored on the floor.

Over-Door Racks

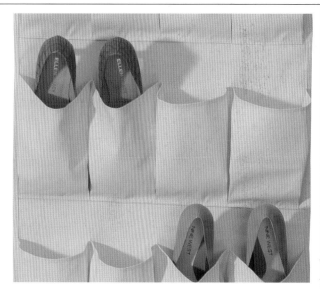

- To make the most of the vertical space in your bedroom, use an over-door shoe rack.

- These racks are available with pockets or loops of metal. Slip your shoes into a pocket or over a metal loop.

- Avoid a cluttered look by installing an over-door rack on the inside of your closet door.

- To keep the rack from moving each time you open the door, attach the bottom of the rack securely to the door.

ENTRYWAY

Find organizing recommendations for your entryway based on how you use the space

The best ways to make the most of your home's front hall or entry depend on what that space is like for you and how you use it. If it's the site of frequent comings and goings, you'll want to arrange it differently than you would if it were mainly seen by guests and delivery people. Choose the definition that most accurately describes your space, and then read specific tips below the photo.

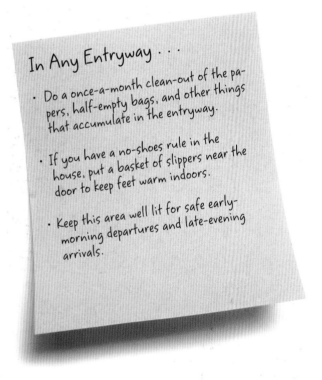

In Any Entryway . . .

• Do a once-a-month clean-out of the papers, half-empty bags, and other things that accumulate in the entryway.

• If you have a no-shoes rule in the house, put a basket of slippers near the door to keep feet warm indoors.

• Keep this area well lit for safe early-morning departures and late-evening arrivals.

Busy Port

The front hall in my home is the family's main entry and exit. I need storage spots for the things that get dropped here every day, like backpacks and coats. I also want to keep this space as neat and organized as possible to avoid chaos when we leave the house and come home.

In a Busy Port . . .

• Get your family involved in planning and setting up storage here so that they'll be more invested in using it.

• Use storage furniture and supplies that blend with your hallway's decor to make the space feel more cohesive and less cluttered.

• Designate space for each person in the family to drop off and pick up bags, jackets, papers, and other everyday essentials.

Occasional Entry

The front hall in my home isn't our primary entryway, but we do use it for visitors, deliveries, and carpool pickups. I need simple storage here for a few jackets, shoes, and umbrellas, as well as a spot for the work, school, and practice supplies we grab when carpools pull up outside. I want to keep this space neat and clean for visitors and would love a spot for them to hang their coats.

Open Space

My front door is the main entry into the home, and it opens directly into a room, not into a hallway. I need storage here that doesn't take up much space or look out of place, but that can hold our coats, bags, and shoes. I want to keep this space well organized to avoid feeling overwhelmed as soon as I walk in the door.

In an Occasional Entry . . .

- Use a simple bench and hook rack as spots to get things like coats, bags, and lunchboxes ready for carpoolers.

- Keep hooks (or hangers in the closet, if you have one) empty for guests' coats.

- Liven up the space and give delicate decorative items a safer home by displaying them here, rather than in busier areas of the house.

In an Open Space . . .

- Opt for one or two pieces of storage furniture that can serve multiple functions.

- Consider using a folding screen, a curtain, or another simple divider to create some division between the front door and the rest of the room.

- Store only the essentials (everyday coats, bags, and accessories) here to keep the space from feeling cluttered and overwhelming.

FOYER

Create an uncluttered, welcoming entrance to your home with organizing systems for everyday essentials

The foyer is often the first thing you see when you come home and your final glimpse when you leave. It's also the space where the stuff of everyday life—mail, keys, bags—comes and goes. The busy nature of this part of the house means it's one of the most likely places to gather clutter and slide into chaos. Luckily, with some simple organizing systems, you can keep your foyer looking great and functioning smoothly.

Start by thinking about how you currently use this space, as well as how you'd like to be able to use it. How would you like things to look and feel when you open the front door? What would you like to be able to store in

Easy Organizing Systems: Basic Storage

- If you don't need to store a lot in your foyer, a simple table or small cabinet unit works well as the basis of your storage system.

- Choose a unit that fits comfortably in the space without impeding traffic and that meshes with the room's decor.

- Set up bins, baskets, or other containers on top of the unit for things that will collect here, such as keys and small electronics.

Cubbies and Seating

- Make the most of the space in your foyer with wall-mounted storage units.

- Look for a unit with cubbies and hooks so that you can easily stash things like hats, packages to mail, and books and also can hang jackets and keys.

- A bench beneath the cubby is a convenient spot for resting bags; one with additional cubbies will offer even more storage.

your foyer—coats? shoes? incoming and outgoing mail?

Also think about who uses the room. Is it primarily reserved for guests' arrivals, or does the whole family use it on a regular basis? Do the kids dump their stuff here when they get home from school?

Keep the answers to these questions in mind as you plan the space and set up systems for the things that come through it.

Next, take some time to sort and weed the stuff that's cur-rently in your foyer. Put away anything that has a home else-where, and get rid of what you no longer want, use, or need. The things that remain will help you determine what sort of storage you need.

Choose the furniture and containers for this space based on the size and layout of the room, how you want to be able to use it, and how much you need to store. And be sure to pick things you don't mind looking at—you'll be seeing a lot of them.

Shoe Storage

- Keep the floors in the rest of the house clean by in-stituting a no-shoes-inside policy. A comfortable bench with shoe storage placed near the front door helps make this policy easier to stick with.

- Even if you do allow shoes inside, a bench and rack in the entryway makes chang-ing shoes or taking off wet or muddy ones a snap.

- Assign each family member a section of the rack to avoid confusion about whose shoes are whose.

Kids' Storage

- Large, sturdy baskets give kids a spot to store backpacks, sporting goods, and other supplies in the entryway.

- Label each basket with the name of the owner. For an extra dose of fun, let kids create their own labels.

- If you need to clear out the entryway when guests come over, simply move the baskets to a nearby closet or to the kids' rooms.

SMALL ENTRYWAY

Maximize storage in small spots to create a clean, clear, inviting entrance to your home

If your home doesn't have a separate foyer, chances are your entryway shares space with another room, such as a hallway or a living room. Even when you're working with limited space, though, you can still create an organized, efficient, welcoming area inside your front door with some creative storage ideas and tools.

Before making any changes to your entryway, create a list of what the space is currently like (clear? cluttered? busy? frustrating?) and how you'd like it to be. Also give some thought to what the space needs to provide, such as storage for coats and bags or a spot to stash mail before you have a chance to open it.

Shelves and Hooks

- Save floor space and create a spot for coats, bags, and umbrellas by using wall-mounted hooks for hanging these entryway essentials.

- Options range from a basic peg rack to a unit that has hooks and shelf space. Choose one based on what you have to hang and whether you need flat storage space as well.

- If you choose a unit with shelf space, use baskets or bins to contain small items like hats and gloves.

Kids' Storage

- Give kids a place to store bags, sports equipment, and other things they need near the front door by hanging sturdy baskets in the entryway.

- Put matching labels with the kids' names on the baskets, or let each child create a label.

- To clear the entry during slower times of the year (like summer and school vacations) or when guests come over, take down the baskets and stash them in a closet or in the kids' rooms.

With a general plan for the space in mind, do some weeding: Clear out everything except the things you need or regularly use there. Decluttering is especially important in small spaces, so be tough on your things. Deciding what to keep and what to toss can be difficult, but it's a crucial step in creating a calm, welcoming space.

After you've gotten rid of unwanted and unused stuff, start planning some specifics for the space based on how it's laid out, how you want to be able to use it, and what you need to store there. Choose furniture, containers, and organizing supplies that help define the entryway without overwhelming the space.

Once you've set up the organizing systems here, take time to put things away when you get home, deal with mail at least once a week, and help others in the family get used to the systems so that they work for everyone. Keeping your entryway streamlined and uncluttered will make coming home more pleasant.

Maximized Wall Storage

- If you need storage space for more than a few things, look for a wall-mounted unit with shelves or cubbies and hooks.

- Use the hooks for keys, coats, umbrellas, and light bags, and use the shelves or cubbies for things to take out of the house (such as packages to mail or books to return), accessories like hats and gloves, and larger bags.

- Keep small items organized by storing them in bins or baskets.

Shoe Storage

- Keep shoes easily accessible in the entryway without devoting a lot of space to them by using an upright shoe holder.

- These units are tall and thin and have broad drawers for storing shoes; they're a good option if you have more vertical space available than floor space.

- Use a few units side by side for busy entries, and assign each family member a drawer or two.

IN-AND-OUT CENTER
Keep track of what comes and goes with organized systems for mail and other essentials

The entryway is usually the first point of contact for things that come into the house, such as mail, school papers, and keys; it's also the final gathering spot for these things before they go out. As such, it can become an area in which papers accumulate, important things get lost, and junk seems to grow on its own. With a few simple systems for the things

that enter and leave your home, you can bring calm and order to this space.

To create an in-and-out center that works well for you and your family, you first need a clear idea of what you'd like it to do. So start by taking a look at what tends to accumulate each day in your entryway, where that stuff winds up, and

Mail Sorting Station

- Keep mail from piling up on flat surfaces, and stop losing important pieces, by setting up a wall-mounted sorting system.

- Hang three letter sorters (or one three-part sorter) where mail comes into the house.

- Use one sorter for important mail with deadlines attached (such as bills); the second for letters, event notices, and other important-but-not-urgent items; and the third for magazines, newsletters, and catalogs.

- Put bins on the floor for mail to shred and recycle.

Kids' In-Boxes and Out-Boxes

- Designate spots for the papers kids bring to and from school with personalized in-boxes and out-boxes.

- Use wall-mounted sorters with two pockets, one labeled To School and the other From School. Put a name label on each sorter.

- Have kids put papers like permission slips, tests, and PTA newsletters in the From School pocket for Mom or Dad to review.

- Put anything kids need to take in the morning in the To School pocket.

why it lands where it does. Also give some thought to what you'd like this area to do, such as providing a designated spot for things each family member needs to take out of the house each morning or offering space for you to drop keys and sunglasses when you walk in the door.

Next, scan the area with an eye toward weeding out anything there that you no longer want, use, or need or that should be stored somewhere else in the house. If possible, get the whole family involved in this process; you'll have fewer decisions to make on your own, and each person will be more invested in making this space into one that works for everyone.

With the space decluttered, choose the organizing tools you'll need to create your system. Once those are in place, work on making it a habit to use them each day, and encourage others in the family to do the same.

Essentials Station

- Stop the mad search for keys, sunglasses, and other essentials by setting up a specific home for them near the door.

- A tray, bin, or basket on a hall table is a good option; if you don't have a table, look for a small basket that can hang from a wall hook.

- Each time you come in, remember to drop your essentials in their designated spot so that they'll be there when you're ready to head out again.

Checklist for Leaving

- Remind yourself of the things you need to take when leaving the house and of safety checks (stove off, windows closed) by posting a checklist on a dry-erase board near the door.

- Change your lists based on where you're going and what's scheduled for the day.

- Before you leave, take a moment to run through the checklist (or delegate this task to an older child).

85

HALL CLOSET: COATS AND JACKETS

Make your hall closet an oasis of calm, order, and easily accessible outerwear

Hall closets tend to be where every coat and jacket a family ever owned winds up, sometimes never to emerge. This can mean a battle of wits each time you open the closet door. Transform this space with a bit of decluttering and a few organizational tweaks, and stop fighting with your outerwear.

How to make the best use of your hall closet depends on its size, how much you need to store there, and what else (other than coats and jackets) you'd like to be able to keep in the space.

Start organizing coats and jackets by sorting through them. Get family members involved by having them try things on and voting on which outerwear they want to keep. Set aside

Maximize Hanging Space

- Make the most of the hanging space in your closet by using double-hung rods.

- These help avoid dead space below short coats and jackets and are especially useful if you have kids: Hang their outerwear on the lower rod so that it's easy for them to grab what they need.

- Be sure to leave some long-hanging space in the closet for trench coats and other long jackets.

Door Storage

- Put the back of your closet door to use with a hook rack that mounts directly on the door or hangs over the top of the door. (If you choose an over-door model, secure the bottom of it so that it doesn't move each time you open or close the door.)

- Use the hooks to hold lightweight coats such as windbreakers and fleece jackets, and reserve the rod for heavier items.

- Hooks are also a good option for holding things like scarves and umbrellas.

for donation anything that no longer fits or doesn't get worn. Pull out anything that needs to be cleaned or fixed, and toss coats that are beyond repair.

Unless you have extra space in your hall closet, don't use it to hold out-of-season items; move these to storage in a guest room closet or another out-of-the-way spot.

With a clear sense of how many coats and jackets you have, you can start planning hall closet storage that will keep your outerwear neat, organized, and accessible.

Wall-Mounted Storage

- In closets that are long and narrow, wall-mounted storage is a more efficient option than hanging rods.

- Hang a series of peg racks at varying heights on the wall. Be sure to mount these racks so that items hanging from one won't cover the things on the rack below it.

- Mount racks for kids low to the floor so that they can easily reach their things.

- Use one rack per family member to keep everyone's things separate.

Coat Racks

- If your hall closet doesn't have space for coats, or if you don't have a hall closet, use a coat rack to store outerwear.

- Choose a rack that's sturdy and has space enough for the things you need to hang, including scarves and umbrellas.

- Double up storage on each hook if you need to, but be sure to hang less frequently worn items under the coats and jackets you use every day.

HALL CLOSET: EVERYTHING ELSE
Clear the clutter and create smart storage to make your hall closet a functional, orderly space

Coats and jackets aren't the only things that take up space in hall closets. Chances are you also use this area to store accessories (like hats and gloves), bags, umbrellas, shoes, and more. And unless you have a comfortably large space to work with, your hall closet might be so full that you dread opening it. It's time to lose the dread and gain more storage by getting this area organized.

What's currently in your hall closet? What should be there but isn't? What's there that belongs somewhere else in the house—or out of the house entirely? How would your closet

Storing Accessories

- Put the closet door to use and create storage space for accessories by hanging over-door shoe pockets.

- Use the pockets to hold scarves, gloves, hats, and other things that tend to get lost in coat pockets or at the bottom of the closet.

- Soft shoe pockets prevent snags in knit accessories and can help keep things clean.

- Assign each family member specific pockets, reserving the lower pockets for kids.

Storing Bags

- Prevent a heap of bags on the floor of the closet or in the entryway by installing hooks on the back of the door or along the walls.

- Be sure to choose hooks that are sturdy enough to hold heavy bags (like full backpacks) and long enough so that bags don't slip off.

- If family members have multiple bags, use horizontal hook racks, and assign one rack per person.

look and feel if it really worked for you? Your answers to these questions will help you figure out the best storage solutions for this space.

First, though, get back in touch with the stuff in your closet. Take a look at each thing there and decide whether to keep it or get rid of it. Stuff you no longer want, use, or need, or that's broken beyond repair should go into your giveaway pile.

When you've decided what things to keep, figure out which items should be stored in the hall closet and which should go somewhere else. Remember, it's best to keep things close to where you use them, so consider moving anything you don't need near the front door to another spot.

Finally, based on what you want to store in the closet, choose organizing tools that fit the space and make it easy to stash (and find) what you need. Then get in the habit of using them each time you open the closet door.

Using Shelves

- If your closet has a shelf, use it to store baskets or bins that hold loose items.

- Corral things like accessories, lightbulbs, and pet items in containers and stash them on the shelves. Label the containers so that you won't have to take them down to see what's inside.

- Use high shelves (like the ones above closet rods) to store things you don't have to access often; use lower shelves for everyday stuff.

Storing Shoes

- The closet can be a good spot for shoe storage if you don't have space in your entryway or would rather keep shoes behind closed doors.

- A simple basket is a good option if you don't have many shoes to store. Look for a low, broad basket to avoid having to dig for the pair you want.

- For multiple pairs, look for shoe shelves, which are long and narrow. If possible, stack these shelves for additional storage.

MUDROOM AND LAUNDRY ROOM

Identify what your utility areas are like to determine the smartest ways of organizing them

How you set up and organize your mudroom and laundry area depends on what those spaces are like and how you want to be able to use them. Read the following descriptions and choose the one that most closely defines your utility spaces, and then look for specific tips below the photo.

In Any Utility Area . . .

- If your mudroom or laundry area tends to get and stay damp, put a dehumidifier there to help prevent mold growth.

- Don't have a mudroom? Put a waterproof mat near your primary entry during wet weather to collect drippy shoes and clothes.

- If you store your cat's litter box in the mudroom, install a pet flap in the door leading to the rest of the house.

Dual-Purpose Space

My laundry area and mudroom are in the same spot. I need a way to set up my laundry space so that clean clothes stay that way. I also want a place to put wet clothes and shoes where they'll dry quickly, rather than sitting around damp for days.

In a Dual-Purpose Space…

- Use shelves or a table in the laundry area to hold baskets of clean clothes, rather than putting them on the floor.

- Put racks and hooks for wet, muddy shoes and clothes near the dryer so that they'll dry more quickly.

- Keep rags and a bottle of simple cleaning solution handy to clean off particularly dirty shoes and boots.

Separate Spots

My mudroom and laundry area are in different parts of the house. I want to be able to use my mudroom as a utility and cleaning zone and a wet entry space. I need a way to keep dirty clothes and socks that are shed here from sticking around long-term.

Small Spaces

My mudroom and laundry area are separate and are tucked into small spaces (like a back porch, a kitchen nook, or the basement). I need super-efficient storage in these spaces for wet stuff and laundry supplies. I want to keep each of these spaces contained to avoid cluttering the surrounding room.

In Separate Spots . . .

In Small Spaces . . .

- Space and plumbing permitting, install a utility sink in your mudroom so that you can rinse off muddy shoes and boots, fill cleaning buckets, and take care of other wet, messy tasks.

- Keep a laundry basket or hamper in the mudroom to collect wet, dirty clothes.

- Store basic stain-removal supplies in the mudroom to treat grass, mud, and oil stains before you have a chance to put the affected clothes in the laundry.

- Make the most of tight spots by using walls and doors to hang storage units and hook racks.

- Look for foldable or collapsible storage bins, tables, and shoe racks so that you can keep them out of the way when they're not in use.

- If there aren't doors separating your utility areas from the surrounding rooms, hang curtains or use a folding screen to divide the space.

WET AREAS AND PET CARE

Create designated spots for wet, muddy tasks and stashing pet care supplies

There are certain things better done in a mudroom or utility area than inside the house; taking off wet, muddy clothes and shoes and storing pet supplies are two such tasks. Designating spots for these in your mudroom goes a long way toward keeping the rest of the house cleaner and less cluttered because you won't have to worry about dirty footprints tracked inside or giant bags of pet food taking up other valuable storage space.

Making a few small improvements to your mudroom will help keep the space neat, orderly, and useful. Before creating new systems for the room, though, it's well worth taking the time to weed out the things that are currently there.

Shoes and Boots

- Keep wet, muddy shoes and boots from making a mess of the mudroom by setting up drying pans for them.

- A simple, inexpensive option is cooling racks—the kinds you normally use for cookies—set inside jellyroll pans. The racks give shoes dripping room, which helps them dry more quickly.

- Sturdy rubber mats with ridges also work well. Look for a mat with ridges high enough to prevent shoes from sitting in puddles.

Shelves and Racks

- If you have wall space, use it to mount a set of sturdy, waterproof shelves and racks.

- Hang damp (but not dripping) coats and jackets to speed drying, and stash slightly wet footwear on shelves.

- A mudroom shelving unit is also a good spot to store things you normally put on or take off in this room, such as raincoats, work boots, and sports shoes.

- Choose a customizable unit so that you can create storage for other mudroom essentials.

Mudrooms often become catchalls for stuff that doesn't seem to belong anywhere else, so they tend to be cluttered and a bit chaotic. Sort through the stuff (yes, all of it) that's there. Toss anything that's garbage or that's broken and is unlikely to be fixed. Create a donation box for things you no longer want, use, or need, and set aside things that should be stored elsewhere in the house, basement, or garage.

After you've weeded, divide up the space based on what you use the room for—taking off wet boots, storing pet sup-plies, hanging jackets—and how much storage you need for each function. Be sure the areas you establish are logical and convenient; for example, the spot for removing muddy shoes should be as close to the door as possible.

With your space plan in mind, choose some simple, sturdy organizing tools and supplies for each area. Many of these supplies are very inexpensive (or free, if you already have them on hand in the house), and they do a lot to help keep the mudroom organized and functional.

Pet-Care Area

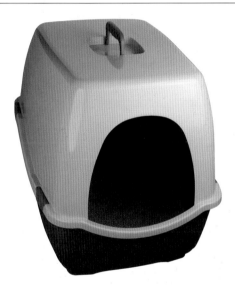

- Keep pet-care supplies and accessories together and out of the way by storing them in the mudroom.

- Transfer bulky supplies like dry food and kitty litter from their original bags into sturdy, waterproof cans, such as small garbage cans. Label each can with its contents and store a plastic or metal scoop in each.

- If your mudroom is warm enough, use it as the location for a litter box.

- Hang a row of pegs or hooks on the wall near the door to store leashes and collars.

Organizing Smaller Supplies

- Use a small cabinet unit for small pet supplies like toys, bones, brushes, canned food, and medications.

- Store loose supplies (such as small toys or medication packages) in baskets or bins inside the cabinet. Label these containers if it's not clear at a glance what's inside.

- Put a lock on the cabinet if your pets tend to be inquisitive or if you have young children.

RECYCLING
Create an organized recycling area to make it easier and neater to go green

As our awareness of the importance of recycling increases, and more communities develop or improve their recycling programs, the need for efficient, easy-to-use recycling storage at home grows. Creating a designated space to store recyclables inside the house means you don't need to trek out to the garage each time you empty a jar of pasta sauce or finish reading the newspaper—which, in turn, probably means that recycling will seem like less of a chore.

A mudroom or utility area is the perfect spot for a household recycling station—even a simple one that requires nothing more than a pair of standard kitchen trash cans. Choose a system that will work for you based on the size of

Dividing Recyclables

- If your recycling program requires that cans, bottles, and papers be separated, collect them in different containers or in a container with different sections.

- Use color-coding (red for bottles, yellow for cans, green for paper, for example) as an extra reminder of what goes where. If you're using separate containers, label each one.

- To conserve space in your mudroom, opt for one large container to collect all recyclables if they don't need to be kept apart.

Wheeled Bins

- Make it easier to transfer your recyclables to the garage or the curb by collecting them in wheeled bins.

- Look in home stores for bins or small trash cans with wheels, or make your own by attaching casters to the bottom of a regular bin.

- A bin with a lid decreases the chances of things spilling out when you roll it out of the house.

94

your mudroom, how many recyclables you generate each week, and how you need to prepare the recycling for pickup or drop-off.

Set up your system in an area that's waterproof and easy to clean, such as on an uncarpeted floor. In addition to bins for storing cans, bottles, and paper, stock your recycling area with the things you need to get your recyclables ready to leave the house: paper bags to carry empty cans, for example, or twine to bind newspapers and magazines together.

MAKE IT EASY

Wondering whether you can recycle yogurt containers and aerosol cans in your community? Want to know a safe way of disposing of dead batteries or unused paint? Visit Earth911, a clearinghouse of information on local recycling, reuse, and disposal programs. (See the Resources section in the back of the book.)

Just the Basics

- If you don't need a lot of space for your recyclables and/or don't have a mudroom, use a few simple kitchen trash cans as your recycling system.

- Choose trash cans that fit easily in the storage area (in your utility area or under the sink) and are large enough that you won't have to empty them daily.

- Use a paper grocery bag to line the paper recycling can; you'll avoid a mess when you transfer the bag to your curbside bin.

Easy Organizing Systems: Recycling Chart

- It can be hard to remember what is and isn't recyclable in your area. Jog your memory and keep nonrecyclables out of the mix by posting a recycling chart above your bins.

- Ask your waste management company or local government if they have a pre-printed chart. If not, create your own.

- As an additional reminder, consider labeling each of your recycling bins with a list of what can and can't go in it.

UTILITY AREA

CLEANING SUPPLIES

Simplify your cleaning routine and keep your family safe with effective storage solutions

Cleaning supplies often seem especially tricky to keep organized: they come in many different packages, sometimes cause more messes than they solve, and need to be kept in a safe spot. Because the same supplies can be used throughout the house, it's hard to figure out the best spot to store them, which means they're often scattered.

Take some of the stress out of cleaning, avoid clutter, and keep potentially dangerous potions out of the wrong hands by creating a central cleaning supplies storage area.

Choose a spot that allows you easy access to supplies for quick cleanups and, ideally, that provides enough room to store all of your cleaning necessities (including mops and

Mops and Brooms

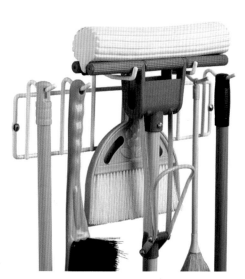

- Use a wall-mounted rack to keep mops and brooms off the floor and stored together in one spot.

- Look for a rack that has enough slots or hooks to hold your mop, broom, dustpan, and other floor-cleaning tools.

- Hang the rack high enough to keep it out of kids' reach but not so high that you have to strain to access it.

Cleaning Caddy

- A cleaning caddy with a handle makes it easy to store supplies and to carry them around the house.

- Look for a caddy that has enough space to store your basic supplies and tools and that has a handle you can easily grip with wet gloves or hands.

- Opt for a caddy with compartments, which will let you keep wet supplies separate from dry ones (like dust rags).

brooms) together. If you have pets or young children, be sure to select a spot that will be out of their reach.

Before storing anything, go through the supplies you have. Consolidate duplicates, recycle or toss empty containers, and reconsider whether you truly need multiple bottles and formulations. Multipurpose cleaning solutions can do many jobs, and household basics (like vinegar, lemon, salt, and baking powder) can often take the place of more complicated products.

After you've weeded, look for organizing tools that will help you keep your supplies neat, safe, and ready for use.

ZOOM

In recent years, natural cleaning supplies have become more effective, less expensive, and easier to find. As a bonus, many of them are concentrated, which means that a small bottle goes a long way. It's worthwhile giving a few earth-friendly basics a try.

Wall Racks

- Put empty space on a wall or the back of a door to good use by installing a narrow rack for cleaning supplies.

- Look for one with sturdy shelves that won't bend under the weight of full bottles and that attaches securely to the wall at both the top and the bottom.

- Store heavier items on the lower shelves and lighter things up higher.

- Use clips or hooks to hang rags, brushes, and dusters from the bottom of the rack.

Simple Habits for Staying Organized: Cleaning Checklist

- Taking care of basic cleaning tasks on a regular basis—and scheduling more intensive ones a few times a year—can help you keep a neater house with less stress.

- Remind yourself of what to clean and how often with a cleaning schedule and checklist. See the Resources section for some sample checklists.

- Post your checklist near your supply storage area, and consider laminating a shortened version of it to stash in your cleaning caddy.

UTILITY AREA

LAUNDRY: WASHING

Make laundry less of a chore with intelligent storage and a few simple supplies

An organized laundry area probably won't make you love doing laundry (unless you already do), but getting your laundry room in order will make doing the wash more efficient and less stressful. It will also help bring a measure of calm to an area that can often feel cluttered and chaotic.

Step one in organizing your laundry space is clearly defining what that space is, whether a separate room, a nook off the kitchen or bathroom, or part of a mudroom or utility area. (If you wash your clothes at a self-service laundry, use the tips in this section to create portable solutions you can take with you to the Laundromat.)

Prep

- Use separate baskets to hold clothes for separate loads. Break baskets into categories based on how you do your wash: by clothing type, by color, or by family member.

- Choose portable baskets for easy sorting anywhere in the house.

- If you share the laundry area, label baskets by category so that each person can sort correctly.

- Use collapsible baskets if you're pinched for space. When you're not using them, fold and stash them on a shelf or next to the washer.

Laundry Supplies

- Store your supplies together in the order in which you use them: pre-treatment sprays first, then detergent, then bleach, then fabric softener.

- Keep large bottles in a spot that lets you dispense the amount of product you need without having to lift the container. Another option is to transfer the cleaner or softener to a smaller bottle or box.

- If you buy in bulk, keep unopened bottles on a separate shelf to avoid the chance of having multiples open at once.

When you've defined what your space is, decide what needs to be there, such as baskets, detergent, and fabric softener. Next, figure out what doesn't need to (and shouldn't) be there: outgrown clothes, things that belong elsewhere in the house, stuff that's piled up over time and become clutter. Get these things out.

Finally, set up systems that make the most efficient use of the space, give you enough room to prepare clothes for laundering and get them in the washer, and provide storage for the supplies you use. If others in the house help with laundry, make sure they know how to use your systems, too.

On laundry day, get in the habit of taking care of the full task—collecting clothes, washing, drying, folding, and putting away—in sequence to prevent piles of damp clothes on top of the dryer or stacks of clean things that never seem to make it back to where they belong.

Containers for Small Items

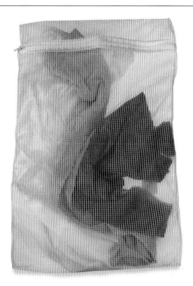

- Mesh lingerie bags are useful not only for washing delicates but also for keeping small items (like socks or children's underwear) from scattering in the washer.

- Another option is to safety-pin small things together before tossing them in the wash.

- Lingerie bags are dryer safe, so you can transfer them directly from the washer without emptying them.

Laundry Hints

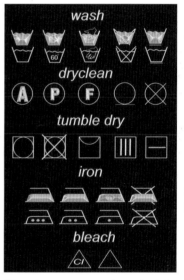

- Keep a list of laundry tips, stain removal techniques, and other clothing care information handy by posting a bulletin board in your laundry area.

- You can also use this board to tack up buttons, thread, and other supplies for quick repair.

- If you don't have wall space for a bulletin board, use a small three-ring binder; sheet protectors can keep papers from getting wet and can corral small items like buttons and safety pins.

LAUNDRY: DRYING, FOLDING, IRONIN

Get clean clothes ready to wear quickly and easily with designated spots for drying and ironing

Cleaning clothes gets you only partway through the laundry process. Drying and folding are equally as important as what happens inside the washer; in some cases, you'll also need to take out the ironing board before you can officially consider laundry day over. Creating designated spots for the tools, supplies, and spaces you need for drying, folding, and ironing makes these tasks quicker, easier, and more efficient.

Ideally, your main laundry area will also have room for the follow-up tasks, so you won't have to move clothes to a different part of the house to finish working with them. Space-

Air-Drying

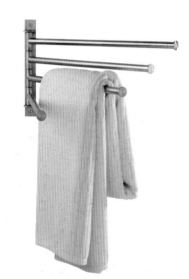

- Drying racks speed the process of drying clothes by air and are useful to have if you regularly wash delicates and other items that can't go in the dryer.

- If you need lots of space, look for a freestanding rack that folds up and can be stored behind a door or next to the washer.

- Racks that attach to the wall make the most of small spaces by folding out when you need them and folding flat when you don't.

Hanging Space

- A simple closet rod installed under a shelf in the laundry room provides space to hang clothes after they've been ironed or that need to be air-dried.

- If you plan to use the rod for drip-drying clothes, be sure at least part of it hangs over a waterproof surface.

- Use a wall-mounted hook rack if you don't have space for a rod.

savers like wall-mounted racks and fold-down tables let you store your other necessary supplies in the same spot as your washer and dryer without having to cram.

Select the tools you need based on how much space you have to work with and what type of care you normally do. If you very rarely air-dry clothes (or do so mainly on a clothes-line), you probably won't need drying racks, but these are useful gadgets to have on hand if you have several pieces of clothes that can't go in the dryer.

If you do a lot of ironing or need to be able to easily iron a wide variety of fabrics (from cotton pants to poly-blend blouses), you'll want an advanced iron, but a basic model will do if you tend to iron only a few clothes. The same goes for your ironing board: Invest in one you truly love if you use it a lot, or choose a simpler version if you're only an occasional ironer.

Make your overall goal creating a system that's uncluttered and that lets you work through your laundry tasks easily.

Folding Space

- Folding clothes is easiest on a broad surface such as a table.

- Create folding space in your laundry area without cluttering the room by installing a flip-up table on the wall.

- Pull the table out when you need it and flip it back against the wall when you don't.

- A flip-up table can also provide extra workspace and storage for supplies while you're doing laundry.

Ironing Space

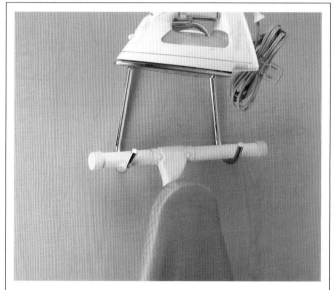

- Keep your ironing board and iron accessible but out of the way on an over-door or wall-mounted rack.

- Choose a rack that's sturdy enough to hold your board safely, with a secure spot for the iron so that it won't fall when you open and close the door.

- If you prefer to leave your ironing board set up—and have enough space to do so—be sure not to use it as a collection point for anything other than clothes that need to be ironed.

LIVING ROOM
Discover the best way of organizing your living room based on what happens there

Not all living rooms are created equal—or used in the same way. You'll need different storage solutions if you spend a lot of time in your living room than you will if you reserve it as a spot for entertaining guests and observing special occasions. From the list, choose the living room profile that best describes how you use this space, and then read targeted tips below the photo.

Everyday Entertainment Zone

My living room is where the family gathers to play games, watch movies, look at photos, and generally spend time together. I need storage that will keep things like board games and DVDs from being scattered around the room. I want the room to be a reflection of my family, with a warm, welcoming feel.

In an Everyday Entertainment Zone . . .

In Any Living Room . . .

- Keep very fragile items in display cabinets or on high shelves, and secure them with museum wax. Even if you don't use your living room often, you don't want to risk a favorite piece being broken.

- Use folding screens to create divisions within the room or to hide anything you don't want guests to see.

- If your living room has different zones—the reading zone, the bar zone, and so on—set them off with different area rugs.

- Each time the family gathers here for games or movies, assign one person to be responsible for putting things away and tidying up the room when you're done.

- Keep storage for things like movies and games within kids' reach.

- Do a board and video games audit once a year with the family; weed out games that the kids have outgrown, that never get played, or that are missing several pieces or parts.

Guests-Only Spot

I use my living room only when I have company and for special family celebrations around the holidays. I need storage for entertaining supplies so that I don't have to look all over the house for them. My living room should feel like a special, slightly formal place, not like just another room.

Reading and Relaxation Space

My living room is the place I go to relax with a book, some music, or a movie. I need a way to keep my reading material organized, and I want easy access to my CDs and tapes. I'd like this room to surround me with good memories and a sense of peace.

In a Guests-Only Spot . . .

- If your living room has doors, keep them closed when you're not using the space so that it stays cleaner and doesn't become a magnet for clutter.

- To give the room a more formal air, don't allow things like toys and newspapers to accumulate.

- Use this space for storing party supplies and special occasion linens; you'll clear space in other parts of the house and will reinforce the fact that this is a room for celebrations, not for everyday use.

In a Reading and Relaxation Space . . .

- Place reading lamps on the floor or on tables near your favorite reading spots.

- Think of the room as your own personal museum, and rotate "exhibits" of collectibles and memorabilia on a regular basis. Have your kids help you with this so that they can learn a bit about family history.

- Reserve your bookshelves for books (and perhaps a few decorative items); store games, gadgets, and other items elsewhere.

PHOTOS AND MEMORABILIA

Keep reminders of the past safe, organized, and accessible with simple supplies and a storage plan

Photos and memorabilia are among the most valuable things in many homes. They also tend to accumulate fairly quickly, which can lead to clutter and damage if there aren't smart storage systems in place to accommodate these items. Organizing your photos and memorabilia, and creating displays of those things that are most meaningful to you will help keep them safe and make them easier to enjoy.

Before getting started on setting up systems for storing and displaying memorabilia, think about which mementos are really important to you and which aren't. Remember that the more things you keep, the more difficult it will be to find and enjoy the ones you truly love. Ask yourself if it's really worth holding

ORGANIZING YOUR HOME

Displaying Photos

- Personalize the decor in your living room by displaying photos that are special to you.

- Show one or two framed photos if you want to emphasize them.

- For a less formal display, frame several snapshots

and show them together. Use frames of similar colors and materials to keep things from looking cluttered and to bring a sense of cohesion to the display.

- Wall-mounted shelf ledges are an easy way of creating more flat space for photo displays.

Storing Photos

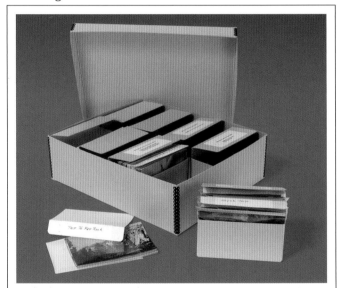

- Keep photos not on display safe and organized by storing them in photo boxes.

- Many boxes have inserts and dividers that let you create categories or groups for hundreds of photos.

- Choose boxes made of photo-safe materials, such

as acid-free paper. Storing pictures in containers not meant for them (like shoeboxes) causes damage and fading.

- If you have old photos that are brittle, cracked, or damaged, bring them to a restorer, who may be able to repair them.

onto every birthday and holiday card you've ever received, for example, or whether it would make more sense to create a small album of only those cards with sincere, personalized sentiments from people you're fond of.

After you create some guidelines for what to keep and what to let go of, start weeding. Aim to get rid of things like blurry, unidentifiable, or duplicate photos; gifts and trinkets you've received from others but don't enjoy; and anything that brings back bad memories, such as angry letters or photos of people you no longer want to be associated with. Set aside the pictures and objects you'd like to keep.

How you store the things that remain will depend on how much you have, what condition they're in, and what you want to do with them: Display them, put them in scrapbooks or albums, or simply box them up for safekeeping.

Get your mementos organized so that they can be the positive connections to the past they're meant to be, rather than a source of stress and clutter.

Creating Albums

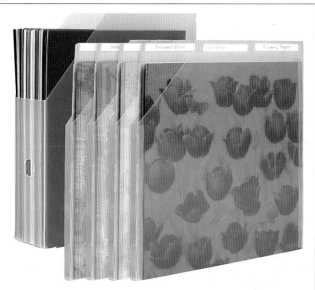

- Highlight special photos and mementos without framing them by putting them in a scrapbook or album.

- This allows you to interact with your mementos in ways you're not able to when they're stored in boxes.

- Keep scrapbook supplies and pages organized in page holders or files, which are sized specifically for album pages.

- If you like the idea of scrapbooks but don't have time to create them yourself, consider hiring a professional to lend a hand.

Shadowboxes

- Shadowboxes, which are essentially frames with deep storage space, let you keep three-dimensional memorabilia safe and on display.

- You can use shadowboxes to highlight one or two particularly meaningful pieces or to create a collage of an event, such as a trip.

- Look for shadowboxes at art supply stores or frame shops.

- If you have old or fragile memorabilia you want to display, bring them to a professional framer.

COLLECTIBLES
Organize and display your favorite collections to liven up and personalize your space

ORGANIZING YOUR HOME

Collections add richness to our lives and, when displayed, can convey our personality and interest to others. Of course, they can also be a major source of clutter. A truly organized collection is one that you enjoy and have stored and displayed in a way that integrates it with the rest of your home, rather than allowing it to take over the house entirely.

Step one in getting your collections in order, then, is reconnecting with the things you already have and committing yourself only to those you love. Collect things because doing so brings you pleasure and satisfaction, not because someone else has told you to or has handed down an unwanted collection you feel obligated to keep.

Fragile Collectibles

Flat Collectibles

- Keep collections of china, glass, crystal, and other fragile materials in a cabinet with doors to keep them clean and safe.

- Choose a cabinet with enough space to display your selected pieces without crowding them; you might consider one with closed cabinets or drawers beneath to store items you don't want to display.

- Use museum wax to keep things in place on shelves—especially important if the cabinet is in a high-traffic area and could be bumped.

- Stand items like maps, postcards, and scarves upright for display by framing them.

- Hang framed pieces of a collection on a wall—possibly with a decorative element with a similar theme—or group them together on a shelf.

- If you have more pieces than you can display at one time, swap out the items in your frames a few times a year. You'll enjoy a larger part of your collection and will keep your living room decor fresh.

Also be wary of collecting things as an investment strategy. Unless a professional appraiser you know and trust can assure you that a specific collection will appreciate in value, chances are good that it won't, and it may end up costing you far more than it's worth.

Sort through your collections with the goal of getting rid of anything you don't enjoy collecting, as well as anything that's broken beyond repair, that has no value to you, or that you have duplicates of. The things that are left after you've weeded will help you determine how much storage you need and what you'd like to put on display.

The best ways of storing and showing your collections will depend on what they are. For example, ceramics require much different care than postcards or wooden figurines. Choose methods and tools that let you safely display a few pieces of your collection and keep the others neat and organized in storage.

Small Collectibles

- Small three-dimensional collectibles like shells, thimbles, and butterflies work well in deep frames or shadowboxes.

- Group collectibles together for a more interesting display and to save space. Consider storing different items—butterflies and eggshells, for example—in the same frame for an unusual twist.

- Hang framed collections on a wall or set them on shelves.

- If you're not sure how to safely prepare your collectibles for framing, bring them to a frame shop.

Using Wall Space

- If you don't have space for your collectibles on existing shelves, use shelf ledges on the wall for displays.

- Ledges are ideal for oddly shaped items, as well as those you want to highlight, such as unusual bottles or wood sculptures.

- These shelves come in a variety of shapes and sizes, and you can mix and match them to accommodate different pieces.

- Look for ledges that are sturdy enough to securely hold the things you want to display on them.

ENTERTAINING SUPPLIES

Organize your living room to make it a welcoming spot for guests and family members alike

The living room is meant to be one of the main places in the house for entertaining guests. Often, though, this room gathers clutter, which means we don't want guests to see it, which in turn means it's where things cleared out of the kitchen, dining room, or family room get stashed when company calls, which— you guessed it—means that clutter builds up even more.

It's time to reclaim your living room, not only as a spot for welcoming guests but also as a comfortable place for family members to gather on less formal occasions.

The first step toward achieving this is clearing out the things that shouldn't be there. This includes not only large items—such as pieces of furniture that have migrated here

Entertaining Supplies

Party Supplies

- If you enjoy entertaining guests, set aside space in your living room for some basic supplies, such as bar glasses, nonperishable snacks, and cocktail napkins.

- A bar cabinet is a good option for storing all of these supplies in one central spot. Look for one that fits the room and has shelves and dividers inside for organizing bottles and supplies.

- Use a smaller piece (such as a bedside table with a cabinet and drawer) if your living room is compact.

- Keep your party supplies contained and organized to make it easier to plan your next celebration. Knowing what supplies you have on hand also decreases the chances of buying duplicates.

- Create a storage box for each type of party you have: kids' birthday parties, holiday open houses, and so on. Stock each box with paper goods, decorations, and favors; if you have blank invitations, store them here.

- Label boxes by event type, and store them on a shelf or in a cabinet.

from other rooms—but small stuff as well: unread books and magazines, holiday decorations that never got put away, toys and games your kids have outgrown.

Sort through everything in the living room and get rid of anything you no longer want, use, or need. Put things that should be stored elsewhere back where they belong.

With the space cleared, you're ready to plan how you want to use it. Think of what you do here (or used to, if you don't currently use the room) and what you wish you could do here, and designate spots for those activities. For example, if you want to be able to use the space for parties as well as for family game nights, plan storage for entertaining supplies and board games.

Once your living room feels comfortable and functional again, work to keep it that way. Use the space on a regular basis in order to make it a room that's truly living, rather than dead space at the heart of your home.

Games and Activities

- Create a designated spot— a shelf, drawer, or cabinet— to store board games and cards to prevent lost pieces and to keep the living room neater.

- Replace broken or damaged board game boxes with Game Savers, plastic containers designed to hold boards and game pieces. Game Savers are sturdy and stackable.

- Corral loose pieces that don't have boards in small containers with lids. Label each container.

Central Storage

- If you don't have space in your living room for multiple pieces of storage furniture, opt for one larger piece in which you can store bar supplies, party goods, and games.

- A unit with a combination of shelves, drawers, and cabinets will give you the most storage flexibility.

- Designate specific spots for specific things: games in one drawer, for example, and party supplies in another.

READING MATERIAL

Create a comfortable, organized, clutter-free spot for enjoying your favorite reads

A living room with comfortable seating and good light is a great spot for reading, and for storing reading material. Too often, though, the things we want to read (or feel we should read) pile up rapidly with nowhere to go and little chance of being enjoyed anytime soon. These stacks can quickly become overwhelming.

Create your ideal reading nook by choosing a spot you enjoy, clearing it of the things you don't want to read or won't ever have time to read, and setting up effective storage for those books and magazines you truly love.

Before you start sorting, make some agreements with yourself. Give yourself permission to let go of books you've

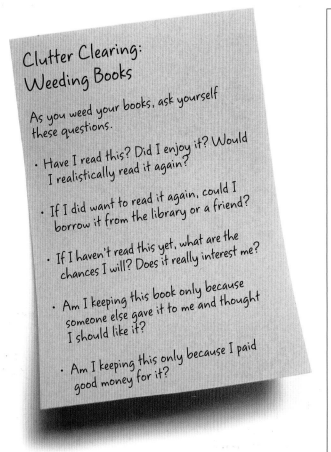

Clutter Clearing: Weeding Books

As you weed your books, ask yourself these questions.

- Have I read this? Did I enjoy it? Would I realistically read it again?

- If I did want to read it again, could I borrow it from the library or a friend?

- If I haven't read this yet, what are the chances I will? Does it really interest me?

- Am I keeping this book only because someone else gave it to me and thought I should like it?

- Am I keeping this only because I paid good money for it?

Book Storage

- Invest in some sturdy, spacious bookshelves to keep your favorite books together and organized.

- Choose shelves that look good in the room and that have enough space to hold your favorite volumes.

- Use bookends or heavy decorative objects to keep books upright on shelves that aren't closed on both sides.

- Keep your shelves stable by storing the heaviest books on the lower shelves and lighter volumes up top.

been keeping only because you feel like you should read them (*War and Peace,* anyone?), not because they truly capture your interest. Allow yourself to donate or recycle magazines that have been piling up for months; if you haven't had the chance to read them by now, that opportunity probably isn't coming (especially if more periodicals arrive in the mail each month). And give yourself the chance to pass along books you've read but aren't likely to read again. Create a list of these books so that you can remember what you enjoyed and how much reading you have under your belt.

With these agreements in mind, do some weeding. Focus on the goal of creating a reading spot where you can store your favorites, keep handy the things you're reading now, and stash the stuff that's next on your reading list. Get rid of anything that's simply clutter or that you're not interested in, and then plan storage for the reading material you want to keep.

Alternate Book Storage

- If you don't have space for bookshelves, or if you need room to store oversize books, use a coffee table.

- Put one or two decorative books on top of the table for a nice visual touch (they're called coffee table books for good reason); store other volumes on a shelf below.

- Look for a table with drawers or a small cabinet to stash smaller books like paperbacks.

Magazine and Newspaper Storage

- Keep magazines and papers from collecting on flat surfaces throughout the house by creating a designated spot for them in the living room.

- Choose a magazine rack that fits near a comfortable chair or sofa, or that mounts on a nearby wall.

- Use the size of your magazine rack as a way to prevent a backlog of periodicals: As soon as the rack fills up, it's time to recycle older issues to make room for the newer ones.

MUSIC, MOVIES, AND VIDEO GAMES

Set up smart storage to make your entertainment center the fun spot it's meant to be

The living room can be a great spot to gather for listening to music, watching movies, or playing video games. However, the supplies and gadgets those activities require—discs, tapes, consoles, controllers, cables—can easily become a daunting pile of clutter. To keep your entertainment center a fun and accessible spot, clear out what you don't need there

and set up storage for what you do.

Start by weeding out the CDs you no longer listen to, movies you're unlikely to watch again, and video games your kids (or you!) have outgrown. As you weed, remember that music and movies are among the easiest things to rent or borrow, and it's probably not worth keeping them around unless

Music Racks

- Keep CDs neat and organized by storing them in a music rack. These units are available as cabinets, shelves, and open racks.

- A music cabinet is a good option for keeping discs behind closed doors, which lends the room a cleaner, less cluttered look.

- Choose a unit with shelves (either open or in a cabinet) if you want to be able to separate your music into categories.

Disc Binders

- If you have limited storage space, or simply don't want to store CDs or DVDs in their original cases, use disc binders.

- These binders come in a variety of sizes and have separate pockets for each disc. Look for pockets made of material that won't scratch

or damage your discs, such as paper or Safety-Sleeve, a soft mesh material.

- You can use binders to divide discs into different categories, such as classical music or kids' movies.

they're tried-and-true favorites. If you need an extra incentive to get rid of things like CDs and DVDs, consider selling them; you'll clear out space and make some cash.

After you've sorted and weeded, take a look at the things you have left, as well as the space available for storing them. Aim to keep entertainment supplies as close as possible to where you use them: CDs near the stereo, for example, and DVDs within easy reach of the TV.

················ GREEN ● LIGHT ··············

Keep your entertainment center clutter-free and expand your movie-watching options by subscribing to a rental-by-mail service like Netflix or GreenCine. Video gamers can check out Gamefly, which rents games for a wide range of systems. (See the Resources section for links.)

Entertainment Centers

- Keep music, movies, and games together—and in the same spot as your stereo and TV—by storing them in an entertainment center.

- Look for a unit that has space for your electronics (TV, DVD player, game console, and so on) as well as storage shelves, drawers, or cabinets for discs and supplies.

- A unit with closed storage spaces or shelves on the side rather than the front will decrease visual distractions when you're watching TV or playing a video game.

Gaming Supplies

- Store video games and supplies (such as cables and controllers) together in a drawer or on a shelf.

- Corral controllers and accessories in bins to keep them from getting lost or tangled.

- Get everyone in the family who uses the game console into the habit of putting games back into their boxes and stowing controllers after playing.

DINING ROOM

Maximize your dining room's organization and efficiency based on how you use the space

For every household that has regular casual meals in the dining room, there's one that uses the room for special occasions throughout the year, and another that reserves the space for entertaining guests occasionally. Organizing tips for the dining room depend on what the space is like in your home. Choose the description that fits best and find targeted tips here.

In Any Space . . .

- A dining room table with drawers is a neat, uncluttered, and space-saving way to increase storage in the room.

- Keeping a tablecloth or runner on the table at all times can help protect it, and can be a deterrent to clutter pile-ups.

- Choose linens and serving pieces you can use for multiple occasions, rather than having full sets of items for each specific holiday or event.

Anything and Everything Spot

My family uses the dining room regularly, and it's not a formal part of the house. When we're not eating here, I use the space as a home office—a place to pay bills and sort mail. I want to be able to switch easily between functions, and I need storage space for both dining and office supplies.

In an Anything and Everything Spot . . .

- Create a designated storage spot in a hutch or sideboard for your non-dining-related supplies so that you can easily clear off the table at the end of the day.

- Look for a hutch or sideboard with multiple drawers and cabinets so that you can easily divide it into different storage sections for different types of supplies.

- If you don't have a lot of storage space, use a rolling file cart as a portable office.

Small Space for Special Occasions

I use my dining room to entertain friends throughout the year; at other times, I want the space to be clean and uncluttered. My dining room is big enough for a table and chairs but not for a hutch, so storage can be a challenge. I need a spot to keep the special linens, dishes, and decorative pieces I use when I have guests over.

Formal Entertaining Room

My dining room is reserved for formal entertaining a few times a year. At other times, my family and I generally don't use the space because I don't want the room to get cluttered. I want to keep my dishes, linens, and serving pieces together and well organized so that they're easy to find when I need them.

In a Small Space for Special Occasions . . .

- Use a convertible dining room table with leaves that fold into it. When you're not using the room, fold up the table to save space.

- Keep the table decorated with a simple centerpiece at all times to make the space look special, even when it's not in use.

- If you don't have space for a sideboard or hutch, use sturdy bookshelves; store plates, linens, and decorations in decorative boxes or baskets on the shelves.

In a Formal Entertaining Room . . .

- Invest in a hutch or sideboard large enough to hold all of your dishes and supplies. One with multiple drawers and cabinets is best.

- If you have additional storage space available in the dining room, use it for items you don't have space for elsewhere, such as extra kitchen linens.

- Store items together by occasion—for example, your Thanksgiving turkey platter, carving accessories, and gravy boat—so that it's easy to locate all of the items you need for an event.

DISHES AND CHINA

Organize and protect your special occasion dishes so that you can enjoy them for years to come

Fine dishware can make special occasions even more so and can bring a sense of celebration to everyday meals. By organizing and protecting your best dishes, you'll make it easier to find them when you want them and can help keep them safe from cracks and chips.

The first step in getting your china organized is deciding which sets and pieces you'd like to keep. As with other things throughout the house, your fine dishes should be useful, meaningful, and enjoyable to you. If you have pieces you rarely (if ever) use but have been holding onto because they were a gift or because

China Cabinets

- A china cabinet is a great way to keep dishes together, especially if you have large sets. Look for a cabinet with sturdy shelves and doors that open and close smoothly.

- Use a hutch or sideboard if you have small sets or only a few special pieces.

- Choose a cabinet with glass-front doors or open cabinets if you have pieces for display.

- If you have pets or young children, look for cabinets with locking doors, or add door latches to keep your china safe from paws and small hands.

Displaying Dishes

- Putting special dishes on display lets you store them and add to your dining room decor at the same time.

- If you have space, use plate stands, which keep pieces upright. Choose stands that are sturdy enough to support each piece.

- You can also hang plates on the wall. Wall-mounted plate holders come in a variety of sizes, shapes, and materials. Select the plates you want to display; then look for a holder that fits them. Be sure to mount your holder securely onto the wall.

they're reminders of past events, consider letting them go. You'll clear out space for the things you do use, and you'll give someone else the chance to appreciate the items you pass along.

Once you sort your dishes and choose the ones you want to keep, it's time to create storage systems for them. How you store your pieces depends on how many you have, how often you use them, and how fragile they are. Dishes you pull out regularly should be easy to access, while pieces you use less often can be stored in padded containers and out of the way.

When you're happy with how you've stored your china, create a storage map that details what goes where. This list will make it easier to find what you need when you're ready to entertain, and to put things away when you're done with them. Keep your map in a central spot (such as a drawer in your hutch), and share it with anyone who'll be lending a hand with pre-party prep.

Stacking Dishes

- Stack dishes of the same type—salad plates, dinner plates, and so on—to keep them organized. If you have multiple sets, divide pieces by collection first, and then by type.

- Use felt or a few sheets of paper towels between each dish to prevent cracks and chips.

- Shelf expanders let you make the most of your storage space; stack dishes both on top of and underneath these gadgets. Choose expanders made of sturdy metal, which can bear the weight of heavy china.

Padded Storage

- If you have sets of china that are especially fragile or that you don't often use, keep them organized and protected by storing them in padded containers.

- These containers are made of fabric and come in a variety of sizes and shapes. You can find padded containers for different types of dishes as well as for cups, glasses, and serving ware.

- Pin tags to your padded containers with a note on what's in each one.

117

GLASSWARE

Be ready to serve up drinks at a moment's notice by keeping your glassware organized

Most of us have several kinds of cups and glasses floating around the house. If you find yourself searching high and low for wineglasses before a party, or having to extract your fine crystal from a jumble of plastic tumblers, it's time to get organized. Keeping your special occasion glasses separate from your everyday ware helps prevent breakage and makes getting ready for your next soireé a snap.

Start by collecting the glasses you use for entertaining or for special occasions in one spot. With everything together, you'll be better able to get a realistic overview of what you have, which in turn will help you decide what to keep.

Hanging Glasses

- Wineglass racks are an easy way to keep stemware organized and protected.

- If your dining room storage furniture doesn't have glass racks built in, install your own racks under shelves or inside cabinets. Another option is a freestanding wine rack; look for a model that has space for storing glasses.

- Choose a glass rack with an opening that fits the width of your glasses' base. Install it so there's enough space below and to the side to keep glasses from hitting.

Storing Glasses in Cabinets

- Store other glasses directly in a cabinet. Choose one that's not in the center of the room's traffic flow so that it's less likely to be bumped or jostled.

- To maximize space, store sturdy glasses in two stacks: one directly on the cabinet shelf, and the second on a tray resting on the first stack. Use a shelf liner or felt to protect the bottom stack.

- Store wineglasses base-down. The base is the strongest and most stable part of the glass.

Next, think realistically about how you entertain, and how often. If you frequently have guests over for formal parties, it's probably worth holding onto an array of glasses. If you entertain only once or twice a year, though, or tend to have more casual events, a smaller selection is a better option, especially if your storage space is limited. With these guidelines in mind, start weeding. Get rid of glasses you don't use, need, or like, as well as any that are chipped or cracked.

Then set up storage for the glasses you're keeping. Put similar types together (wineglasses with Champagne flutes, for example), and store them where they'll be easy to access but out of harm's way, such as in a sideboard or a corner cupboard. When things are in place, consider labeling the insides of cabinet doors or the edges of shelves to indicate what goes where. This will make the process of putting things away easier.

And when you're ready to put glassware away after you've used it, make sure it's completely clean and dry: You'll keep it from getting musty and won't have to wash and dry it again the next time you want to use it.

Displaying Glasses

- If you have small, delicate, or unusual glasses, consider putting them on display. Displaying glasses provides an easy storage solution and adds to the decor of your dining room.

- Create an inviting tableau by putting a special bottle of liquor on a tray with related glassware, such as brandy snifters or cordial glasses.

- Use extra space in a glass-front cabinet to show off special glasses. Arrange them as you'd like, and secure them to the shelf with a dab of museum wax under the base of each glass.

Protected Storage

- Protect especially fragile or rarely used glassware by storing it in boxes or bins.

- For stemware, cut a divided wine case so that it's just slightly taller than your glasses, and store one glass in each divided section of the case. Tape a piece of cardboard to one edge of the case to serve as a lid.

- Consider padded storage boxes for smaller or more fragile pieces. A stemware-size box can hold wineglasses and taller bar glasses, while a box meant for teacups is a good option for small glasses.

119

LINENS

Keep napkins and tablecloths organized so that they're always ready to protect and decorate your table

Table linens add a special touch to meals, and they also help protect your table from spills and scratches. Getting your tablecloths, place mats, and napkins organized makes it easier to find what you need and to get your table ready for dining in a snap.

Step one is to sort through your linens and decide which to keep. Gather together all of your table coverings and cloth napkins—even those that are stored elsewhere in the house (with holiday decorations, for example). As you sort, unfold each piece and check it for tears, wear, or stains. If something is damaged beyond repair and you can't hide the trouble spots (camouflaging a rip under a centerpiece, for example), it's probably time to let the piece go. The same holds for ta-

Using Drawers

- A drawer in a sideboard or hutch is a convenient place to store dining room table linens. Line the drawer with shelf paper to keep linens fresh and to prevent snags.

- Measure your drawer and calculate how many linens you need to store there. If you have several table-cloths, fold them in a fairly compact way to fit as many as you can; if you have only a few, store them folded more loosely.

- Store linen sets together in stacks so that it's easy to pull out an entire set at once.

Using Baskets

- If drawer space is at a premium, use baskets or bins to store linens on shelves or on top of a hutch.

- Look for containers that are large enough to store the linens you have and fit easily on the shelves or surfaces you plan to use for storage.

- Use baskets with cloth linings to prevent snags and keep linens clean. Draping a large dinner napkin inside an unlined basket offers the same protection.

- Separate linens into baskets by type (napkins, round tablecloths, etc.) or by set, and label each basket.

blecloths that aren't the right size for your table and anything you don't like or never use.

Once you decide what to keep, fold each piece carefully. If you have sets of matching linens, store them together. Keep old or fragile linens safe by wrapping them loosely in acid-free tissue.

After using table linens, launder dirty pieces as soon as possible to prevent stains from setting, iron as needed, and fold them neatly. Carefully organizing and storing your linens can help keep them usable for years to come.

MAKE IT EASY

Pin a handwritten label to each tablecloth with a description of its size, shape, and pattern or theme—sixty-inch round rosebud print, for example—so that you don't have to unfold multiple linens to find the one you want. You can also label napkin or place mat sets.

Hanging Linens

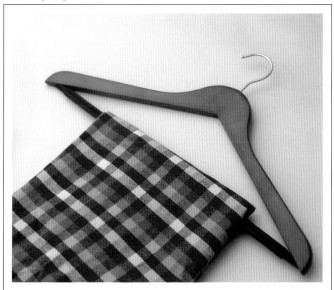

- Use extra rod space in a hall closet to hang large or bulky tablecloths, which can take up a lot of drawer or shelf space when folded.

- Fold the tablecloths carefully and drape them over a pants hanger with a non-slip coating on the crossbar. To protect delicate linens, slip them inside a suit bag (ideally made of fabric) before hanging them.

- To store napkins or place mats on a closet rod, attach them to skirt hangers with padded clips.

Rolling Linens

- Consider rolling your linens rather than folding them to maximize storage space in drawers or baskets. Rolling also helps prevent wrinkles and creases.

- To roll a napkin or tablecloth, fold it in half or in thirds lengthwise then roll it up from one end to the other. Make adjustments as you work to keep your roll tight and symmetrical.

- Slip a napkin ring around napkins to keep them rolled, and tie tablecloths loosely with thread or ribbon.

SERVING WARE

Keep platters, trays, and serving dishes at the ready with a simple organizing system

Serving pieces liven up a dining table—and, of course, make it easy to transport food from the kitchen. Keeping these pieces organized helps prevent breakage and maximizes the storage space in your dining room. Plus, when you know what pieces you have and where to find them, it's a snap to pull them out for your next special meal.

Start by collecting all of your serving pieces—bowls, platters, trays, and large plates—together. Do a quick sort by type (all bowls together, for example) in order to see how many of each you have. Then do some weeding. Put in your Donate pile anything you don't like or use, as well as anything you have too many of. Toss (or repurpose for nonfood use) any

Displaying Serving Ware

- Putting serving pieces on display saves on storage space and adds a sense of flair to your dining room's decor.

- Hang large, flat pieces (such as platters and trays) on the wall with sturdy plate holders or prop them up in a cabinet or on top of a sideboard with sturdy plate stands.

- Pieces with more depth, like bowls and pitchers, are better off on shelves or other horizontal surfaces.

- If you have several pieces from the same set, try displaying them together on a shelf for dramatic visual impact.

Storing Heavy Pieces

- Store very large or heavy serving pieces safely in low or chest-height cabinets. Avoid storing them in high cabinets that you need to reach overhead to access.

- Drawers in a hutch or sideboard can be useful for storing broad, flat serving pieces (such as platters),

but be careful not to store too many heavy items in the same drawer, which can cause the bottom of the drawer to warp or crack.

- Use baking sheet racks or tension rods to create vertical storage for heavy pieces in a cabinet.

pieces that have significant scratches, chips, or cracks.

Next, create a storage plan based on how many and what kinds of serving pieces you have and how often you use them. Stash things you use on a regular basis in an easy-to-access cabinet, with lesser-used pieces in higher or lower spots. If all of your serving ware shares one storage space, keep everyday items in front so that you don't have to reach over other pieces to get at them.

Finally, create a storage map—a list of each piece and its location—and keep it in a convenient spot so that you can easily find the items you need come mealtime.

MAKE IT EASY

After taking out your serving ware (for big meals or celebrations), clean out the cabinets and drawers in your dining room. With the serving pieces out of the way, dust the storage spaces and replace drawer or shelf liners. Then do a quick round of weeding to make sure you still want and use the things you're keeping.

Stacking Serving Ware

- Stacking serving ware maximizes storage space and helps keep like items together (platters with platters, for example).

- Use felt pads, several sheets of paper towels, or cloth napkins between stacked items to help avoid scratches and chips.

- Always be sure to place the heaviest items at the bottom of a stack, and layer things according to size.

- Because it's so fragile, bone china shouldn't be stacked with anything but other bone china.

Other Storage Options

- If you're pressed for space in the dining room, or if you have several pieces of serving ware you use very rarely, look to other areas of the house for storage.

- Slip flat pieces inside padded envelopes and stack them in a sturdy plastic storage bin. Label the bin and stash it in an out-of-the-way spot, such as the basement or the back of a large closet.

- Put extra space in your kitchen, pantry, or living room to use as a spot for storing serving pieces you don't use frequently and don't have room for in the dining room.

123

SPECIAL OCCASION ITEMS

Keep special dining supplies organized for more enjoyable, less stressful celebrations

Holiday-themed china, linens, and serving pieces—as well as items that are so special they're only used on certain occasions, such as an anniversary dinner—deserve storage solutions that will keep them organized and easy to find but out of the way of everyday supplies.

Before you decide where or how to store your special dining pieces, take a look at what you have. Gather these items together and group them by occasion to get a clearer sense of what you have, and then sort through them. Keep things that you use at least yearly, as well as pieces that are espe-

Storing Holiday Supplies

- Make it easy to find supplies for certain holidays by storing them in colored bins. Choose colors that will make you think of each holiday: orange and black for Halloween, for example.

- Label each with its contents and the holiday, and store with your seasonal items.

- If you don't have decorations or serving pieces specific to certain holidays, store items together by their color to mix and match later.

Storing Small Items

- Keep small accessories (such as napkin rings, place card holders, and table decorations) together and organized by storing them in bins or boxes.

- Choose clear containers if you're planning to store them inside drawers or cabinets. Use decorative bins or baskets if you'll be storing them in the open.

- Sort items together by type (napkin rings) or by occasion (New Year's Eve dinner supplies), and label each container accordingly.

cially important to you; let go of items you don't use, like, or want, as well as those that are damaged beyond repair.

If you have pieces that can do double or triple duty—say, a green serving bowl that could be used at a Christmas dinner, a St. Patrick's Day party, and an Easter brunch—consider giving away similar pieces that are specific to only one event or holiday. The same holds for linens: You can use tablecloths, napkins, and placemats in standard holiday colors at events throughout the year, rather than having to keep on hand sets with colors,

patterns, or themes appropriate only to a single holiday.

After you weed, think about storage. Aim to keep the supplies you use for each holiday or event together in one spot so that it's easy to find everything you need. If you don't have space in your dining room cabinets for special occasion items, store them in sturdy bins or boxes elsewhere in the house. Be sure to keep a list of what's where—that way, you'll be able to grab what you need for your celebration when the time comes.

Vases and Candles

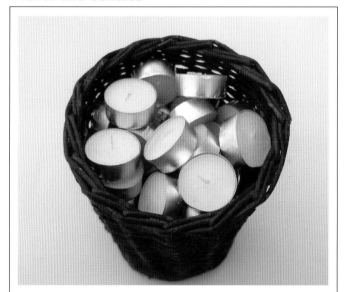

- If you have multiple vases, store them in cardboard wine cases, which come with dividers. Remove dividers as necessary to accommodate vases of different sizes; label the cases and store them in a cabinet or closet.

- Keep loose taper candles in check by storing them in empty cardboard tubes from rolls of paper towels or toilet tissue. Empty tissue boxes or small baskets are useful for holding votives and tea lights.

- Corral candlesticks and votive holders in a basket or bin stored in a cabinet or drawer.

Displaying Items

- Putting holiday and special occasion dining ware on display adds a festive touch to the dining room.

- If you have serving ware for holidays and occasions throughout the year, set up a rotating display. Designate a few spots (on the wall, in a glass cabinet, in the center of the table) as exhibit spaces to show off platters, pitchers, and other items related to the event you're celebrating.

- When one holiday or event is over, update your display with items related to the next celebration on the calendar.

HOME OFFICE

Choose the most accurate description of your home office space for customized organizing tips

Whether your home office is its own room decked out with a full set of furniture and equipment or a nook in another room in the house, keeping it organized will help make the space more efficient. Read the three descriptions here, choose the one that most accurately describes the type of home office you have, and find specific recommendations for your space below the photo.

In Any Space . . .

- Buy only as many office supplies as you can conveniently store. In small spaces, limit bulk purchases to supplies you'll go through quickly to keep clutter from accumulating.

- Every home office should have a quality cross-cut paper shredder, file storage large enough to hold your necessary papers, and a time and task management tool (paper or electronic) you're comfortable with.

- Give kids their own homework spots—ideally separate from your office—to avoid tussles over desk space and supplies.

Separate Home Management Center

My home office has its own room, and I use the space primarily for office tasks. This is the space where I manage household affairs, from paying bills to tracking family members' schedules, so I tend to spend a good deal of time here. I need organized storage in my office for lots of papers and supplies.

In a Separate Home Management Center . . .

- Invest in a comfortable chair and desk; they'll make it more pleasant to spend time here. Also make sure the lighting in the room is adequate.

- Set up a filing system that has plenty of room to add new papers and files as needed. Keep new folders and labels close by to make creating files a snap.

- If you have unused closet space in the room, use it to stash supplies you don't need directly on or around your desk.

Part of a Multipurpose Space

My home office shares space in a room that's sometimes used for other things, like hosting overnight guests or letting my kids entertain when their friends come over. The office space needs to be easy to corral and keep tidy so that it doesn't overtake the room, and I need compact and super-efficient storage for my office supplies.

Nook in Another Room

My office isn't really an office; it's part of another room (a corner of the kitchen, a nook under the stairs, an unused hall closet). I need to maximize space here without making things too cramped, and I'd like the office to blend in with the rest of the room as much as possible.

In Part of a Multipurpose Space . . .

- Consider using a folding screen to block off the office portion of the room when you need to use the space for another purpose.

- Look for a desk or a separate drawer unit that blends with the room's decor and has space to store both files and supplies.

- Use a low cabinet or a set of shelves in a closet to store extra supplies and gadgets. Storage that's behind closed doors helps keep the room neat.

In a Nook in Another Room . . .

- Consider using an office armoire or hutch. You'll have a designated workspace, and when you're done working, you can hide everything behind closed doors.

- Look for multipurpose equipment—such as a printer that can also scan things and make copies—to save space.

- Think vertical: Whenever possible, use doors and walls to hang things like simple supply shelves and a bulletin board.

PAPER: SORTING AND WEEDING

Take control of your papers and files by clearing out what you no longer need

Many people name paper as one of their biggest organizing frustrations, and with good reason: It's perhaps the only thing we get more of every day, whether we want it or not. Luckily, with a few straightforward sorting techniques and an effective storage system, you can get your papers under control, which will save you time and stress.

The first step in getting papers and files organized is sorting through them and deciding which ones you need and which you don't. Because this process involves making decision after decision, it's helpful to create some guidelines about what stays and what goes before you start weeding. These guidelines can help make the entire sorting process smoother and more effective.

Gathering Papers

- Before you sort, gather papers from other parts of the house to get an accurate sense of how many and what types of papers you have.

- Use a box or bin to keep everything together. If you find papers that require your immediate attention (like bills you need to pay), put them in a separate box or folder, but keep them with the rest of your gathered papers.

- As you collect, pull out and shred or recycle anything that's clearly junk.

Questions to Ask

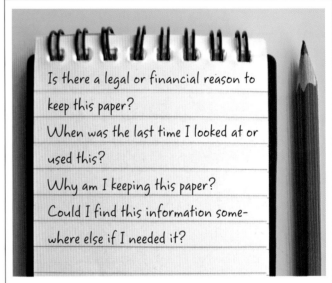

Is there a legal or financial reason to keep this paper?

When was the last time I looked at or used this?

Why am I keeping this paper?

Could I find this information some-where else if I needed it?

- In addition to the guidelines you create for what to keep and toss, ask yourself some additional questions to make those decisions.

- The questions above can get you started. Here are a few more: Is the benefit of keeping this paper worth the effort of storing it?

What's the worst that would happen if I got rid of it?

- If I've been indecisive about keeping this paper, what additional info do I need to make that decision?

Your guidelines should answer the questions, "Do I need to keep this? If so, how long?" for each kind of paper you have. You might decide, for example, that you want to keep all utility bills for one year and that you want to hold onto your kids' report cards indefinitely. It's also worth creating guidelines for things like periodicals, catalogs, clippings, event calendars, and correspondence.

Many (if not most) of the papers that accumulate in the average home are related to taxes and finances. It's a good idea,

then, to ask your CPA or tax preparer for guidance on how long to keep financial papers. Requirements can vary from person to person, so ask your financial professional if there are any special requirements that apply to you.

Once you establish your sorting and weeding guidelines, you are ready to get started. Keep on hand a shredder (or a bag for shreddables), a recycling bin, Post-it Notes, empty file folders, and an empty banker's box or file drawer to temporarily store files as you sort.

Sorting and Categorizing

- With all of your papers in one spot, start sorting. Use your guidelines and Questions to Ask to decide what you need or want.

- When you decide to keep something, write a category on a Post-it Note to describe the paper—Utility Bills, Articles to Save, Vaca-

tion Ideas, and so on. Put the Post-it on a folder and put the paper inside.

- Don't worry about creating perfect categories. Your main goal at this point is to get rid of papers you don't need.

Shredding and Recycling

- Many of the papers you'll toss probably will have sensitive personal information (such as bank or credit card account numbers) on them. To help avoid the danger of identity theft, shred these papers.

- Shred anything that includes your Social Security number,

any sort of financial account number, private identifying information about you (like your mother's maiden name), and any sensitive medical information.

- Also shred things like pre-approved credit card or loan offers. Recycle everything else.

PAPER: FILING

Set up a customized filing system to get—and keep—your papers under control

After you sort and weed your papers, you're ready to set up a filing system that provides easy access to the papers you need. There are several different types of filing systems to choose from; the method that's best for you depends on what you need to store, what sort of home office you have, and how you think. The following guidelines will help you choose the right system for your needs.

Start by taking a look at how much paper you're left with after sorting and weeding. If you have only a few folders, you'll probably be fine with a single file drawer or a portable file tote. If you have many folders, though, you'll probably need more drawer space or several bins.

Arranging Files

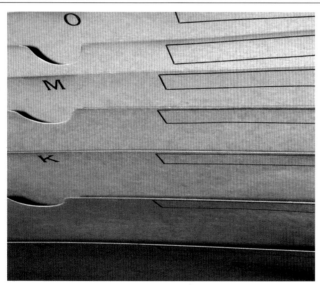

- Regardless of the physical file system you use, there are several different options for categorizing and arranging your files.

- Filing alphabetically is one of the most common methods. Sort your files alphabetically either by the broad categories they be-

long to—such as Banking, Family, Insurance, Travel—or by the name you've given each specific folder.

- Another option is to arrange files by how often you use them, with the folders you grab most often in the most easily accessible spot.

Desktop File Storage

- A desktop file holder is a good option if you have a small number of files or if you want to keep certain folders out and easily accessible.

- Unless you regularly deal with all of the papers that accumulate on your desktop, opt for an upright file holder over a horizontal version; it's easier to lose or forget about papers when they're stacked horizontally.

- Use labeled file folders in the sorter to keep papers separated by categories.

Also consider what types of paper you need to store. Things like tax returns from prior years can probably go into archival storage—a box in a closet, say—so you won't need space for them in your active files. Be sure to plan space, though, for the files you'll use often, such as folders for your current financial information.

The size and location of your home office also help determine the best filing system. If you have a separate room and lots of space, a multidrawer filing cabinet is an option; if your office shares space in another room, you'll need a more compact system.

Finally, take into consideration how you think when it comes to looking for information. Do you want folders to be out and visible, or would you rather store them in a drawer? Does it make more sense to you to sort files alphabetically, chronologically, or based on how often you use them? Create a file storage system that makes sense to you and that lets you find information quickly and easily.

Wall-Mounted Storage

- Put vertical space, such as a wall or a door, to use by hanging paper sorters.

- These units come in a variety of sizes and materials; choose one that's large and sturdy enough to hold the papers you need to store.

- Wall-mounted units are a good way of separating current files into categories, such as Bills to Pay, Follow-ups, and Ongoing Projects. Use several one-pocket sorters, or one with multiple pockets, to keep categories divided.

Portable File Storage

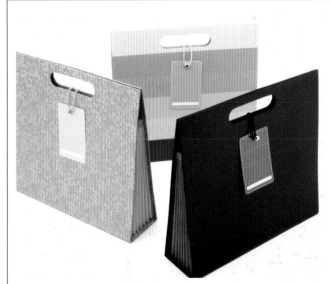

- A portable file tote is a good option if you have limited office space or if you need to transport files between your home office and another location.

- Totes come in a variety of sizes. If you need to transport files, opt for a smaller model that will still be easy to carry when it's full. Make sure the tote has a sturdy handle and a lid that closes snugly.

- If your files will stay in one place, select a tote that's roomy enough to fit all of your papers.

DESK

Clear it off and get it organized to create a pleasant, efficient workspace

Desks often wind up as catchall spots for things that don't have other homes (or that have migrated away from their homes). Clearing off your desk, and using some simple techniques to keep it organized and free of clutter, will make it a more pleasant place to work and will make the time you spend at it more efficient.

Get things under way by sorting and weeding the stuff that's currently on your desk. Set aside anything that belongs elsewhere so that you can return it to its rightful spot. Toss or recycle things that are clearly junk (and if you don't have a trash can and a recycling container near your desk, add them to the list of things you need in an effective workspace). Put

Storing Paper

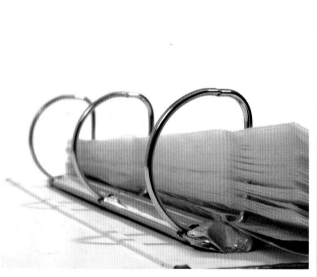

- Reserve the space on and around your desk for active papers; stash those you're not currently working with in a file cabinet or tote.

- Use a desktop file sorter to contain and organize things like bills, event reminders, and papers you need to follow up on. You can also store these things in a three-ring binder with sheet protectors.

- A bulletin board hung above the desk is another good option for stashing active papers. Tack up things like appointment cards, event invitations, and bills to pay.

Storing Supplies on the Desk

- Keep your main workspace neat by using containers to corral supplies. For your desktop, choose jars or boxes that are large enough to hold your essential supplies but small enough that they don't overcrowd the desk.

- Simple jars work well for holding pens, scissors, push pins, paper clips, rubber bands, and the like.

- Also try a container of supplies for each regular task: A bill-paying jar for example, might have stamps, clips, a pen, and a small calculator.

in your Donate pile anything you don't need, use, or want. As a general rule of thumb, if it's been sitting on your desk unused for more than a few months, you probably don't need to keep it.

Once you weed, look at what's left. The best solutions for storage on, in, and around your desk will depend on how much stuff you have and what it is. If you have lots of supplies, you'll need space in drawers or containers to hold them all. If you use your desk mainly for paperwork, you'll want plenty of easily accessible storage for papers and files.

Decide what goes where based on what things you need closest at hand while you're working at your desk. Supplies you use on a regular basis—such as stamps, address labels, pens, and your checkbook, if you use your desk for paying bills—should be within arm's reach when you're sitting down. Store less frequently used supplies out of the way so that they don't clutter up your workspace.

Organizing Desk Drawers

- Basic desk drawer trays or dividers will keep the supplies you store there from getting jumbled together every time you open the drawer.

- Take a look at the supplies you need to store, measure the drawer, and choose dividers that fit.

- Keep different kinds of supplies—especially small ones like paper clips and tacks—in separate divider compartments.

- You can also keep supplies organized within a drawer by keeping them in their original boxes.

Simple Habits: Keeping the Desk Organized

Maintaining organization on your desk is easy with a few regular habits:

- Each day, take a minute to put supplies away, toss trash, and recycle unneeded papers.

- Once a week, pay and file bills, deal with any active papers on the desk, make sure things are in order within the desk drawers, and tackle your shredding pile.

- Monthly, replace near-empty supplies and reconnect with everything on your bulletin board or in your file sorter to make sure things there are still current.

OFFICE SUPPLY CLOSET

Save time, space, and money by keeping your office essentials organized

Office supplies often come in greater quantities than you can use in an average week (or month), which means that you need to find somewhere to stash the rest of that ream of paper or the other eleven pens in the pack until you're ready to call them into service. Having an orderly, organized office supply area makes it easy store and retrieve things, which

means there's less chance you'll waste money on buying more of the supplies you know you have but can't find.

Organized storage starts with weeding out the stuff you don't want, use, or need, as well as supplies that are past their prime (such as dried-out pens and rusted paper clips). Be realistic about how many supplies you truly use and need on

Using Bins

Office Supplies
pencils, tape, rubberbands, markers, paper clips

- Boxes and bins are useful for storing loose supplies like pens, clips, envelopes, and rubber bands.

- To maximize storage space, choose containers that have lids and are stackable. Clear bins are a good option, because they let you see at a glance what's inside.

- You can create your own bin using shoeboxes or other sturdy boxes with lids. For a personalized touch, wrap them in decorative paper.

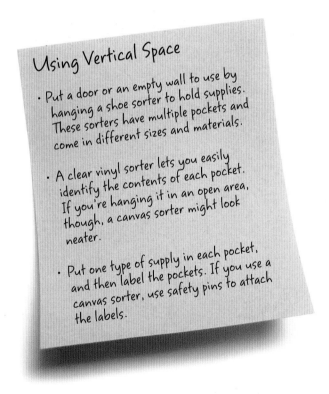

Using Vertical Space

- Put a door or an empty wall to use by hanging a shoe sorter to hold supplies. These sorters have multiple pockets and come in different sizes and materials.

- A clear vinyl sorter lets you easily identify the contents of each pocket. If you're hanging it in an open area, though, a canvas sorter might look neater.

- Put one type of supply in each pocket, and then label the pockets. If you use a canvas sorter, use safety pins to attach the labels.

hand; unless you have generous storage available, keeping more than a few months' worth of supplies may be more of a headache than it's worth. If you have excess supplies, put them to good use by donating them to a school, a nonprofit organization, or a religious institution.

After weeding, look for a convenient spot to store your supplies. If your home office is a room with a closet, consider using a set of shelves inside the closet. In a room with no closet, use bookshelves or a credenza near your desk. If your office is part of another room, use part of a nearby cabinet or closet, or mount a few sturdy shelves near your workspace.

Divide your supplies into categories such as paper and stationery, writing tools (pens, pencils, markers, erasers), and fasteners (staples, clips, rubber bands); put each category in its own container. Look for containers that fit in the storage space; if the containers will be in the open (on wall-mounted shelves, for example), find ones that work with the room's decor.

Storing Filing Supplies

- Keep empty hanging file folders organized and easy to access by storing them in a banker's box or portable file tote.

- Use one of the folders to hold supplies like tabs and labels. Label that folder so that you can find your supplies quickly.

- Store manila folders in their original box, or divide them up and store them with the hanging folders.

Storing Paper

- Use file trays to keep blank paper out of the way but easily accessible, and to separate different kinds or colors of paper.

- Look for trays that stack to make the most of your storage space, and choose ones that are sturdy enough to hold a ream of paper without warping.

- If you have several kinds of paper, tape a sample of each type of paper to the edge of the tray it's in to make it easy to find what you need.

135

FAMILY SCHEDULE

Create an effective household calendar to keep tabs on your family's activities and tasks

As life gets busier—and it always seems to—it becomes more important than ever to find a way of tracking all the things you and the other members of your household need to do. Creating a central spot for your family's schedule (or your own schedule, if you're not tracking others' activities) and choosing a calendar system that works for you will make

it easier to stay on top of events and dates.

Selecting the system that's best for you starts with determining how many schedules you need to track each week. If there are kids in your house, chances are you'll want to keep tabs on their activities and events, which will require a calendar with extra capacity; you might also want to note what's

Dry-Erase Calendars

- A calendar on a dry-erase board is highly visual and easy to update. Look for a board printed with a blank weekly or monthly calendar, which you can fill in and then erase when the week or month is through.

- Tend to plan in advance? Use two calendars side by

side so that you can see what's happening currently and what's ahead.

- If you're tracking several people's schedules, use different colored pens to distinguish one person's activities from another's.

Paper Calendars

- Paper calendars are easy and inexpensive options.

- If you don't need something portable, choose a wall calendar and post it in a communal spot. If you want to be able to take your calendar with you, use a planner book.

- If you're tracking several schedules, consider a calendar specifically designed as a family planner, which has several different blocks per day. Use the primary space for your own schedule or to list activities everyone's involved with, and devote the secondary blocks to specific family members.

on your spouse's or partner's schedule for the week. On the other hand, you might need to keep track of only your own schedule, possibly with a few notes on household-wide events (such as a family vacation), in which case a simpler calendar might do.

Your calendar choice also depends on whether you prefer an electronic tool, such as a PDA or a Web-based scheduler, or an analog tool, such as a wall calendar or a whiteboard. Also take into consideration whether you need your calendar to be portable or whether it can remain in one spot.

Once you select a calendar, sit down with everyone involved and do some schedule weeding: Take a realistic look at each person's activities, and ask whether those activities are enjoyable, beneficial, and worth continuing. Strongly consider letting go of activities and events that don't meet at least one of those three criteria.

Finally, enter into your calendar the information you want to track, and set aside time each week to update it so that you can stay on top of dates.

Electronic Calendars

- If you're tech-savvy, consider an electronic calendar. These include Outlook, iCal, and the scheduling programs built into PDAs and many cell phones.

- Electronic calendars let you easily enter, modify, and share information. You can schedule recurring events (such as a weekly soccer practice) and can color-code different types of activities or schedules for different family members.

- Be sure to back up your data regularly if your main calendar is on a PDA or other portable electronic device.

Online Calendars

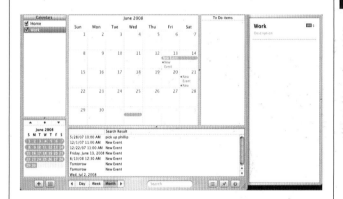

- Online calendars have many of the same benefits as electronic calendars. In addition, they allow you to access your schedule information from any computer connected to the Internet.

- Many free Web-based e-mail programs, including Gmail, Yahoo! Mail, and MSN, offer free online calendar programs.

- These programs include features such as e-mailed reminders and the ability to transfer information about an event (such as date, time, and location) from an e-mail message directly to the calendar.

HOME TECHNOLOGY
Get targeted organizing tips for the technology in your home based on your setup

Technology opens up our worlds, but it also requires careful organizing: What to do with those cords, cables, boxes, discs, and manuals? For ideas on how to get the computers, peripherals, and gadgets in your house in order, read the profiles here, choose the one that best describes your home, and find specific recommendations below the photo.

In Any Space . . .

• Keep the box and packing material that your computer or printer came in only until the warranty expires. After that point, you can safely recycle them.

• When you're ready to replace your electronics, get rid of the ones you're no longer using so they don't become clutter. See the Resources section at the back of this book for information on recycling electronics.

• Sort and weed your tech-related discs, boxes, and manuals each year and get rid of the ones you don't use.

Central Computing Spot

There's one central spot in our house with a computer that everyone in the family uses. We need a way of keeping each person's files on the computer separate and a way of dealing with the discs and boxes that come with the software we install. This space is active, but I'd like it to be more orderly and less cluttered.

In a Central Computing Spot . . .

• If your computer's operating system allows, create a separate account for each family member who uses the machine.

• Another option is to set up a folder for each person in the computer's main Documents directory.

• Consider scheduling time slots for computer use to avoid fights. Post a sign-up sheet near the computer at the start of each week, and let family members request the times they want.

Personal Computing Spaces

There are a few different computers in our home: The kids each have one in their room for their use, and I have my own machine. I want to be able to keep the basic supplies for all of our computers—the software, the extra printer paper, and so on—in one location, rather than having them spread throughout the house.

Anywhere There's a Seat

The main computer in my house is a laptop, and I tend to move around with it. I want one central spot for things like supplies and manuals but would like to be able to work from anywhere in the house. I'd love it if, at the end of the day, I could tuck everything computer-related neatly away.

In Personal Computing Spaces . . .

In Anywhere There's a Seat . . .

- Set up a basic computer network so that you can share an Internet connection and a printer among several machines. Call your local electronics store to ask for help with network setup.

- Store all the electronics boxes together in one place (ideally a garage, basement, or attic). If you lack space, collapse the boxes and store them flat.

- Create a central supply location near your main computer to avoid having to look in multiple rooms for the discs, cables, or supplies you need.

- Use a hutch or an office armoire as your home base. When you're done with your computer, put it away and close the door.

- To cut down on clutter, download software from the Internet whenever possible, rather than buying packaged versions.

- Go wireless, both with your Internet connection and with your printer. You'll be able to work on your computer as normal regardless of where you are in the house.

SOFTWARE, GAMES, AND MANUALS

Keep your computer software and games easily accessible with an organized system

Software and games are the things that make computers useful and fun. By getting the discs, manuals, and accessories that go along with these programs organized, you'll be able to know at a glance what you have and to keep computer-related clutter from piling up. In addition, if you ever need to re-install a program, you won't have to waste money on

purchasing it again because you can't find it—it'll be right at your fingertips.

Get ready to organize your computer programs by gathering together all of the discs, packages, and user guides you have. If other family members have software or games stored near their own computers, ask them to pitch in on this process. With every-

Disc and Manual Binder

- If your programs have accompanying user guides, store the discs and manuals together. A three-ring binder with sheet protectors and tabbed dividers is a good option.

- Choose a sturdy binder with a spine that's at least two inches wide. Slip a disc and the guide that goes with it into a plastic sheet protector.

- Use tabbed dividers to separate programs by type or by the computer on which they're used.

Accordion File

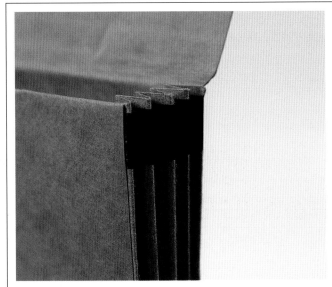

- An accordion file is another good way of storing discs and manuals together. Choose a file with both a bottom and sides that expand to maximize capacity.

- Label the tabs on the file with what you've stored in each pocket so that you can easily find what you want.

- If you have only discs to store, look for an accordion file normally used to hold checks or receipts.

thing in one spot, match up the disc, packaging, and manual for each program, and then start weeding. Pull out any programs you don't use (especially if they've never been or aren't currently installed on your computer), as well as any that are out-of-date and any discs that are too damaged to be used.

If the software or games you're getting rid of are current, consider donating or selling them. (Note, though, that many programs can't be registered to more than one user and shouldn't be passed along if you've already used them.) Recycle anything that's old or damaged. (See the Resources section at the back of the book for information on safe disc disposal.)

Now decide how to store the programs you want to keep. Unless you have lots of storage, don't store programs in their original boxes, which can take up lots of space. (If you need to keep the boxes, collapse them and store them flat; stash Styrofoam and other packing materials in sturdy trash bags.) Instead, try storing them in a binder, a notebook, a small box, or a drawer.

CD Notebook

- A CD notebook, with pockets for individual discs within a binder, is a good option if you only need to store discs.

- If the programs you're storing require product keys or registration numbers for installation, store these numbers in the notebook pocket with the related disc.

- Keep your CD notebook on a shelf or in a drawer near your main computer.

Hanging File

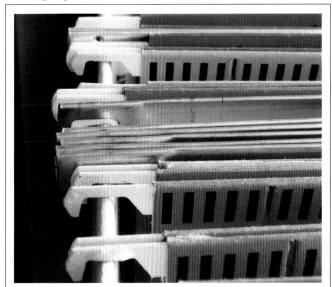

- Put extra space in a filing drawer to use by storing software and manuals there.

- Hanging folders with closed sides prevent things from slipping out and getting lost in the drawer.

- Store software either individually in separate folders or together in one larger folder. Look for a folder with a box bottom, which has a wider base that flattens out to create more storage within the file.

- Store discs inside the manuals that go with them, and secure the two with a rubber band.

CORD AND CABLE MANAGEMENT

Take control of your computer cords and cables to cut down on clutter

ORGANIZING YOUR HOME

Regardless of the kind of computer you have, there's probably a tangle of cords connecting it to a power supply, a printer, a keyboard, a mouse, and other accessories and peripherals. Getting these cables organized and under control makes the space look less cluttered and makes it easier to take care of your computer.

Start by turning off your computer and anything connected to it. Then choose a cable and follow its trail to find out what its purpose is. As you figure out where each cable goes and what it's for, label it—Computer Power, Printer-Computer Connector, and so on. Write your label on a bread bag clip or on a strip of paper looped around the cable.

Cable Snakes

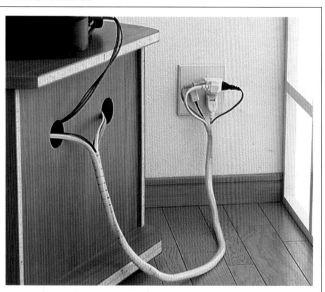

- Cable snakes are hollow plastic tubes designed to enclose a bundle of cables. They're useful for keeping cables bunched together rather than spread out.

- Most cable snakes can be cut to fit the length of the cables you're working with. It's generally a good idea

to fill the cable snake first and then cut off the excess length.

- To fill a snake, gather your cables together and slip them into the opening. Some snakes come with a tool designed to make this process easier.

Cable Clams

- Cable clams are plastic or rubber spools with outer "shells" that snap down over the cable rolled inside. They are great for taking up the slack in cables that are too long.

- Clams come in several different sizes, so measure the length of your cables first.

Remember that thick cables (like power cords) will take up more room when they're rolled.

- To use a clam, wind the excess length of a cable around the spool, and then close the shell.

Once you identify each cable, start unplugging them. Be sure you know what's what before you disconnect things so-that you won't have to spend time trying to figure out where a mystery cable is supposed to go. Next, reconnect one end of each two-end cable to get a sense of how many cables are connected to each device and how best to route them. Bunch cables that go to and from the same place (such as the connectors for your keyboard and mouse, both of which

go from your computer to your desktop). To prevent tangles, roll or bundle cables that are longer than they need to be. Use simple tools like cable snakes, cable clips, and twist ties to keep cords from spreading out around your workspace.

Finally, reconnect the other end of each cable. Be sure to plug power cables into a surge protector, rather than directly into an outlet, to prevent outlet overload and to protect your electronics in the event of a power surge or sudden outage.

Cable Clips

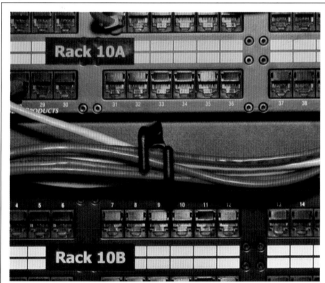

- Cable clips attach to flat surfaces (such as a wall or desk) and help control thinner cords, like USB cables and phone wires.

- Clips help route cords in a certain direction (a phone wire toward a jack, for example) and keep cables from dangling. They're also

useful for keeping in place cables you might frequently connect and disconnect.

- Choose clips wide enough to hold the cables you're working with, and follow package instructions for mounting them.

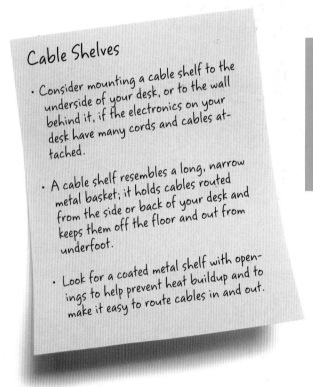

Cable Shelves

- Consider mounting a cable shelf to the underside of your desk, or to the wall behind it, if the electronics on your desk have many cords and cables attached.

- A cable shelf resembles a long, narrow metal basket; it holds cables routed from the side or back of your desk and keeps them off the floor and out from underfoot.

- Look for a coated metal shelf with openings to help prevent heat buildup and to make it easy to route cables in and out.

E-MAIL: SORTING AND WEEDING

Take control of your in-box by doing some electronic decluttering

For many of us, e-mail is an indispensable tool. It lets us communicate quickly and easily, brings news and information, and keeps us in touch with what's happening around the corner and across the world. Getting your in-box organized can help make e-mail even more useful and effective by making it easy to find what you need and keep on top of things you need to do.

As with everything else, organizing your e-mail begins with sorting and weeding. By clearing out messages you don't want or need, you'll get rid of clutter (of the electronic variety) and make it easier to focus on messages that are actually important to you.

Start with the oldest e-mail messages. Delete any that are outdated or no longer useful or relevant, or that you've never

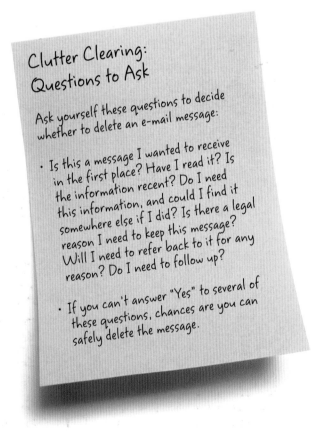

Clutter Clearing:
Questions to Ask

Ask yourself these questions to decide whether to delete an e-mail message:

- Is this a message I wanted to receive in the first place? Have I read it? Is the information recent? Do I need this information, and could I find it somewhere else if I did? Is there a legal reason I need to keep this message? Will I need to refer back to it for any reason? Do I need to follow up?

- If you can't answer "Yes" to several of these questions, chances are you can safely delete the message.

Outdated E-mail

- Delete e-mail messages with information that's out-of-date, including notices about past store sales, invitations to events that have passed, and news updates from more than a week ago.

- If you're keeping these messages because you need to

follow up on them—calling a friend and apologizing for not being able to attend a party, for example—add the tasks to your To Do list and delete the messages.

- Get in the habit of checking for and deleting outdated messages every week.

read (such as old e-newsletters). Also be sure to delete all junk mail, or spam; there's never a reason to keep these messages.

As you weed, look for ways to stem the flow of new e-mail. Unsubscribe from mailing lists that send you messages you're not interested in or newsletters you don't read. Ask friends and family to limit the messages they forward to you to only those they're sure you'll be interested in. Finally, be very careful when giving out your e-mail address on Web sites to keep spam at bay.

Newsletters and Updates

- Most e-newsletters and updates are sent out on a regular basis. They're meant to be read within a certain time frame, and after that point, the info they contain is probably stale.

- Delete newsletters and updates you received more than a week ago but haven't read. If you've read the message, keep it only if it contains information you won't be able to find somewhere else.

- If you're overwhelmed with e-mail, don't subscribe to any daily updates or messages.

E-mail to Keep

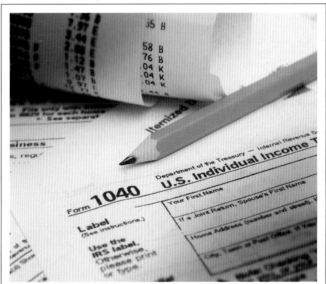

- Some e-mail messages are worth keeping indefinitely, including Web site user account information, legal messages (such as a notice that a tax return you've filed online has been received), and messages with important financial info (such as e-receipts you plan to deduct from your taxes).

- Rather than keeping these messages in your in-box, move them to folders. (See page 146 for information on creating e-mail folders.)

- To be extra safe, print a copy of any message you absolutely need, and keep it with your paper files.

145

E-MAIL: ORGANIZING

Organize your in-box so that you can quickly and easily find important messages

After you weed your e-mail in-box of messages you don't want or need, it's time to organize it so that you can keep track of important messages and find the information you need without having to dig. Think of your in-box as you would your physical desktop: When it's functioning smoothly, it should hold only the things you're currently working on or interested in. Everything else should be in a logical, convenient storage spot that's out of the way but easily accessible when you need it.

How to organize your in-box and any accompanying folders depends on the e-mail program you use, how many messages you receive each day and need to store when you're done with

ORGANIZING YOUR HOME

E-mail Folders

- Folders are a convenient way of storing e-mail messages you want to keep but don't need in your in-box.

- Most e-mail programs allow an unlimited number of folders, but start with only a few. You can create more folders once you're in the habit of using them.

- Determine the types of folders needed: basic task-related folders (such as In Process, Waiting on . . . , and Follow up), folders for the people who e-mail you regularly, folders for tasks and projects you're working on, or a combination of those systems.

Color-Coding

- Many desktop e-mail programs include a color-coding feature, which lets you distinguish messages from certain senders or with certain subjects by using different colors.

- You can set up the color-coding feature so that, for example, any message from a member of your family is listed in blue in your in-box, while messages from co-workers are listed in green.

- Refer to the Help section of your e-mail program for specific instructions on using color-coding.

146

them, and how comfortable you are with technology. You don't need an elaborate, multilevel system of folders if you use e-mail primarily for personal correspondence and receive only a few messages per day, but such a system might be helpful if your in-box includes work-related messages and you have a steady flow of e-mail coming in throughout the day.

In addition to folders, tools like color-coding, keywords, and flagging or starring messages can help you customize your e-mail program so that it works well for you and is easy to keep organized.

········· YELLOW ● LIGHT ·················

Save paper and ink and nip clutter in the bud by being very selective with the e-mail messages you print out. Unless you need a message for your legal or financial records or want to share it with someone who doesn't have e-mail access, you probably don't need to print it.

Flagging Messages

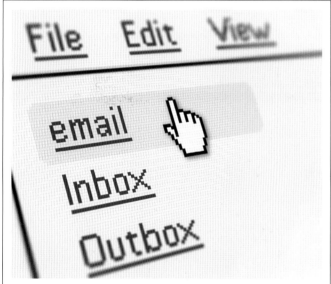

- Another way to make certain messages stand out in your in-box is by flagging or starring them. Almost all e-mail programs have a flag/star feature.

- Flagging is useful for marking messages that require action, that you want to read again, or that are related to a specific task or project.

- You can sort the messages in your in-box so that those that are flagged or starred appear on top.

Using Keywords

- Some e-mail programs let you add keywords (or tags) to your e-mail messages. You can then sort or search messages by keyword to easily find what you want.

- You can add whatever keywords you'd like, from names to projects to types of tasks.

- As with e-mail folders, you can create unlimited keywords. Start with a few basics, and then add to your list as you get used to using them.

ELECTRONIC FILES

Organize the files on your computer for an uncluttered desktop and easy access to the information you need

Take a look at your computer desktop. Can you see the beautiful scene you've chosen as your background image, or is it lost behind a flurry of icons? Computer clutter may not take up any physical space, but clearing it out can be just as satisfying as cleaning up a messy desk or an overcrowded closet. Further-more, organizing the files on your computer makes it easier to find what you need and to store new documents you create.

Start the organizing process by tackling what's on your computer desktop. Look at the files, programs, and shortcuts here and ask yourself whether you need and use them. De-

Desktop Folders

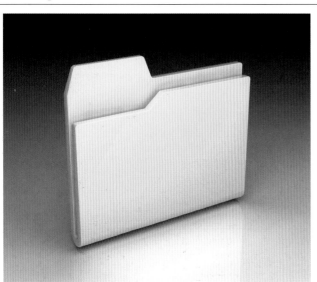

- Your computer desktop serves the same basic purpose as your physical desktop: It's a place to keep the programs you use often and to store documents you're currently working on.

- Reserve your computer desktop for shortcuts to frequently used programs.

- Keep folders on the desktop to a minimum: a To Do folder to hold files related to active projects and tasks, your main Documents folder, and a Photos folder to store pictures.

Documents Directories

- Your main documents directory is the filing cabinet of your computer. As with a filing cabinet for paper, keeping this directory organized makes finding and storing things much easier.

- Consider using the same file categories and names on your computer that you do for your paper files, as long as those categories are relevant in both places.

- Create subfolders on your computer to make things even easier to find; within a folder called Family, for example, you might have subfolders called Mom and Dad, Kids, and Pets.

148

lete any documents or files you don't need, as well as short-cuts to programs you don't use. (A shortcut is a program icon with a small arrow in the bottom corner; deleting a shortcut doesn't delete the program itself.)

When you're done with the desktop, move on to your main documents folder. (On PCs with Windows, this is usually called My Documents; on Macintosh machines, it's called Documents.) Take a look at the documents and folders here, deleting those you don't need, as well as any duplicates.

After weeding, create a set of file folders on your computer. Think of these as similar to folders in a filing cabinet (see page 130): Divide them into categories that make sense to you, label them, and sort documents into them.

Finally, keep your computer organized by taking the time to save documents and files to the right folders, rather than letting them accumulate on the desktop or "loose" in your main documents folder. You'll keep things uncluttered and will be able to find what you need in a snap.

Desktop Search

- Another way of finding files and programs on your computer quickly and easily is by using a desktop search tool.

- These tools let you look for documents and applications by typing in search terms, just as you would with an Internet search engine.

- A desktop search tool creates an index of the files on your computer (including music, photos, and e-mail messages) on a regular basis, so you can easily search for even new files.

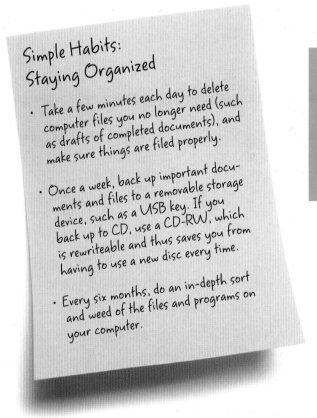

Simple Habits: Staying Organized

- Take a few minutes each day to delete computer files you no longer need (such as drafts of completed documents), and make sure things are filed properly.

- Once a week, back up important documents and files to a removable storage device, such as a USB key. If you back up to CD, use a CD-RW, which is rewriteable and thus saves you from having to use a new disc every time.

- Every six months, do an in-depth sort and weed of the files and programs on your computer.

149

YOUNG CHILD'S ROOM

Find customized organizing recommendations for your little one's room

An organized, orderly, inviting room for a young child gives him or her a great start. Whether your little one has her own room or shares space with a sibling, you can create a comfortable spot for her and storage for the things she needs. Read the descriptions here, choose the one that best describes your child's room, and find specific recommendations below the photo.

In Any Space . . .

- Opt for décor that can grow along with your child. Choose paint or wallpaper in a basic, child-friendly color, and decorate the room with age-appropriate wall hangings and pictures.

- Keep clutter to a minimum by being selective about the child-care gadgets you purchase. Wherever possible, opt for basic, multifunctional gear over highly specialized supplies.

- Store future clothes for the child sorted by weight rather than by age.

Spacious Room of Her Own

My child has her own room with plenty of space for furniture, toys, and clothes. I don't want to fill the room so much that it starts to feel cluttered. I need storage ideas to keep things neatly tucked away but easy to get at so I don't have to scurry for diapers at changing time or dig for clothes when it's time to get dressed.

In a Spacious Room of Her Own . . .

- Don't buy extra furniture just to fill up open areas of the room. Remember that although baby furniture may not fill the space, the pieces your child will use as she grows (such as a bed and a desk) will take up more room.

- Bring a sense of cohesion to the space by choosing coordinating storage containers, such as a set of matching baskets on shelves for storing toys.

- Use hanging sweater bags in the closet to store extra diapers, crib linens, and clothes.

Smaller Spot

My child's room is small and cozy, so I want to be sure I'm making the most of the space. Finding enough storage can be tricky; I don't want the space to seem messy just because it's small. I want to make this room warm and welcoming but not overwhelming.

Space Shared with a Sibling

My child shares a room with her sibling, so it's extra important that the space is well planned and organized. I want to create a spot within the room that's just hers and want to be sure we avoid confusion in terms of which toys and clothes belong to which child.

In a Smaller Spot . . .

In a Space Shared with a Sibling . . .

- Put the walls to use for extra storage. Use wall-mounted shelves to hold bins of toys, folded clothes, and stuffed animals.

- Consider using an armoire as your central storage unit. Add a rod for hanging clothes, and use dividers to separate things in the unit's drawers.

- Use closed bins or boxes under the crib to store things like bedding and clothes to grow into.

- Consider using two different colors of paint on the walls—one shade for one child's half of the room, and a second shade for the other's.

- Color-code hangers and storage containers by child so that it's easy to tell at a glance what belongs to whom.

- Space permitting, put beds on opposite sides of the room, rather than side by side, to give each child her own area. In a small space, mount a curtain from the ceiling between the beds for privacy.

BABY GEAR

Keep baby's supplies neat, accessible, and in order with simple organizing systems

Babies require a lot of specialized furniture and gear, from a changing spot and a crib to diapers and bath supplies. Smart furniture choices save you from having to purchase a whole new set as your child grows, and organized storage for gear both large and small helps keep your baby's room uncluttered while giving you easy access to the things you need.

Start the organizing process by gathering baby gear from throughout the house in one spot to get an accurate sense of what you have. With everything together, do some sorting and weeding. Dispose of anything that's unusable (broken, empty, or damaged beyond repair), and set aside things your child has outgrown or doesn't need.

Convertible Furniture

- Stock your child's room with convertible furniture whenever possible, choosing pieces that you can use for other purposes as the baby grows.

- Rather than buying a changing table, use a dresser with a changing platform on top; you'll have more storage space and won't have an extra piece of furniture when your baby grows out of diapers.

- Also consider a convertible crib, which can be modified into a bed.

Decluttered Cribs

- Having too much stuff in a young child's crib is dangerous. Keep toys and stuffed animals to a minimum, and rely on a single blanket.

- A mobile hung above the crib well out of baby's reach is an effective way of providing comfort or stimulation without adding clutter.

- When your baby is old enough to push herself up, remove pillows, toys, and bumper pads from the crib so that your child can't use them as step stools for climbing out.

If you plan to have more children and you have sufficient storage space, you might want to save things that are in good repair for your next child; otherwise, donate them to an apropiate charity, such as a women and children's shelter.

After you weed, sort the things that remain by type and use—for example, all changing supplies together. Next, decide on the best place to store each type of thing; keep things as close as possible to where you use them. Once you know how much you have and where you'd like to store it, choose a container that will keep it all corralled.

Storing Small Supplies

- A hanging supply holder keeps small supplies like diapers, creams, burp cloths, rattles, and teething rings corralled. By putting wall space to use, you'll save room elsewhere.

- Another option for small gear is over-door shoe pockets, which can hold toiletries, small toys, and diapers.

- If you have shelf or surface space, consider using decorative baskets or bins to store supplies.

Storing Gear on the Go

- Keep your diaper bag and stroller storage space organized so that you can quickly find the essentials when you need them.

- Create a checklist of diaper bag must-haves. Check it before leaving the house; when you get home, clear out trash and anything that belongs elsewhere, and re-stock the bag.

- Don't let the storage compartments on your stroller become catchalls. Use them to hold things you need in transit, but clear out the nonessentials once you get home.

CHILD'S ROOM

TOYS: SORTING AND WEEDING

Give your child room to grow by letting go of unwanted, unneeded, and unused toys

Toys tend to be one of the biggest causes of clutter in young children's rooms. By being selective about the toys and stuffed animals you keep for your child, you'll not only keep the room more organized, but also help reinforce from a young age the idea that more isn't always better.

Very young children can't sort and weed on their own, of course, so you'll need to take care of the process. Toddlers and preschoolers can help by selecting a certain number of favorites—or you can watch their play habits to see which toys they pick up again and again.

Start weeding by collecting toys from throughout the house, including any in diaper bags, strollers, or the car. With

Broken and Damaged Toys

- Toys that are broken or significantly damaged should be among the first things you get rid of when weeding.

- These toys should be thrown away, not donated, as they pose a danger to any child.

- Toys made with lead paint or other harmful substances are also risky for young children. Keep a few of these as decorations, far out of the child's reach, if you can't stand to part with them.

Toys with Small Parts

- Toys with small or moving parts generally aren't suitable for babies and toddlers. Look on a toy's tag or box for guidelines on the appropriate age range.

- Box up and set aside toys you want to keep until your child gets older. Before storing these toys, though, consider whether they're unique or valuable enough to be worth the storage space.

- Toys with strings and cords are also inappropriate for a young child because they can be strangulation hazards.

all of the toys in one spot, divide them by type: stuffed animals, rattles, games, blocks, and so on. Set aside for donation or disposal any that your child doesn't play with or doesn't like, as well as a few of each type your child has in abundance. Toss any that are broken or otherwise unsafe.

If you're planning to have another child, create a box of toys to pass along, but limit yourself to saving only toys that are clean and in very good condition. Label the container and store it in an out-of-the-way spot.

GREEN ● LIGHT

If you're expecting a child, ask for clutter-free baby gifts instead of the usual parade of toys. Savings bonds, certificates for free babysitting, and contributions to a college savings fund are all great ways to celebrate a baby's arrival and will be remembered far longer than another stuffed animal or rattle.

Unused Toys

- Regardless of her age, your child probably has toys she has never played with (even though they're age-appropriate).

- These toys are good candidates for donation. Bear in mind that there are children who have no toys; put your child's unused items into good hands by donating them to an agency that serves kids.

- If your child doesn't like a toy, there's rarely a good reason to keep it, even if it was a gift or was expensive.

Toy Multiples

- If you have multiple versions of certain types of toys, cull them and add several of each type to your Donate pile.

- Most young children don't need more than a small handful of toys; if put in front of a dozen stuffed animals, they'll choose one.

- Take the opportunity to teach your children at a very young age that a smaller collection of high-quality things is better than a large number of unremarkable things.

155

TOYS: ORGANIZING
Create organized storage for your child's toys so that they're out of the way but easy to access

After you sort and weed your child's toys, it's time to create effective storage for them. Getting and keeping toys organized helps prevent clutter in your child's room and can help her learn the basics of putting things away.

When thinking about storing baby toys, focus on what would be most convenient for you and any other caregivers. Your baby won't be taking out or putting away her own toys, so the storage you create needs to work well only for the adults in the household. Most baby toys are fairly simple and don't have many parts, so simple bins, baskets, and shelves should do the trick.

If your child is a toddler, involve her in the process of figuring out where and how to store toys. Getting kids to share

Storing Books

- Many children's books are irregularly shaped, which means they are hard to store on standard bookshelves. In addition, storing books spine-out on shelves doesn't let your child easily see what she has.

- A better option is a book rack that stores volumes with their covers facing forward. Look for a rack that's sized for kids' books.

- Another choice is to store books upright in a box or basket. Your child can flip through, look at each cover, and choose the book she wants.

Using Containers

- Divide different types of toys into various containers, and store the containers on open shelves or in a cabinet.

- When storing toys for babies and infants, keep containers at adult height so that it's easy for you to get things out and put them away. Use containers with lids if you want a less cluttered look.

- When your child is old enough to retrieve toys on her own, use colorful open bins on low shelves to allow her to reach them by herself.

the responsibility of caring for their own things at a young age will make them more invested in taking care of their stuff (and perhaps even keeping their rooms clean!) as they grow up.

Toy storage for toddlers should be easy for children to understand and access. Toddler toys start to get more complex than infant toys and may have several parts, so look for storage that will make it simple to store all of the components of a toy in the same place.

Often, the least effective way of storing toys is in a toy box. In these boxes, smaller toys tend to filter to the bottom and can be hard to find; further, trying to store toys of several different shapes or sizes in the same box makes the box's storage space less effective. A better bet is to use different containers for different types of toys.

Once you organize the toys, get yourself—and your child—in the habit of putting things away once playtime is through.

Labeling for Non-readers

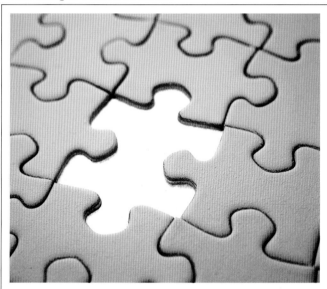

- Help your child find and put away her toys by using visual labels on toy containers.

- Take a photo of a sample of the box's contents (say, a few puzzle pieces for a container of puzzles), and attach it to the front of the box. Write the name of the toy on the photo to help your child start to identify words.

- Take the time to teach your child to look at the label on each box to identify the contents.

Labeling for Readers

- When your child starts to read, replace the photo labels with verbal labels.

- Be sure to write labels clearly and large so that they're easy for young readers to understand.

- Let your child practice writing by having her copy the words you write on each label. Each time she goes to look for a toy, she'll be able to identify what's in each box by reading both your writing and her own.

ORGANIZING CLOTHES

Make getting your child dressed easier by creating smart organizing systems for clothes

Take away some of the stress of getting your child dressed each day (or several times a day) by organizing her clothes so that they're neat and easy to find. When you can get your hands on the pieces you want in a matter of seconds, you can keep your focus on your kid.

An organized system for your child's clothes starts with some sorting and weeding. By culling pieces you no longer want or need, you'll clear space for the clothes your child actually wears. Get things under way by gathering clothes from throughout the house, including the diaper bag, the laundry room, and the car.

Once you have everything in one place, sort through

Storing Baby Clothes

- Most baby clothes, because they're so small, are best stored folded in drawers, bins, or other containers.

- Drawer dividers keep different kinds of clothes—onesies, shirts, socks, pants—separated within a drawer. You can also use these dividers to hold clothes on a shelf.

- If you have clothes on hold for your baby to grow into, store them in bins labeled by age or weight. Keep the bins on shelves or in the closet until you're ready to use them.

Hanging Clothes

- As your child grows, she'll probably have a more elaborate wardrobe; in addition to folded clothes, make space for hanging clothes.

- Maximize closet space by using a double-hung rod, a second closet rod that hangs off the main one.

- If you want to use hanging space to store clothes your child will grow into, separate clothes for different sizes or ages with closet rod dividers, like those you see on store racks.

it. Set aside anything your child has outgrown or never wears and anything you don't like (unless your child is old enough to express an opinion and the item in question is a favorite). Consider donating these clothes to charity or to a friend, neighbor, or relative with a younger child. Toss or cut into rags clothes that are torn, stained, or damaged beyond repair.

If you plan to have another child and want to save some clothes, choose only pieces that are special and in good condition, and be sure they're completely clean before put-ting them in storage. To keep clutter to a minimum, limit the clothes, toys, and supplies you save for future children.

After you weed, create a storage plan. Put your own convenience first when it comes to storing clothes for babies and infants; above all, it should be easy for you and other caregivers to find and put away clothes for very young children. If your child is old enough to dress herself (at least partially), be sure the storage systems you create let her access her clothes.

Storing Basics

- A great way to store basics like underwear, socks, and T-shirts is in an over-door shoe holder, which has multiple pockets. Hang it on a door or on the wall.

- Divide each row of pockets by category—top row for shirts, second row for under-wear, and so on—and tuck clothes into each pocket.

- Get toddlers and preschoolers involved by storing things like socks and underwear in the bottom rows; kids can choose and put on their own essentials each day.

Kid-Height Closets

- Involve an older child in her own dressing by install-ing a kid-height rod in the closet. (The second rod in a double-hung rod system will do the trick.)

- Use this low rod to hang ev-eryday clothes. Keep special occasion wear stored out of reach.

- Separate clothes by type, and consider using a dif-ferent color hanger for each type (red for shirts, green for pants, and so on) to make it even easier for your child to find what she's looking for.

MEMORABILIA AND ARTWORK

Keep treasured pieces organized so that you and your child can enjoy them for years to come

Memorabilia and artwork from early childhood—a baby blanket, an essential stuffed animal, a finger-painted masterpiece—are sweet reminders of growing, learning, and changing. They're also representations of a time that, for many parents, grandparents, and other caregivers, goes by much too quickly. It can often be tempting to keep every memento of

a child's young life in an effort to hold onto the pleasures of those days. The more memorabilia you have, however, the more likely they are to become clutter.

Organizing your child's memorabilia lets you focus on the pieces that are truly meaningful and special and lets you strike a balance between keeping reminders of the past and

Memorabilia Displays

- One of the nicest ways to honor memorabilia is to put them on display.

- Show off a single piece, or create a curated collection around a specific event or theme, such as the birth of your child, her first day at preschool, or visits from her grandparents.

- Shadowboxes, which are like deep picture frames, are a good choice for scrapbook-like displays. You could also use a special bulletin board or a few small wall shelves.

Storing by Year

- Create a time capsule of each year of your child's life by storing memorabilia from that year in a labeled box.

- Use the same kind and size of box each year. This makes the boxes simple to store, and it also provides guidelines: If you fill up a

box halfway through the year, reconsider how much memorabilia you're keeping for that year.

- As your child gets older, consider letting her decorate her memorabilia box, so even the container itself will be a memento.

enjoying your child's life in the present.

One of the main steps in getting things organized is choosing what to keep and what to let go of. Before you do this, though, spend some time deciding what qualifies as special memorabilia and artwork. Give special weight to one-of-a-kind mementos like a comfort blanket, your child's absolute favorite stuffed animal, and the paper showing her first attempt at writing her name on her own. Be more selective in keeping the artwork she brings home from preschool every day, birthday cards from casual friends or neighbors, and her second through two-hundredth try at perfecting her signature.

As you sort, consider creative ways of keeping the memory of an item without having to keep the item. For example, you might take a series of digital photos depicting your child's finger paintings and make these photos into a slide show on your computer.

Finally, choose a way to safely store or display the pieces you want to keep, and get in the habit of going through this memorabilia collection each year to keep it organized and under control.

Framing Artwork

- Create a rotating display of your child's artwork with a series of wall frames or a magnetic frame on the refrigerator door.

- Set a time limit for each piece; rotating displays every few weeks or once a month will let you enjoy many works of art throughout the year.

- When you change displays, consider whether you want to keep the pieces you're taking down or whether you could photograph them and let go of the originals.

Storing Artwork

- Use a clear plastic bin to collect artwork throughout the year. Choose a bin that's large enough to hold 3-D pieces (such as those made with paper plates, straws, or popsicle sticks).

- At the end of the year, sort through the pieces you've accumulated and transfer the ones you want to keep to a smaller bin. Label that bin with the year and your child's name and age.

- Put the main bin to use again for collecting the next year's works.

161

OLDER CHILD'S ROOM

Create a space for your child to grow and thrive with these specialized ideas

As children grow, they can become more involved in organizing their own rooms and can help decide how to arrange the space. For targeted ideas on how create a comfortable, organized room for your child, and on tasks he can do to take responsibility for his space and his things, read the descriptions here, choose the one that best describes your child's room, and read the related recommendations below the photo.

A Spacious Room of His Own

My child has his own bedroom, which has space enough for his furniture and all of his things. I want to be sure, though, that the stuff doesn't expand to fit the space, and I want things to have designated homes so that my child learns to put things away.

In a Spacious Room of His Own . . .

- Take advantage of the room's spaciousness by dividing it into zones for sleeping, reading and doing homework, playing, and getting dressed.

- Use small area rugs, or a larger rug with varied patterns, to delineate the room's zones.

- Give the room a cozy (but not cramped) feel by using a low dresser and low bookshelves rather than taller versions.

In Any Space . . .

- Involve your child as early as possible in taking care of his clothes and toys. Model the habits you want your child to develop, and he'll be likely to follow your lead.

- Until your child learns where things belong, label storage containers, dresser drawers, and closet shelves; labels with both words and pictures can be especially helpful.

- Use simple box frames on your child's walls to display his artwork, which can easily be swapped out from time to time to create new displays.

Smaller Spot

My child has his own room, but it's fairly small, and we have to be creative to fit his furniture and belongings in without making the space feel cramped. I'd like to be able to maximize storage in the room, and I want to keep on top of how much stuff accumulates so that the space doesn't get cluttered.

Space Shared with a Sibling

Two of my children share a room. It's important to divide the space in a way that gives each of them some privacy and allows them each to take responsibility for their own things. Though the room has to hold several pieces of furniture to accommodate both kids, I don't want it to feel cramped or crowded.

In a Smaller Spot . . .

In a Space Shared with a Sibling . . .

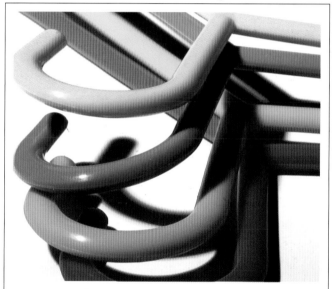

- When your child is old enough, consider a loft bed, which has sleeping space above a nook for a desk or play area.

- Mount wall shelves for storing books and toys. These take advantage of vertical space but don't pose a tipping danger.

- Create a rotating supply of toys: Decide how many to keep out at one time (perhaps as many as can safely fit on a few shelves), and put the others in an out-of-the-way spot. Every few months, switch the toys.

- Use storage furniture to divide the space in two. For example, try pushing two bookshelves together back-to-back in the center of the room; they'll create separate areas and will give each child personal storage space.

- Consider two identical sets of furniture in different woods or colors to keep the room feeling cohesive while visually dividing the space.

- Use color-coded hangers in the closet so that you and your kids can tell at a glance which clothes belong to each of them.

163

TOYS: SORTING AND WEEDING

Help your child clear out toy clutter for a more organized, more enjoyable space

As children grow, their tastes in toys change and mature, and old favorites are set aside as newer and more exciting toys come on the scene. Helping your older child sort and weed his toys will teach him the importance of letting go of unused, unwanted, unneeded things—and, of course, will help keep his room and other play areas of the house more organized.

Before you start the weeding process, make clear to your child that it's not a punishment, but rather is intended to help him enjoy his room and his current toys more by getting rid of the things that he doesn't use. You might want to let him choose a charity to which he can donate the toys he's letting go of, so he'll know that the stuff he's giving away will be used by children in need.

Outgrown Toys

- Letting go of toys that are too young for them can help kids celebrate their growth and maturity.

- If your child has younger siblings, encourage him to give his outgrown toys that are still in good condition to them. He'll still have the toys around but will get to experience sharing them.

- Another option is to give outgrown toys to a younger friend, neighbor, or relative or to donate them to charity.

Broken or Damaged Toys

- Ask your child to get rid of toys that are broken, damaged, or missing enough pieces to make them not worth playing with.

- Some manufacturers offer replacement parts for things like games and other toys. If one of your child's favorite toys is missing pieces, try ordering replacements.

- Throw away items that are broken, badly damaged, or made with potentially dangerous materials (like lead); these shouldn't be passed along to other children.

When you're ready to weed, work with your child to gather toys throughout the house in one spot, and then sort them into type. (I strongly recommend weeding your child's toys only with his involvement.) Encourage him to choose a few favorites from each category and to set aside the rest for donation. Other giveaways should include toys he's outgrown, doesn't play with, or doesn't like. Throw away anything that's broken beyond repair or dangerous to use.

If your child wants to hold onto a few of his outgrown toys as memorabilia, choose a specific container to store them in; limit what he can keep to that container, and store it in an out-of-the-way spot.

Go through the sorting and weeding process at least once a year with your child to keep clutter from accumulating; scheduling a session before gift-giving holidays like birthdays and Christmas will help clear out space for new toys.

Unused Toys

- Encourage your child to let go of toys he's had for a while but doesn't use or doesn't like.

- Learning to weed out unused and unneeded things will help your child avoid accumulating clutter of other forms as he grows up.

- If your child tends to receive toys he doesn't use as gifts for birthdays or other holidays, ask friends, relatives, and other givers for alternative presents, such as a special outing or a contribution to a savings account.

Toy Multiples

- If your child has several different versions of the same kind of toy, encourage him to choose one or two and give away the rest.

- Consider establishing specific containers or shelves as spots for storing different kinds of toys. One shelf might be for storing games, for example, and another for storing puzzles.

- The limited storage space for each type of toy will help determine how many toys can be kept—as many games as fit on one shelf, for example.

TOYS: ORGANIZING
Help your child create a fun, effective system for organizing games and toys

Once your child weeds his toys and chooses the ones he wants to keep, it's time to create a system for keeping them organized. By setting up designated toy storage, you'll make it easier for your child to find the toys he wants, keep all of a toy's pieces together, and put away his toys quickly.

As with the sorting and weeding process, it's very important to involve your child in the organizing process. Allowing him to make decisions about how and where to store toys makes him more invested in maintaining the systems you create. If you set up a toy storage system with no input from your child, he may be less likely to want to know how to use it.

Boxes and Bins

- Boxes and bins are useful for storing toys, especially those that are oddly shaped or have multiple parts or pieces.

- Choose containers that let you divide toys into categories and store them together. You might have a box for building toys, for example, and another for exploration-related toys. Label each bin.

- If you have a toy box, use it for large, single-piece toys, such as stuffed animals. Smaller toys or those with multiple parts tend to sift to the bottom and are hard to retrieve.

Doll Storage

- Use a shelf and a series of boxes to store your child's dolls and their related accessories.

- Put dolls on display so that they're easy to find but don't get tangled up with other toys. Stash clothes and accessories in clear, stackable bins with lids; label each bin with its contents.

- If your child collects figurines, store these on a higher shelf in the same unit to keep them safe.

166

Start the process by dividing the items your child wants into categories that make sense to him. He might choose to separate things by type (games, trains, puzzles) or by theme (all toys related to trains, all toys related to exploring, and so on).

Once things are separated, look at toy quantities, and think about the best places to store things. If there's a central play area in your house, such as a family room, it might make sense to store toys there; if your child tends to play mainly in his room, on the other hand, it's best to keep his toys there.

Of course, if you have several children who share toys, store the items in a central spot, and make sure everyone pitches in to help keep the system organized.

Work with your child to build the habit of putting things away in the right spots when he's done playing. Set a good example by taking care of your own things, but resist the temptation to take over the job of putting toys away. This is a great opportunity to instill in your child a sense of respect and responsibility for his belongings.

Storing Small Toys

- Keep small toys and accessories organized by storing them in over-door shoe pockets. Hang the pockets from a door or on the wall.

- Sort toys into pockets by category, and then label each pocket. Get kids involved by having them create their own labels (use white mailing label stickers).

- If your child has younger siblings, be sure to store toys and accessories with small pieces in pockets that are out of the little ones' reach.

Storage Furniture

- Depending on storage location, you might choose a unit that has space for your child's toys, books, and games all in one spot. This will make it easier to find toys.

- For multiple children, consider using one unit to store most of their toys in one central spot (such as a playroom). Divide the unit by child, age, or toy type. Let each child keep a few toys in his own room for private playtime.

- For safety, attach toy storage furniture to the wall, and be sure to store the heaviest items near the bottom of the unit.

ORGANIZING CLOTHES

Help keep rooms neater and make dressing easier with organized clothes storage

Getting your child ready for school in the morning and out the door dressed in something you can stand may require more than organizing his closet and dresser, but that process can definitely help. When his clothes are organized, easy to find, and easy to put away, your child can spend less time digging for the shirt he wants and more time on things like eating breakfast and—dare to dream!—putting away his laundry.

To create a clothes organizing system your child can use on his own, it's important to involve him in every step of the process. If you set up a system on your own and then request that he use it, there's a good chance he won't, either because

ORGANIZING YOUR HOME

Using Drawers

Using Shelves

- One of the easiest ways to store kids' clothing is folded in drawers. Choose a low dresser with broad drawers for younger children so it's easy to reach; older children can graduate to a taller model.

- Use drawer dividers to keep different types of clothes separate.

- To help a child remember what goes where, use labels—with words or pictures, or both—on the front of the drawers. Let your child design and create his own labels if he'd like.

- Another option for storing folded clothes is a series of open containers on shelves.

- Choose clear, sturdy containers, and look for a deep shelving unit so bins don't stick too far off the front.

- Divide clothes into bins by type, by occasion, or by day of the week. This last option is useful if you want to make morning routines easier; your child can simply pull out the day's outfit from the appropriate bin.

- Get your child involved in making labels for these bins.

it's too simple or too complex or just because he's not invested in it in any way. Get your child on board by explaining the benefits of getting organized and by emphasizing that the process isn't intended as a punishment.

Start the organizing process by sorting and weeding your child's clothes, including things like shoes and outerwear. Encourage him to give away anything that no longer fits, that he doesn't like, or that he rarely (if ever) wears. Put these items in a donation pile; toss anything that's too damaged to wear and can't be repaired.

Older children might prefer to do their sorting and weeding with a friend or a sibling rather than a parent. Let them! Kids might be more inclined to take the advice of their peers when it comes to which clothes look good and which are passé, so encourage your child to choose a weeding partner he'll actually enjoy working with.

After weeding, help your child figure out ways to store the clothes he wants to keep so that he can easily find them and put them away again.

Hanging Clothes

- Make the most of your child's closet space by installing a system that has at least one closet rod and a few shelves.

- Use a double-hung rod in a young child's closet or in part of an older child's closet to maximize hanging space.

- Keep a small step stool handy to help a young child reach hanging clothes.

- Put the back of a door or part of a closet rod to use for storing shoes in over-door shoe pockets or a rod-mounted shoe holder.

Seasonal Storage

- Keep out-of-season clothes from cluttering your child's closet and dresser by storing them in bins.

- Go through your child's clothes for the season that's just passed. Get rid of anything he's outgrown, hasn't worn, or won't fit into the following year.

- Store the rest in a sturdy bin on a closet shelf or another out-of-the-way spot. (Be sure the clothes are clean before you store them.) Label the bin with the season.

169

MEMORABILIA

Help your child preserve his favorite memories with organized storage for memorabilia

Parents collect and store memorabilia of a child's infancy and preschool years, but as the child grows, he starts to gather his own mementos. Helping him decide which ones to keep and how to store them will make it easy to enjoy these pieces for years to come.

Young children have limited life experiences and therefore might be more inclined to hold onto more of the memorabilia they collect; as children grow, though, they're often willing to be more selective about what they gather and keep, as they have assurance that they'll continue to experience new things. Give your child gentle guidance over the years about choosing which mementos to hold onto and which to let go.

ORGANIZING YOUR HOME

Simple Storage

- Use a basic banker's box or other simple container to collect memorabilia throughout the year.

- If you use a cardboard box, have your child decorate and label it with his name and the year; let him decorate with stickers and adhesive labels if you use a plastic bin.

- Store the bin in a convenient spot in his room and encourage him to put things in it as he collects them. Once a year, or when the box fills up, go through it with him to decide what to keep long-term.

Scrapbooks and Albums

- Help your child mark a particularly memorable year or event with a scrapbook or album.

- If your child wants to create the album himself, help him choose the supplies, and lend a hand with tasks like taping and gluing. You could also have him select the memorabilia he wants to include and then make the album yourself.

- Creating a scrapbook at the end of each year can be an enjoyable way of reviewing what happened that year and organizing memorabilia at the same time.

The first step is deciding what to keep. Help your child make these decisions by asking questions like these: Does this thing remind you of a particular person or event? Does it bring back good memories? Does it mean something special to you? Do you have other things that are just like it?

Generally speaking, mementos worth keeping are those tied to specific people or events (grandparents, a family vacation); those that help your child remember and understand life experiences, whether positive or negative, such as losing a tooth or losing a pet; or those that bear positive memories for your child.

After your child has decided what to keep, help him determine the best way to store or display his memorabilia so that he can enjoy them and keep them safe. Divide the things he wants to keep by type (birthday cards, photos), by year or age, or by event. Have him choose a few items to display, and store the rest in boxes or bins.

Finally, set aside time each year to go through the mementos your child has accumulated and to update his storage bins to keep his memories organized.

Displaying Memorabilia

- Displaying recent or particularly special pieces of memorabilia lets your child enjoy them every day.

- Set up a bulletin or magnet board for posting recent photos, cards, and other mementos. Make time once a month or so to change what's displayed and to store items that get taken down.

- For longer-term displays, try framing things like photos or collages, or create shadowboxes for specific events like a special trip or birthday.

Long-Term Storage

- Set up bins or boxes to store memorabilia that your child wants to keep long-term.

- Divide things into containers by type (cards, photos), theme (school, camp), event, or person (friends, family). Have your child decorate and label the bins.

- Use plastic bins or boxes made of acid-free cardboard, which will prevent photos and other papers from disintegrating.

171

SCHOOLWORK AND PAPERS

Help your child create simple systems to organize important projects and papers

Kids generate lots of papers and projects while in school. Help your child create systems and habits for keeping this stuff organized so that it doesn't take over his room (or other parts of the house) and, more importantly, so that he can stay on top of what's happening in school.

To set up the most effective organizing system, you need to know what kinds of papers and projects—and how much of each—your kid has to store. Work with him to gather things from his desk, his backpack, and other places in the house.

With everything in one spot, start sorting. Have him describe things as he goes through them, and divide them into categories by the class or event they're for. Encourage him

Keeping Papers Visible

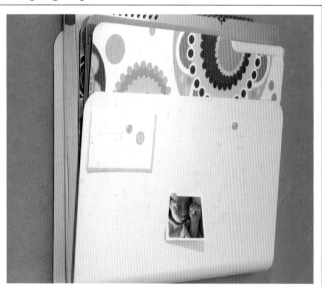

- Wall-mounted paper sorters keep current schoolwork visible, organized, and easily accessible. Hang the sorters near your child's desk or homework spot.

- Use one sorter pocket per class, labeled with the name of the class and/or teacher.

- Have your child sort papers into the relevant pockets when he gets home from school each day, and then check each pocket when it's time to do homework. Once he finishes an assignment, he can store the completed paper in his binder or a folder.

Using Binders

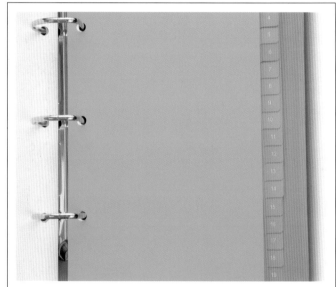

- Three-ring binders are very common and useful school organizing accessories.

- For a binder to be as effective as possible, organize it in a way that makes sense to your child: by class, by teacher, by paper status (homework to do, complet-ed homework, and so on), or by some other category.

- Use tabbed dividers to create sections within a binder. Look for dividers with built-in pockets so that your child can easily stash papers that aren't hole-punched.

to get rid of papers he no longer needs, including things like drafts of reports and simple tests from past years.

As he decides what to keep, create piles and label them with Post-it Notes. You'll get a sense during the sorting process of how much storage your child will need for each class or category.

Once things are sorted, brainstorm the best ways to store them. Keep papers for current classes in binders or folders, and store those from past school years in a box or file drawer. Use portfolios for artwork and bins for 3-D projects.

Finally, help your child develop habits to stay organized both throughout the week and throughout the school year. Encourage him to schedule a few minutes each day to clear out his backpack and put things away, and a few minutes once a week to deal with anything that's accumulated on his desk. At the end of each school year, set aside time to sort through, weed, and store papers and projects—a great way to celebrate finishing a grade and starting vacation.

Storing Artwork

- Store big and bulky art porjects and posters in an artist's portfolio.

- Portfolios are very large folders or envelopes designed to hold flat works of art. They come in a variety of sizes and materials.

- For transporting artwork, look for a leather, nylon, or heavy cardboard model. For storage, a simple paperboard model works.

- Label portfolios with your child's name and the year(s) of the work.

Archiving Papers and Projects

- Use plastic or sturdy cardboard bins to store papers and projects long-term.

- Create a bin for each grade or age. Add things to it throughout the year and after sorting/weeding school papers once classes are through.

- Have your child decorate and label the bin, or create a label with a current photo of your child.

- Make a folder to hold special school papers (like essays and important tests) from each class; store the folders in the bin.

ATTIC

Create an effective, clutter-free storage room with these targeted tips

Whether your attic is a comfortable, fully finished room or a tiny crawl space, you can turn it into an effective storage spot. Read the descriptions here, choose the one that best describes your attic, and find detailed recommendations and ideas below the photo.

Large, Simple Space

My attic has plenty of space, but it's not fancy. I want to create storage that will keep my stuff safe no matter how hot, cold, damp, or dusty it gets up here. I also need to be able to find what I'm looking for quickly so that I don't have to linger.

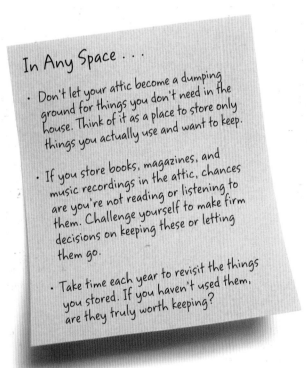

In Any Space . . .

- Don't let your attic become a dumping ground for things you don't need in the house. Think of it as a place to store only things you actually use and want to keep.

- If you store books, magazines, and music recordings in the attic, chances are you're not reading or listening to them. Challenge yourself to make firm decisions on keeping these or letting them go.

- Take time each year to revisit the things you stored. If you haven't used them, are they truly worth keeping?

In a Large, Simple Space . . .

- Use shelves throughout the attic to keep things organized, easy to access, and off the floor. Metal shelves are a good option, as they can stand up to humidity and extreme temperatures.

- Attach large, easy-to-read labels to shelves identifying what's on each one.

- Don't store things like photos, videos, or items made of delicate fabric (such as a wedding dress) in the attic; these can all be damaged by heat and moisture.

174

Finished Room

I have a good-size attic that's finished off and insulated, but I'm not using the space to its fullest advantage. I want to devote part of the room to storage and would like to clear out the other part so that I can use it for something else— perhaps a space to tackle crafts projects, or simply to escape. I need neat, efficient, well-organized storage.

Basic Crawl Space

I don't have much of an attic to speak of—it's really just a crawl space. There's not much room here, and it's somewhat hard to get to, but I'd love to be able to use it for stuff I rarely need, like luggage and holiday decorations. The storage in this space needs to be super-efficient, and I want to be sure I remember what I've put up there.

In a Finished Room . . .

- Consider creating built-in shelves and cabinets around the perimeter of the room for neat, convenient, unobtrusive storage.

- Try dividing the space with shelves or a movable room divider to keep your storage area separate from whatever else you decide to use the room for.

- Don't hold onto things you don't want or use simply because you have space to store them.

In a Basic Crawl Space . . .

- Opt for small or medium storage bins rather than very large ones; they'll be easier to lift and to maneuver through the opening to your crawl space.

- Use vacuum-suction storage bags (such as Space-Bags) to hold extra bedding and linen. The bags com-press their contents to save significant space.

- Create a list of what's stored where and post it near the door or stair hatch so that you'll have a quick way of finding what you need.

SORTING AND WEEDING

Get your attic organization project under way by clearing and decluttering

By getting your attic organized, you'll create room to store things you want to keep but don't need in the main part of the house, and you'll be able to find those things quickly and easily when you want to retrieve them. Organizing the things in your attic can also help protect them from dust, pests, and the elements.

Attic organization starts with rediscovering what's stored there and weeding out things you no longer want, use, or need. Tackle this process on a day when it's comfortable to be in the attic for a few hours at a stretch; if your attic isn't temperature-controlled, you'll probably want to avoid working there when it's very hot or very cold outside. You can also

Sorting and Weeding: Questions to Ask

As you weed, ask yourself the following questions:

- Did I have a good reason for saving this? When was the last time I used it? If I haven't used it in more than a year, why am I keeping it?

- Is this thing truly unique or special, or could I find a replacement if I needed it? Is keeping this item worth the storage space and the effort required to keep it clean?

Sorting Clothes

- Any clothes stored in the attic are necessarily clothes you don't wear regularly. Unless they're out-of-season clothes that you swap out annually, seriously reconsider keeping them.

- If you do store seasonal clothes in the attic, sort through them and make

sure they're still in good condition and still fit.

- Check all clothes stored here for damage such as moth holes or mold. Set aside any that are damaged but can be repaired; throw away damaged clothes that aren't worth fixing.

bring items down from the attic to another part of the house if it's not comfortable to be up there for long stretches or if it's a crawl space that doesn't offer room to work.

Because the attic can be dusty and sometimes dirty, dress in work clothes and consider wearing gloves and a filtration mask if you're sensitive to dust or have allergies. Finally, if you see evidence of pest or rodent infestations (such as droppings or chewed cardboard boxes), call in a pest management company to get the situation under control before you start working.

To begin, set up a Donate box, a recycling bin, a trash bag, and a Move Elsewhere box; if you have a folding card table, set it up as a staging area. Start weeding in the area closest to the attic door, and work your way in. Go through every item and decide what is worth keeping, what belongs elsewhere in the house, what can be passed along to someone else, and what is simply junk. The guidelines below can help with this process.

Sorting Media and Papers

- Donate or dispose of any books that are outdated, damaged, or that you've read and are unlikely to read again.

- Recycle or give away any magazines stored here.

- Weed out vinyl records and cassettes, unless you still have a record player and cassette deck, in which case these recordings should be stored close to your stereo.

- Use the retention guidelines you created in Chapter 12 (see page 128) to decide which papers you need to keep and which you can recycle or shred.

Sorting Furniture

- If a piece of furniture winds up in the attic, chances are you're not going to use it.

- Store only pieces here that are true heirlooms, that have significant value, that you're actively planning to sell, or that you're repairing but don't have space for elsewhere.

- Donate or dispose of furniture you don't like and don't intend to use again, pieces that are broken beyond repair, and pieces you've had for more than a few years but haven't done anything with.

ORGANIZING HOLIDAY GEAR

Make holiday prep easier and more enjoyable by organizing your seasonal gear

The attic is often a convenient spot for storing holiday decorations and supplies. Getting these seasonal items organized eliminates digging for what you need before the next celebration; an organized storage system also helps keep your gear clean, protected, and pest-free.

Start by gathering together the holiday supplies in your attic, as well as any stored elsewhere in the house—a few stray Christmas tree ornaments tucked in with the holiday serving ware in your dining room, for example. (If you've already stored holiday-themed dishes or glasses somewhere other than the attic, feel free to leave them there.) With everything in one place, you'll have a clear sense of how many decora-

Holiday Color-Coding

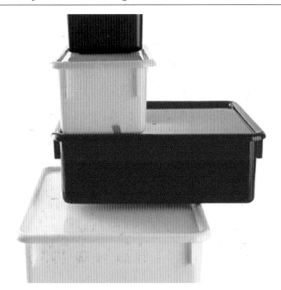

- Use colored bins for an easy way to identify decorations and supplies for different holidays.

- Choose colors related to each holiday—a blue bin for the Fourth of July, for example, and an orange bin for Halloween.

- Give each bin a label that specifically identifies its contents, such as Fourth of July picnic supplies or Easter baskets.

Storing Bins

- Store your bins of holiday supplies on basic metal shelves. You'll be able to lift the lid on each bin without having to move the one on top of it.

- Measure the height of your attic ceiling to be sure you buy shelves that fit. When assembling the unit, put each shelf at a level that will let you easily fit bins on it.

- Use the sides of the shelves to store things on hangers, such as Halloween costumes.

tions and supplies you have for each holiday.

Next, go through your supplies holiday by holiday to decide what to keep and what to let go of. If you didn't use a decoration or supply during the most recent year's holiday, consider giving it away; do the same for things you don't like, have several versions of, or simply don't need. Toss anything that's broken beyond repair.

Once you weed, decide on the most efficient way to store your holiday gear based on how much of it you have and what your attic environment is like.

GREEN ● LIGHT

Keep holiday clutter to a minimum and do something good for the earth by using natural decorations whenever possible. Get creative with plants, flowers, fruits and vegetables, pinecones, and other items that can liven up your house naturally. When the holiday is over, replant, eat, or compost your decorations.

Specialty Bins

Storing Small Decorations

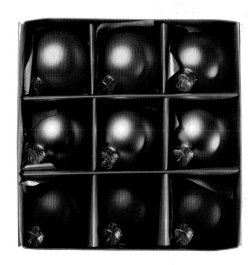

- Many stores sell containers designed to hold specific holiday decorations, such as a divided box for Christmas tree ornaments or a case designed to store a perennial wreath.

- These containers make it easy to store decorations quickly and carefully, because you don't need to modify the boxes to make your decorations fit or worry about things shifting around or being crushed.

- Visit stores after each holiday to find these containers on sale, often for much less than the pre-holiday prices.

- Rather than putting small decorations directly into a larger bin, first put them into smaller boxes so they don't get lost or damaged.

- Divide decorations by type—ornament hooks in one box, extra bulbs for tree lights in another. Label each small box and put them into the main bin.

- If you have only a few decorations for certain holidays, store them all together in smaller boxes and put these smaller boxes in a bin labeled with all of the relevant holidays.

SEASONAL CLOTHES

Make the seasonal clothes swap process fast and convenient with organized storage

ORGANIZING YOUR HOME

Storing out-of-season clothes in the attic clears out space in bedroom closets for the items you and your family are currently wearing. Organizing the clothes you stash in your attic can help keep them clean and in good repair so that they're ready to wear when the next season rolls around.

Get things under way by going through any clothes you already have in the attic. (See page 68 for guidelines on the sorting and weeding process.) Next, take a look at the stuff you've chosen to keep. The best way to store things depends on what types of clothes they are, what they're made of, and who they belong to.

Because many attics are subject to extreme temperatures

Storage Chests

- Use a chest that's made of or lined with cedar to store clothes made of wool, such as sweaters, hats, and mittens.

- Cedar is a natural moth repellent, allowing you to keep clothes pest-free without having to use mothballs, which can leave an unpleasant scent and potentially dangerous residue.

- You can also use a storage chest for blankets, sheets, and other bed linens.

Clothes Racks

- Keep hanging clothes organized and wrinkle-free by storing them on a clothes rack. Buy a freestanding rack or install a closet rod between beams.

- Use zipped storage units on the rack to keep dust and pests away from clothes. These units attach directly to the rod and come in a variety of materials; choose one that will let clothes "breathe," such as canvas.

- If you're storing special clothes (such as formal suits or dresses), store them inside their own garment bags before hanging them on the rack.

and humidity, and because they can harbor pests like moths, it's important that the organizing system you create includes ways of safely storing fabrics like wool. In addition, it's worth making sure clothes are completely clean before you put them in storage; you'll keep pests at bay and will avoid fabric disintegration.

Your clothes organizing system should not only keep clothes safe but also make it easy to retrieve them at the change of seasons and to know which clothes belong to which family member. Store clothes separated by person, or by size, gender, and type (size 2T boys' shorts, for example) if you have several children who share clothing.

Once your organizing system is in place, maintain it each season. Before putting clothes in the attic, be sure you definitely want to keep them and that they're likely to fit the person they belong to by the time the next year comes around. The end of each season is a great time to weed out unwanted, unneeded, unworn clothes to ensure that you're keeping only those that are truly useful or that you really enjoy.

Clothes Bins

- Sturdy plastic bins are useful for sorting and storing clothes for different family members.

- Get a sense of the quantity of clothes for each person before you purchase bins. Aim for one or two bins per person; as you empty the bins at the start of one season, refill them with clothes for the opposite season.

- Label each bin with the family member's name and the size, type, and season of the contents. Store them on a metal shelf unit for easy access.

Keeping Clothes Fresh

- A few simple supplies can help keep the clothes you store in the attic fresh, dry, and protected. Toss a few cedar balls or blocks in each bin of clothes to repel pests. Look for hanging cedar blocks to protect clothes stored on a rack.

- Lavender sachets also deter pests and keep clothes smelling fresh.

- If your attic is prone to severe dampness or humidity, put desiccant packets in the containers, and switch these packets out a few times a year.

ORGANIZING LUGGAGE

Keep a handle on suitcases and bags by creating organized storage for your travel gear

Getting your luggage and other travel gear organized can make preparing for trips easier, which, in turn, can help keep pre-travel stress to a minimum. The attic is often a useful spot for storing travel supplies, but these tips can help you organize your gear regardless of where you keep it.

First, reconnect with what luggage you have and do some weeding. Gather together luggage and travel supplies from throughout the house, including any in kids' rooms. With your gear in one place, sort it by type—all duffel bags together, all wheeled suitcases together—see how many pieces of each kind you have.

Then start weeding. Set aside for donation any bags you

Nesting Bags

- Nesting smaller bags inside larger ones is a convenient way to save space if you have limited room for storing luggage.

- Zip small suitcases inside a larger one, and designate one large duffel bag (ideally one you don't use frequently) as a container for storing duffels and other soft-sided bags.

- If there are pieces you use very frequently—once a month or more—make sure anything nested inside them is easy to remove.

Luggage Racks

- Take a tip from airport shuttle buses and use a simple, sturdy metal shelf unit to store suitcases and other bags.

- When setting up your unit, space the shelves far enough apart so that they can hold luggage stored on its side.

- Attach S-hooks to the sides of the shelves for hanging backpacks and duffel bags.

- Use labeled bins or boxes on the shelves to stash small travel gear like toiletry bags, money pouches, and portable alarm clocks.

don't like, use, or need. If you have multiples in certain categories (several backpacks, say), choose a few favorites and add the rest to your Donate pile. Get rid of bags that are torn or broken, as well as any that are difficult to use, such as rolling suitcases with tiny wheels and unwieldy pull-straps.

After you weed, think about how to store the pieces you want to keep. Try nesting smaller bags inside larger ones, and store lightweight bags with loops or handles (like backpacks and duffel bags) on pegs.

Hanging Bags

- Keep soft-sided bags like backpacks and duffel bags off the floor and organized by storing them on pegs or hooks.

- If you're storing your bags in the attic, use nails hammered directly into the wall or a beam to hang bags.

- If you're using a closet or other area in the house for storage, use wooden pegs or a hook rack.

Toiletries and Supplies

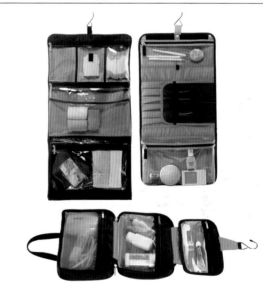

- To make packing easier, keep toiletry kits, carry-on bags, and other travel accessories close to your luggage.

- Save space and frustration when you travel by bringing trial-size toiletries, rather than full bottles. Buy a set of empty plastic bottles and fill them with the toiletries you use at home.

- Store carry-on bags and travel gadgets (such as sleep masks) in a bin or a small bag. Use a luggage tag on the container as a label.

ORGANIZING ARCHIVED PAPERS

Keep old but important papers organized and out of the way with an archival system

Often, the papers and files we need to keep around long-term—such as tax returns and supporting documentation—take up too much space to store in a home office or a household file cabinet. Moving these documents to an out-of-the-way spot like the attic keeps them accessible and helps prevent clutter from building up in other areas of the house. A few simple organizing strategies help ensure that your archived papers are orderly and easy to find.

The guidelines you created on page 128 for what papers to keep and how long to keep them will help you determine which documents and files to store in your archives. Keep a copy of these guidelines handy as you sort and weed any

ORGANIZING YOUR HOME

Banker's Boxes

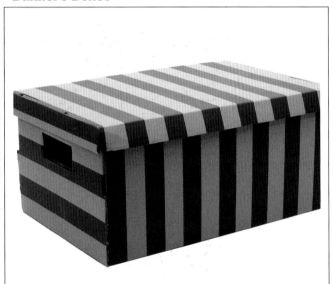

- Banker's boxes—basic cardboard bins with lids—are a simple and inexpensive way to store archived files.

- Store both letter- and legal-size papers and file folders in banker's boxes. If you need to store files in hanging file folders, look for boxes with reinforced edges.

- Clearly label each box with its contents and the year, and store the boxes on a shelf to keep them off the floor, away from pests, and still easy to access.

File Totes

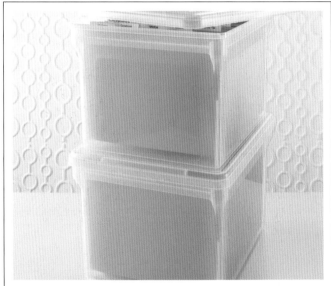

- If your attic gets very humid, or if you've found evidence of rodents, store archived papers in plastic file totes; they won't absorb moisture, and they're much harder for animals to chew through.

- Stacking file totes are a good and relatively inex-pensive option. They're sturdy, have ridges inside for holding hanging folders, and stack easily.

- Use small file totes with handles if you want to store papers for each year separately. Line these totes up sideways on a shelf, and label by year.

papers that are already in your attic, and as you set up an organizing system for the stuff you keep.

Start organizing your archived papers and files by going through anything you currently have in the attic. Recycle or shred papers you no longer need, and sort the keepers into categories that match those you use in your household filing system. If, for example, you store all financial information for one year—bank statements, credit card statements, tax returns, and so on—together in your household files, sort archived papers by year as well.

You might also come across paper memorabilia, such as cards and letters, in the attic. It's helpful to have some retention guidelines for mementos to make sorting and weeding easier. You might decide, for example, to keep only greeting cards that bear truly special sentiments or that you received for milestone occasions, such as a wedding or a fortieth birthday.

After you weed, set up an organizing system. Choose storage containers that will keep your papers and files categorized, orderly, and safe from pests, dust, and the elements.

Storing Memorabilia

- Keep memorabilia safe by organizing them into archival bins and file boxes. These containers are made of acid-free materials, so they won't fade or damage the items stored inside them.

- Sort memorabilia into categories by person, by event, or by year. Store each category in a file folder within an archival file box, or within its own box.

- Put a few desiccant packets in each memorabilia box to help absorb moisture.

Archival Backup

- For an extra measure of security, make digital backups of important papers and store these backups on a CD or USB drive.

- If you have a scanner, you can create these backups yourself; otherwise, take your documents to a print and copy shop, and have the staff scan them for you.

- Keep your digital backups, along with copies of vital records like birth certificates, somewhere outside your home, such as in a safe deposit box or with a trusted friend.

BASEMENT
Turn your basement into an effective storage space with these specific organizing recommendations

Regardless of how large or small, how it's laid out, and whether it's rustic or refined, your basement can be a good spot for storage, as well as a space for tackling projects you don't have room for in the rest of the house. To make the most of your basement, read the descriptions here, choose the one that best matches your space, and find the related suggestions.

Large, Simple Space

My basement has plenty of space, but it's by no means a fancy, finished room. I'd like to use it for storing things that can stand up to a bit of moisture and some chilly temperatures, and I want to be sure that everything is really easy to find.

In Any Space...

- Think of the basement as a storage space for things you actually need and use, not as a dumping ground. Be sure that anything you put in the basement is something you plan to take back out again.

- Label not only boxes and bins but also cabinets and shelves, making it easier for others to find things on their own.

- If you have multiple utility storage spaces—an attic, a garage, and a basement—keep like things together in one spot. Store all holiday decorations in the attic, for example, rather than stashing some in the attic and some in the basement.

In a Large, Simple Space . . .

- Use storage containers with lids that won't get warped or moldy, such as plastic storage tubs. Put them on shelves or pallets so that they won't be affected by any water on the floor.

- Divide your basement into zones based on what's stored or what's done in each space. Create a map of these zones and post it at the top of the stairs.

- Use your basement for tasks that are messy or involve bulky equipment you don't have space for elsewhere, such as painting prep.

Finished Room

I have a finished, insulated basement. I'd like to use it as a place to store stuff as well as a spot for doing other tasks. I want the room to look neat and welcoming, rather than like a standard basement. Although there's plenty of room for storage, I want to use it wisely.

Basic Cellar

My basement is little more than a dirt floor and four walls under the rest of my house. I want to use it as a storage space, but I need to be sure that whatever I put down here doesn't get too dirty or ruined. I also need an easy way of remembering what I've stored here so that I don't have to spend much time looking for things.

In a Finished Room . . .

- Consider installing cabinets (or using freestanding units) around the room's periphery to maximize storage space and minimize clutter.

- Keep similar things together in the same spot: all games in one cabinet, all pantry items in another, and so on.

- If rooms elsewhere in the house serve multiple functions—a dining room that's also a home office, for example—try transferring some of those functions to the basement, where you have extra space and storage.

In a Basic Cellar . . .

- Create an easy-to-clean storage system with sturdy metal shelves and plastic bins that close tightly. When the system gets dusty or dirty, simply sweep it off.

- Maximize your space by installing wall shelves along the stairs; use these for items you need more often, such as extra pantry supplies.

- Post a clipboard at the top of the stairs with an inventory of what you have in the basement and where it's stored. Update your inventory a few times throughout the year.

SORTING AND WEEDING
Take the first step toward an organized basement by clearing out the clutter

Your basement can be a great place to store big, heavy, bulky items that don't belong or don't fit elsewhere in the house; it can also be a good spot for a workbench, a workout room, or, in a finished space, simply a place to hang out. By creating organized systems for the things you need to stash in the basement, you can maximize storage, make things easy to find, and establish this room as an effective multifunction space.

Step one in organizing your basement is sorting through what's stored there and clearing out clutter. Before you start weeding, though, take some time to prepare. If your basement is subject to temperature or humidity extremes, plan

Sorting Tools and Hardware

- You should keep enough tools on hand to support the home repairs and improvements you regularly make. If you're a do-it-yourselfer, you'll need more supplies. Be realistic about how many tools you really need.

- If you have multiples of one type of tool, choose the newest, the best, or a few favorites, and let go of the rest.

- Get rid of any tools that are broken or dangerous to use.

- Toss out rusted hardware, which can't safely be used by anyone.

Pantry and Household Supplies

- If you use your basement to store extra pantry goods, or if you have a root cellar, take a close look at each can, jar, and box.

- Toss anything that's severely dented or damaged, shows obvious signs of spoilage, or is long expired. Bring items with upcoming expiration dates to your kitchen and use them up.

- Set aside for donation any unwanted cans or jars of packaged food that are clean, in good condition, and unexpired to pass along to your local food bank.

your decluttering session during a time when the space will be comfortable to work in for an hour or two at a stretch. Bring lamps or work lights down if the space is dim, and wear gloves and a mask to protect yourself from dirt, dust, and other irritants.

Use a folding table or an empty set of shelves as a space for your sorting boxes. You'll want a bin for donations and one for things that belong elsewhere in the house. Also be sure to have on hand sturdy trash bags and a bin for recycling, as well as a box to stash hazardous materials you're getting rid of.

When you're ready to start weeding, work through the space a bit at a time. Fill your Donate box with anything you no longer want, need, or use that's in good condition; toss items that are broken, expired, stained, or otherwise unusable. Set aside anything that belongs elsewhere in the house (including the garage or attic), and start sorting the things you want to keep into rough categories, such as tools and extra household supplies.

Potentially Hazardous Materials

- Substances like paint, fertilizer, and machine or motor oil require extra care during sorting and disposal. Wear gloves and a mask when handling these materials.

- Get rid of any materials that are damaged or unusable. Also dispose of any cans that are rusted or corroded.

- Don't throw these materials into the trash, as they can cause serious contamination in landfills. Check with your local waste management company for information on safe disposal sites and policies for hazardous materials.

Boxes and Packaging

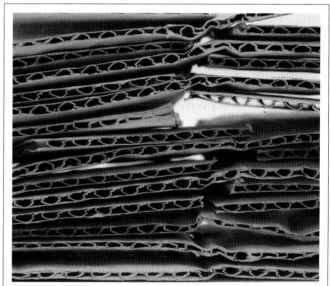

- Get rid of boxes and packaging for any discarded electronics, as well as any that are out of warranty.

- Flatten any boxes you want to keep so that they'll take up less room. Store any box inserts (such as Styrofoam padding) together in a large box or trash bag; use a marker to label which carton the inserts belong with.

- If you choose to keep boxes on hand for shipping, create nested sets of various-size boxes to save space.

PANTRY AND HOUSEHOLD SUPPLIES

Create a convenient, organized storage space for extra pantry supplies and household goods

Using your basement to store extra food, paper products, and cleaning supplies helps keep other areas of the house neater and makes it easy to unload after shopping trips, especially if you buy in bulk. With an organized system for storing these supplies, you'll be able to see at a glance what you have and find what you need quickly and easily.

Organized storage starts with sorting and weeding any food or household supplies you already have in the basement, as well as those you'd like to move here that are currently somewhere else in the house. When sorting pantry items, look for badly dented cans, cracked jars, opened boxes, long-expired packages, and anything that's visibly spoiled; toss all of these. Also pull out any

Stocking Your Shelves

- Sort supplies on your shelves by type, and line them up back to front, with the oldest can or bottle in front and the newest in back.

- If you set up a Use First tray system (see above), sort supplies by type within each tray.

- Store heavy items on the lower shelves to stabilize the unit. Keep cleaning supplies and other potentially dangerous substances out of the reach of kids and pets, but be sure these supplies don't drip or leak onto anything below them.

Tracking Expiration Dates

Item	Purchased	Expires
paper towels	7/3	n/a
soup	8/1	10/8

- Prevent wasted, expired food by keeping track of expiration dates and using your oldest supplies first.

- Mark containers with the purchase date and the expiration date. Get in the habit of doing this each time you restock your shelves; clip a

marker to your shelves to make this process easier.

- If you find you consistently have too much of one thing—too many cans of chicken-noodle soup, for example—make a note on your shopping list not to buy more.

containers that are still in good shape but that you don't want or need, and set these aside for donation to a food bank.

Next, weed your extra household supplies. Give away or dispose of anything you don't want, use, or need. Consolidate partially full bottles or boxes of the same supply, such as two half-full bottles of cleaning fluid. Toss paper goods that have been damaged by moisture or dirt.

Finally, use a simple set of shelves to create a central storage spot for your supplies, and set up your own miniature grocery store.

MAKE IT EASY

Use the cardboard trays that hold flats of soda cans or multipacks of bottles from warehouse stores as dividers for your supply stash. Line the trays up on a shelf and label them Use First, Use Second, and Use Last. Put things that will expire soon in the Use First tray as a reminder to use them up.

Extra Freezer Storage

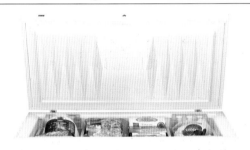

- If you regularly buy more frozen food than you have space for in your kitchen's freezer, use a chest freezer in the basement for additional storage.

- Look for a model with baskets or shelves so that you can divide the space. Store similar foods together—frozen vegetables in one basket, frozen fruits in another—to make it easy to find things.

- Before putting foods in the freezer, label them with their purchase date, as well as a use-by date. Also label what the food is if it's not obvious at a glance.

Home Emergency Kit

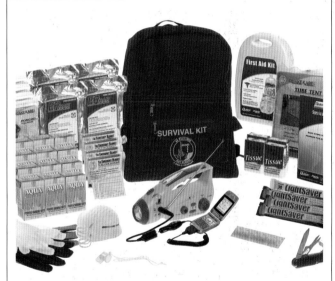

- Depending on where you live, the basement might be a good place to store your home emergency kit, which contains basic supplies in the event of a natural disaster or other emergency.

- Stock your kit with enough water and nonperishable food to last your family several days; also include a first aid kit, flashlights and batteries, and basic protective gear like dust masks. Store your kit in a sturdy, waterproof bin with a tight-fitting lid.

- See the Resources section for more information on what to include in an emergency kit.

EXERCISE EQUIPMENT

Get your exercise equipment in order to create an effective, enjoyable home gym

If your basement is finished and insulated, consider using it as a home gym. Getting your daily dose of exercise will require little more than a trip downstairs, and you'll keep your exercise supplies and equipment from cluttering other parts of the house. (These tips are just as effective if you choose to use another room, such as a guest bedroom or den, as your workout space.)

Before you set up a home gym, give some thought to the types of exercise you enjoy doing. Don't make the mistake of buying equipment for an activity you don't enjoy in an attempt to learn to like it; if you dislike biking, an exercise bike probably won't get you to change your mind. Focus instead on stocking your workout area with gear for exercises you like doing.

Deciding Where Things Go

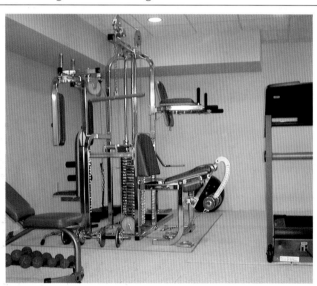

- If your home gym includes a large piece of equipment such as a treadmill or an exercise bike, decide where it will go first, and then plan how to situate other things in the space.

- Take into account things like ceiling height and the location of electrical outlets

when positioning your equipment.

- If you use only smaller equipment or portable supplies like a mat or free weights, you'll need only a bit of clear floor space and a place to store your supplies.

Storing Weights

- Hand weights can sometimes be as effective as weight machines, and, of course, they take up much less space.

- If you have several sets of hand weights, consider storing them on a specially designed weight rack. A set of basic, sturdy metal shelves is another option.

- Keep a collection of smaller weights organized using a low rectangular basket. Line up the weights in the basket by size.

With that guideline in mind, take a look through whatever exercise supplies you currently have, and let go—without guilt—of any you don't like, use, or need. Giving away things you may have purchased with the best intentions but simply don't use will not only clear out clutter, but also help you let go of the negative thoughts that might be keeping you from pursuing a fitness plan you'll stick with.

After you clear out unwanted gear, take a look at the area you want to use as your workout space, and start to create a plan. Be sure to designate space for large equipment, as well as storage spots for things like hand weights, exercise videos, and towels.

Once you've set up and started using your home gym, get in the habit of putting things away after you're done with each workout. You'll keep your equipment and supplies and the room itself in good shape.

Storing Other Supplies

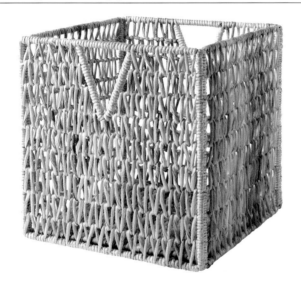

- Use a bin or basket to corral home gym supplies like resistance bands, magazines, and towels.

- If your exercise space is in another room, you can easily move this basket to a corner or a closet if you need to clear out the space.

- An umbrella stand or French bucket (a tall, thin bucket often used by florists) can hold rolled-up exercise mats. Put a flat, heavy stone in the bottom of the container to keep it from tipping.

Exercise Info Board

- Keep yourself motivated by hanging a bulletin or magnetic board for posting exercise information in your workout space.

- Use the board to hold your exercise routine, inspirational photos or quotations, and a chart for tracking your progress.

- If you don't have wall space for an information board, use a three-ring binder instead, and store it in your supply basket.

193

WORKBENCH

Simple home improvements and repairs start with an organized workbench

Whether you're a skilled do-it-yourselfer who loves tackling projects around the house or a person who would prefer to bring in the experts for anything more complicated than hammering a nail, you probably have tools and hardware to store. An organized workbench, whether an actual spot in your basement or a sliver of space elsewhere in the house, can make your home improvement projects easier.

Before you start the organizing process, if you have a garage that also has a work area, ask yourself: Will one workspace be your primary one? Do you want to set up and stock each workspace for different types of projects or tasks (painting supplies in the basement, for example, and woodworking

Planning the Space

- Plan your space so that while standing at your workbench, you can easily access your tool and supply storage spots.

- Use wall space as much as possible. Hang pegboard to hold tools and hardware, and consider installing shelves or cabinets for other supplies.

- Create a secondary workspace where you can store in-process projects and can work on additional tasks when your main workspace is in use.

Using Pegboard

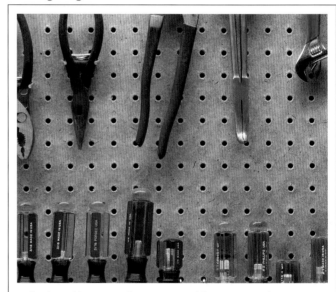

- Pegboard is an easy, inexpensive way of creating organized storage for tools and hardware. Measure the wall above or near your workbench, and have your local hardware store cut a piece of pegboard to size.

- Choose the types of pegs you need based on the things you need to store; options include hooks, loops, and flexible cords.

- Make it easy to remember what goes where on your pegboard by outlining each item in paint or thick marker.

supplies in the garage)? Could you combine the two spaces into one? How can you set up your space(s) to make your work more efficient?

When you're ready to start organizing, begin by sorting and weeding the supplies in your workspace. Give away or toss anything you don't want, use, or need. Throw away anything that's broken or otherwise unusable. And give yourself permission to part with projects you started but didn't finish. If they've been hanging around for a while, chances are you won't return to them.

Once you weed, take a look at the space and the tools and supplies that remain. Your overall goal is to arrange the space so that you have plenty of room to work safely and also have sufficient, convenient storage for the things you need. If you already have a workbench and it's positioned where you want it to be, focus on organizing your tools and supplies; if you don't, add a workbench (or move the one you have) before moving on to the small stuff.

Storing Hardware

- Keep small pieces of hardware like nails, screws, nuts, and bolts organized by storing them in separate containers.

- Empty baby food and spice jars are good options for storing hardware. Label each jar and attach a sample of what's inside to the lid to make identification even easier.

- Look for a rack that attaches to your pegboard and can hold your hardware jars to keep the surface of your workbench clear.

Using Bins

- Heavy-duty bins can hold larger hardware and other supplies that don't fit easily in jars or directly on pegboard. They're waterproof, sturdy, and versatile.

- Stack bins to save room on your workbench, or attach them to a wall panel. (You'll need a panel specifically designed to hold bins.)

- Bins come in a variety of colors, so you can color-code supplies by type or by project. There's also space on the front of each bin for a label.

PAINTS AND CHEMICAL PRODUCTS

Keep potentially dangerous materials organized for a cleaner, safer home

The basement can be a useful place to store things like paint, industrial oils, and pesticides; it's separate from the main part of the house and can weather a few drips and spills. Keeping these substances organized and safely stored regardless of where they are is imperative, because they can be dangerous to humans, animals, and the environment.

Start with sorting through what you have. Gather together paints, industrial lubricants, and other bottles and cans from throughout your basement and garage, as well as any utility closets or other spots in the house. It's worth keeping the supplies you use regularly and paints that match the colors you currently use in your home. Everything else—cans

ORGANIZING YOUR HOME

Safe Storage

- If you have children or pets in your home, a locked cabinet keeps paints and other substances organized and safely out of reach. Look for a cabinet that won't tip and has shelves that can hold heavy cans of paint.

- Another option is a sturdy shelving unit. Choose a metal or heavy wood version; one with shelves that are about two paint cans deep is ideal.

- Use a plastic or cardboard container to corral small cans and bottles so that they won't tip over on shelves.

Identifying Paints

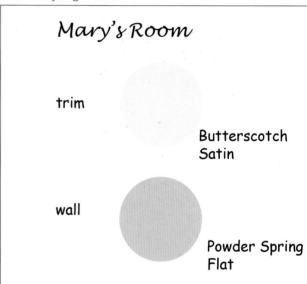

Mary's Room

trim

Butterscotch Satin

wall

Powder Spring Flat

- To easily identify what color paint a can holds, paint a broad swath of it on the lid, and write the color name in marker.

- Remember which paint goes in which room by creating room charts. Using one piece of paper per room, brush on a swatch of that room's paint, indicating where in the room you used it (walls, trim) and the color name. Store the charts in a folder or binder near your paints.

- To replace an exact shade, take the lid (with the paint swatch and the name of the color) with you to the store.

of dried or unneeded paint; any can or bottle that's rusted, cracked, or corroded; or anything you just don't want to keep around the house—should go.

The regulations for disposing of these materials vary widely, so it's important to check with your local city government or waste management company for information on what to do in your community. Avoid putting these materials directly in the trash, though.

After you weed, start creating your storage. Your system should make the things you're storing easy to find and iden-

tify while keeping them away from children and pets. Consider a locking cabinet or a set of sturdy shelves as your main storage space.

Finally, make it a point to return these materials to where they belong after each time you use them, and get in the habit of weeding out unneeded paints and other substances each year. If your community has a household waste drop-off day, schedule your weeding session for a few days before so that you can get the stuff you're ready to part with out of the house and safely disposed of.

Small Storage for Paints

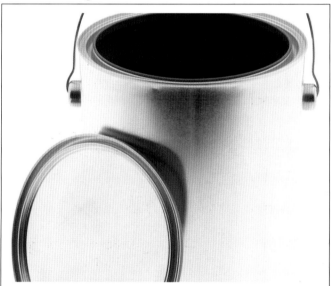

- Rather than storing half-empty gallon cans of paint, decant what remains into smaller containers (available at hardware or paint-supply stores). Paint a swatch on the new lid and label it with the color's name.

- Make touch-ups easy with a paint roller that has a hollow handle. When you're done painting a room, pour the rest of the paint into the handle and label it with the room and color name.

- Use an empty, dry paint can to store brushes, mixers, and standard roller handles.

Commonsense Tips

- Keep a poison treatment chart and the number of your local poison control center posted near your workbench or in the unit you use to store paints and other materials.

- Don't store household or chemical products in food storage containers.

- Read labels carefully to see if there are other substances or materials that shouldn't be stored near a particular can or container because of the danger of a chemical reaction.

GARAGE

Arrange your garage for maximum efficiency based on how you use it

Garages were originally designed to house cars, but these days they seem to hold far more than autos—and sometimes everything but! Regardless of how large or small your garage is, or how basic or elaborate, you can turn it into an efficient spot for storing gear, supplies, and, of course, a car. Read the descriptions here, choose the one that best describes your garage, and find specific tips and recommendations below the photo.

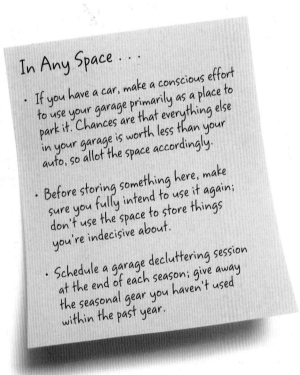

In Any Space . . .

• If you have a car, make a conscious effort to use your garage primarily as a place to park it. Chances are that everything else in your garage is worth less than your auto, so allot the space accordingly.

• Before storing something here, make sure you fully intend to use it again; don't use the space to store things you're indecisive about.

• Schedule a garage decluttering session at the end of each season; give away the seasonal gear you haven't used within the past year.

Simple One-Car Space

My garage was designed for one car, so there's not a huge amount of space to work with. I want to be able to pull my car in each evening without having to worry about running anything over. I'd love to be able to store things here in a way that's really efficient but not crowded or cramped.

In a Simple One-Car Space . . .

• Use the garage's three closed walls for shelves, pegboard, racks, and other organizing systems that will keep things off the floor.

• Consider installing a storage loft above your parking space for things like out-of-season sporting gear. A rolling library ladder will make this space easy to access.

• Look for storage bins in similar shapes, materials, and colors to reduce visual clutter and make the garage look neater.

Multivehicle Spot

My garage has room for at least two cars and various gear and gadgets, but I'm not using the space to its full potential. I'd like the garage to be an efficient storage spot for stuff that doesn't belong or fit in the house, as well as a place to tackle projects and tasks. Overall, it's important that the space feel neat, calm, and under control.

Basic Carport

My garage is actually a simple carport that has a roof but no walls. There's a small, enclosed utility shed in back, but it doesn't have room for much stuff, so I need my storage systems there to be creative and super-efficient. I'd also like to be able to use some of the space outside the shed so that I have more room to work with.

In a Multivehicle Spot . . .

In a Basic Carport . . .

- If you don't have two cars, devote half of the garage to storage and work areas for gardening, home improvements, or other tasks, and reserve the other half exclusively for parking.

- Install a wall-mounted system with customized shelves, racks, workspaces, and cabinets to clear up floor space if you keep two cars in the garage.

- Try painting the floor to make the room look neater and cleaner; choose a paint specifically designed for use on garage floors.

- Mount shelves, racks, and hooks on the outside of the utility shed (on the side covered by the carport), or on the side of the house, to increase your storage space.

- Use these spots for seasonal items: lawn furniture and pool toys in the summer, snow shovels and sleds in the winter.

- Make the storage in your shed easily accessible by using a set of high shelves along only one wall, rather than shelves on parallel walls with little room between them.

199

BULK GOODS

Create convenient, clutter-free storage for the foods and supplies you buy in bulk

Buying food, cleaning supplies, and other household goods in bulk helps save you money and time. Keeping these purchases organized once you get them home makes it easy to keep tabs on what you have, restock when needed, and avoid cluttered storage spaces.

The garage can be a convenient spot for stashing household supplies and nonperishable foods because there's often more room here than there is inside the house. Choose a storage spot that's easy to access when you enter the garage from the house.

Start the organizing process by gathering all of the bulk supplies stored throughout the house that aren't currently

Storage Basics

- A sturdy metal shelving unit is ideal for holding bulk goods, because it can handle a lot of weight and has adjustable shelves.

- Divide the items you're storing into categories such as paper goods, cleaning supplies, and toiletries, and store a different category on each shelf.

- Remove large multipacks (like a three-bottle container of laundry detergent) from their outside packaging to make it easier to grab a single bottle or box of something.

Storing Smaller Items

- Store smaller items such as toiletry bottles in bins to keep them organized and to prevent them from tipping over on open metal shelves.

- Opt for clear bins so it's easy to see the contents. Keep toiletries categorized within the bins by type (shampoo) or by person (Jennie's supplies), and label the containers.

- If your garage is prone to dust, dirt, pollen, or other irritants, use containers with lids to keep the contents clean.

in use. Bring everything to one central spot so that you can see it all together and can get an accurate sense of what you have, and then divide things into categories: toiletries, paper products, canned foods, and so on.

Create a Donation bag or box and fill it with any foods or supplies you don't want or need that are unopened and not expired; bring them to a local charity, or give them to friends and neighbors who will use them. Toss or recycle anything that's gone bad or is too damaged to use. If you notice you're giving or throwing away a lot of a particular thing—a few bottles of a certain shampoo you tried but didn't like, for example—make a note not to buy it again.

Once you weed, look at what remains and decide what to store somewhere inside the house—for example, an extra roll of paper towels in the pantry and a refill bottle of hand soap under the bathroom sink. Also set aside anything that shouldn't be stored in the garage because it could be damaged by extreme temperatures. Then start thinking about a storage plan for the rest.

Storing Cleaning Supplies

- Store cleaning supplies on high shelves, out of children's reach. Keep a step stool close to the shelves if you need a boost to get to things stored up high.

- Line the shelf with cardboard to keep cleaning supplies from dripping on the things stored below.

- Store supplies like aluminum foil, sandwich bags, and plastic wrap on shelves with foods.

Shopping List

- Attach a clipboard with a pen to your shelves with an S-hook, and use it to hold a bulk goods inventory.

- Create a list of the things you normally buy in bulk and the package size you use (for example, four-pack of salad dressing). Next to the list, create a column of checkboxes and title the column "Need to Buy" or "Time to Replace."

- Check the list before you go shopping; once you restock things you needed, print out a fresh copy of the list.

201

SPORTING GOODS

Get the family's active gear organized for a less cluttered, more efficient storage space

Storing sports gear in the garage keeps it from taking up valuable storage space inside the house and also confines the mud, grass, and other stain-makers such gear tends to accumulate to a spot that can handle the mess. Getting your family's sporting goods organized not only keeps the garage neater and more efficient, but also makes it easy to find the right piece of equipment quickly.

Organizing sports gear starts with an audit of all the pieces you have. Take a look through your garage, basement, attic, and closets, and pull out any sporting equipment. If the gear you'll be sorting belongs to other members of the family, get them involved, too. Bring everything together in one spot

Storage Units

- Storage units with open bins are convenient for holding bulky or oddly shaped equipment like balls and helmets. Look for a sturdy wood or metal unit.

- Store similarly sized equipment together—tennis balls in one bin, basketballs

in another—so that you don't have to dig under large items to get to smaller ones.

- If you use the garage to lace up before getting active, look for a unit with a bench top that allows you to sit while you put on shoes.

Storing Gear with Handles

- Put vertical space to use for storing equipment with handles, such as tennis rackets, baseball bats, fishing rods, and hockey or lacrosse sticks.

- Use standard pegboard with ¼-inch holes (which can hold more weight) and sturdy hooks or a wall rack

designed specifically to hold gear with handles.

- If you don't have wall space to spare, choose a compact equipment organizer that sits on the floor. Look for one that's sturdy enough to hold equipment upright without toppling.

and sort it by sport or by type of equipment.

Next, do some weeding. Set aside any gear the family doesn't use or need, as well as anything your kids have outgrown. Donate anything that's clean, unbroken, and in good condition to your local Boys and Girls Club or to Sports Gift, a group that donates sporting goods to kids in need. Toss equipment that's broken or damaged beyond repair.

After you weed, divide the remaining gear by sport, type of equipment, or family member. The best way to categorize your gear depends on how it's used. If the entire family participates in the same sports, it might make sense to split gear by activity, while separating things by person is a good option if your kids each have gear for the activities they're involved in.

If you have limited storage space in the garage, devote it to in-season gear, and store everything else in the basement or attic until it's time to use it again. Do a gear switch-over at the same time you do a seasonal clothes swap to streamline both processes.

Storing Bikes

- Walls and ceilings are great places to store bikes, which tend to take up more than their fair share of floor space.

- Install sturdy bicycle storage hooks in the ceiling if you have limited wall space. Use one hook per bike to store them vertically or two per bike for horizontal storage.

- If you have wall space, mount bike hooks there, or use a wall rack.

- Use a freestanding bike stand to create storage space without mounting anything to the ceiling or walls.

Using Bins and Bags

- Keep gear divided by activity or by family member with sturdy storage bins. Assign a bin to each sport or each person.

- Store bins on a set of sturdy metal shelves. Attach a mop and broom holder to the edge of the unit to hold bats, rackets, and other handled equipment.

- Labeled equipment bags also keep gear sorted and contained, and make it a snap to grab what you need before heading off to a sporting event.

203

TOOLS

Be prepared for simple fix-its or elaborate projects with organized tool storage

It's much easier to do everything from taking care of simple home repairs to undertaking challenging do-it-yourself projects when you don't have to search for the supplies you need. Creating an organized storage system for your tools helps keep your garage neater and makes the time you spend on maintenance projects more efficient.

Start the organizing process by sorting and weeding your tools and related supplies. Gather all of your gear together from wherever it might be stored in the garage, basement, or elsewhere in the house. Separate your tools by type to get a complete picture of what you have.

Then do some weeding. Pull out anything you don't want,

Toolboxes

- Toolboxes range from simple portable models with flip-back lids to cabinets with multiple drawers and compartments.

- If you have only a basic set of tools, or if you want a secondary tool kit to store in a utility closet, use a portable toolbox. Choose one with a sturdy handle and compartments for holding small hardware and accessories.

- A floor cabinet is a good choice if you have a larger tool collection. Look for a cabinet with configurable drawers and compartments so that you can customize it to your needs.

Wall-Based Storage

- Use open wall space in your garage for tool storage. A wall-mounted storage system helps keep flat surfaces (like your workbench) clear and your tools easily accessible.

- If you have many tools, consider pegboard, which can be cut to size. Use board with ⅛-inch holes for storing standard tools, and opt for ¼-inch holes for heavier things, such as power tools.

- A wall-mounted tool rack is a good option if you have a limited number of tools to store or limited space.

use, or need. Set aside things that are in good condition to donate to a local charity or pass along to a friend or neighbor; put broken or badly damaged (and thus dangerous) tools in the trash. If you have multiples of a certain tool, choose a few favorites and give the others away.

After you cull your collection, create a storage plan for the tools you're keeping. The main objectives for any tool storage system should be to keep your gear logically organized, easily accessible, and in good repair. The specifics of your system will depend on how many tools you have and how much space you have to store them in.

If you have a workbench in the garage, wall-mounted storage is a good option; on the other hand, a simple, portable toolbox might be your best bet if you have limited space.

Once your tools are organized, get in the habit of putting them back where they belong as soon as you're done with them. This simple task helps keep your system organized and your tools usable and readily available.

Storing Specific Supplies

- Keep tabs on supplies for specific rooms, projects, or furniture by storing them together in labeled containers.

- For example, after assembling a bedroom set, put the leftover hardware and tools in individual zip-top bags, and put those bags inside a larger bag or envelope. Label the small bags with the piece of furniture they belong to and the large bag with the name of the room.

- Also store instruction booklets, warranties, and receipts for these items with the extra parts.

Project-Based Storage

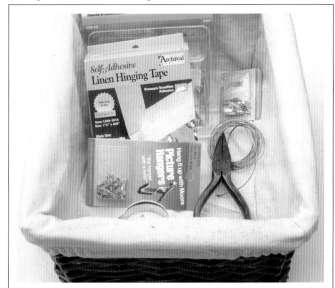

- If you do certain tasks or projects regularly, create a bin for the tools and supplies you need for each.

- For example, you might set up a painting bin to store drop cloths, mixers, paint can openers, roller trays, and so on. A bin for picture hanging might include a hammer, picture hooks, wire, a pencil, nails, and a level.

- Choose sturdy, easy-to-carry bins, and label them by project.

YARD AND GARDEN SUPPLIES

Make it easy to indulge your green thumb by creating uncluttered, convenient storage

Gardening and yard care can be relaxing, engrossing pursuits. Don't let disorganization get in the way of enjoying these tasks; by creating effective storage systems for your yard and garden supplies, you won't have to dig for the tools you need to get started.

The first step toward an organized yard and garden care center is collecting and weeding your supplies. Gather your supplies in one spot so that you can see everything you have, and then sort them by type. Weed out things that are broken, badly damaged, or otherwise unusable, and dispose of them. If you have multiples of a particular item, choose a few favorites, and set aside the rest for

Potting Bench

- A potting bench offers workspace for basic gardening tasks, as well as storage space for tools and supplies.

- Choose from a wide variety of pre-constructed potting benches, build your own, or repurpose an old piece of furniture—such as an armoire or a tall hutch.

- A cabinet beneath the bench's main workspace and a piece of pegboard or a series of hooks above let you keep the supplies you need within easy reach.

Storing Soil and Fertilizer

- Make soil, fertilizer, and mulch easier to use—and prevent moisture damage—by storing them in sturdy plastic or metal containers such as galvanized tubs or small garbage cans.

- Add casters to the container so you can easily move them without having to lift them.

- Attach a scoop to the side or lid of each container so that it won't get lost or buried.

- If you buy in bulk, open bags only when it's time to refill your containers.

206

donation. Add to your donation pile any supplies you no longer want, use, or need.

After you decide which supplies to keep, think about how and where best to store them. Freestanding storage sheds are convenient for large equipment like lawn mowers and wheelbarrows; if you don't have a shed, store these things close to the door in the garage for easy access. Create a gardening zone in your garage with a spot for a potting bench and storage for tools, seeds, and supplies.

Storing Yard Tools

- Keep yard tools organized and safely out of the way by storing them on a wall-mounted rack. Place the rack close to the garage door for easy access from the outside.

- Options include pegboard with hooks, racks that are part of a larger shelving system, and small racks designed to hold a few basic tools like a rake, a shovel, and a pitchfork.

- If you have pets or small children, store tools with their tines facing the wall to prevent injury.

Storing Seeds

- Hang a bulletin board near your potting bench to store seeds. Tack individual seed packets to the board, or slip a binder clip over a pushpin and clip multiple packets of seeds together.

- A seed binder is another option. Slip seed packets into the pockets of a 4x6 photo album (look for one with openings on the top). Include growing notes from past years or other information in the pocket along with the seeds.

- Keep torn or damaged packets in envelopes or zip-top bags so that their contents don't spill.

CAR

Clear the clutter and create smart storage to stay organized on the go

Most of us spend quite a bit of time in our cars—sometimes more than we spend in the less frequently-used rooms in our homes! Given how much time you probably spend on the road, it's worth taking some simple steps to get your car organized and make sure it stays that way trip after trip. Not only is an organized car neater and more enjoyable to be in,

it can also be more fuel-efficient because less clutter means less weight.

Kick things off by doing a car-wide clean-out. Grab a trash bag, a recycling bin, and a box to stash stuff you want to keep but that doesn't belong in the car. Go through every nook and cranny, including under each seat, inside the glove box,

Mobile Office

- If you work out of your car, use it frequently to travel to client meetings, or use the time you're waiting in the car during kids' activities to pay bills or catch up on correspondence, set up a mobile office.

- Use a compartmentalized container on the front seat to store files and papers, basic supplies, and electronics.

- Look for a multipart charger that plugs into your car's cigarette lighter to power several electronics (such as a cell phone, laptop, and MP3 player) at the same time.

Seat-Back and Trunk Organizers

- Create additional storage space with seat-back organizers, which hang over car seats and have multiple pockets that corral things like small toys and games, snacks, and wet wipes.

- Use trunk organizers to control the things you store there. A unit that spans the width of the trunk can hold auto supplies like motor oil and washer fluid, while a grocery bin is useful for keeping bags upright in transit.

- Bungee cords or Velcro strips help keep trunk organizers in place.

208

and in every corner of the trunk. Toss or recycle empty food wrappers and drink bottles, directions you wrote down or printed out but won't need again, and any other trash. Pull out things that belong somewhere in the house (like toys or clothes), as well as anything that's still usable but that you don't want, use, or need.

With the clutter gone, start planning organized storage for the things that belong back in the car.

MAKE IT EASY

Take a tip from UPS drivers and plan your routes so that you minimize left-hand turns. You'll save time by not having to wait for oncoming traffic to clear, you'll save gas by idling less, and you'll help spare the air.

Car Emergency Kit

- A well-stocked car emergency kit can help keep you comfortable and safe in the event of an accident or breakdown.

- Use a sturdy container to hold your emergency supplies, and store it close to the front of your trunk so that it's easy to grab.

- Stock your kit with emergency essentials like a flashlight and extra batteries, blankets, first aid supplies, and water. See the Resources section for a full list of emergency kit contents.

Simple Habits:
Staying Organized

- Each time you return home from errands or activities, take bags, toys, clothes, and sporting gear out of the car, and return them to where they belong. Make each person in the car responsible for his or her own things.

- When you stop at a gas station, take a moment to clear trash out of your car.

- Once every few months, clear out hidden areas like the glove box and the space under each seat, and make sure your emergency kit is fully stocked.

CRAFT ROOM

Find targeted tips on organizing your craft room, no matter what the space is like

Craft areas are by nature full of colorful, creativity-stoking supplies and materials, but that doesn't mean these rooms can't be neat and organized. For specific ideas and recommendations on bringing order to your creativity zone, read the profiles here, choose the one that best describes your craft room, and read the related suggestions below the photo.

Small, Simple Room

My craft area is in its own room, which is fairly small and cozy. I want to be able to keep my supplies organized, visible, and easily accessible without letting them take over, and I'd love room to spread out projects I'm working on.

In Any Space . . .

- Interests can change from year to year, so schedule an annual sorting and weeding session. Reconnect with all of your crafting supplies, toss any that aren't usable, and give away those for crafts you haven't done in the past year.

- To cut down on both expenses and clutter, hold a craft supplies swap party with friends and neighbors.

- Take a few minutes at the end of each crafting session to put away supplies and clean up. You'll keep your space neat and organized with a minimal time commitment.

In a Small, Simple Room . . .

- Use vertical space to hold supplies. Tall wall-mounted shelves are a good option: Their open backs and sides won't make the room feel cluttered.

- Choose a few standardized storage containers to avoid the cluttered look of many different kinds of bins, boxes, jars, and baskets.

- When working on several projects at the same time, lay each one out on a large tray or a piece of finished plywood so you can easily move the entire tray to and from your main workspace.

Full-Size Space

My craft area is a large, separate room with plenty of space for storage. I have lots of supplies for the various crafts I do, and I need to be able to see and get to all of them easily. It would be great to have a dedicated workspace for each craft.

Nook in Another Room

My craft area is a corner of another room that I use for other things, so I don't have too much space to spread out, and I need to be able to put my crafting supplies away easily. I want a sturdy workspace and convenient, organized storage that won't overwhelm the room.

In a Full-Size Space . . .

In a Nook in Another Room . . .

- Divide the room into zones, one for each craft you do. Store the supplies, tools, and equipment for each craft in the relevant zone.

- Mount collapsible tables to the walls to create a distinct workspace for each craft. When you're not using the tables, fold them flat against the wall.

- Opt for clear storage jars and bins for your supplies so that you can easily see what's inside. As a bonus, colorful, varied supplies can serve as the room's decor.

- Consider using an armoire as your main crafting workspace and storage center to keep all of your supplies in one spot and easily hide them away when you're done working.

- A simple card table makes a convenient workspace; it allows you room to spread out and is easy to fold and put away (perhaps behind your armoire) when you're done.

- Keep your crafts area separate from the rest of the room with a decorative folding screen.

SEWING SUPPLIES

Create an efficient sewing space with organized, easy-to-access storage for your supplies

Sewing lets you create unique, customized clothes, bags, linens, and other projects, often for far less than these items would cost in a store. With an orderly, organized sewing space, you'll spend less time looking for the patterns, fabrics, and tools you need, leaving more time for stitching. Organized storage also saves you money because you won't run the risk of buying duplicates of things.

The first step in getting organized is gathering all of your sewing supplies in one spot to assess what you have. Do a sweep of the house to collect sewing stuff from wherever it might be.

Find a large, clear surface (such as the kitchen table) on which you can spread everything out. Divide supplies by type—scis-

Storing Thread

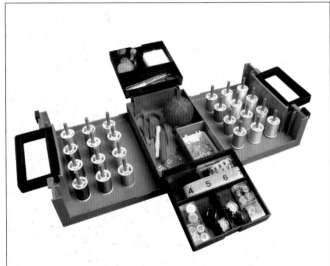

- Put wall space to use for storing spools of thread. A series of peg racks can hold large spools, while a spice rack is a good option for smaller spools.

- If you have drawer space, use it to store thread. A drawer organizer designed to hold spools on their sides

makes it easy to see what's what. (An organizer meant to hold spice jars can serve the same purpose.)

- Sort thread by color or by weight. If you choose to sort by weight, label each rack or drawer organizer section.

Storing Patterns and Notes

- An accordion file helps keep patterns sorted and organized.

- Use a separate file for each item you sew (dresses, shirts, etc.), and stash one pattern in each file pocket. If you keep patterns in their original wallets, you can store several in the same pocket.

- Look for accordion files with tabs for easy labeling.

- Gallon-size freezer bags also work well for corralling patterns. Slip one pattern in each bag, along with its instructions and illustrations; use a large binder clip to keep the bags together.

sors, patterns, thread, needles, buttons, and so on—and then start weeding. Set aside anything you no longer use, want, or need; put supplies that are in good condition in a box for donation to a charity or to pass along to a friend. Toss any pieces that aren't usable, such as tiny fabric remnants, badly torn patterns, bent needles, or hopelessly tangled spools of thread.

If you have multiples of certain things, such as an abundance of pincushions, choose a few favorites and put the rest in your giveaway pile. Holding onto too many supplies is a recipe for clutter.

After you weed, decide how you'd like to store your supplies. You might group them by type, by project, or by size. If you work on sewing projects elsewhere in the house or when you're on the go, you'll probably want to divide your supplies by where you use them: some in your sewing basket, a few in your portable sewing bag, and the majority in your main workspace.

Using Pegboard

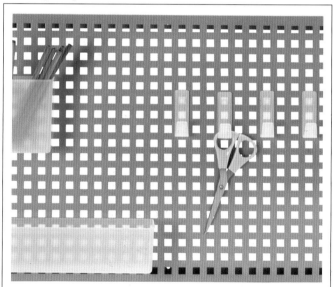

- A pegboard system is a great way to store your essential sewing tools and supplies. Have a piece of board cut to fit a wall near your worktable.

- Before hanging the board, lay it out on a flat surface and arrange the supplies you want to store on it;

- then trace each tool with a marker or a paint pen.

- Use clear jars designed to be hung on pegboard for storing buttons, snaps, and other notions.

Storing Fabric

- If your sewing space has a closet, store fabric there. Fold large swaths of fabric over sturdy wood or metal hangers (or clip them to slacks hangers), and store them on the closet rod. Sort your fabrics by color, weight, or material.

- Store smaller fabric pieces in clear, labeled bins on shelves nearby.

- Use wide, low drawers to stash folded fabric if you don't have a closet. Label the outside of each drawer to make it easy to find what you're looking for.

213

QUILTING SUPPLIES

Keep your quilting supplies and projects organized for a neater workspace

Whether they're heirlooms passed down through generations or bedding used every day, quilts are enjoyable both to use and to make. By setting up an organized workspace and supply area for your quilting projects, you'll keep your crafts room neater and spend less time looking for what you need so you can focus your effort and energy on creating quilts.

An organized quilting area is one that's clutter-free, so start by gathering all of your supplies together and weeding them out. Toss or give away fabric swatches you don't like or have kept around for several years but haven't used. Also cull your stores of thread, needles, batting, and notions. New quilting supplies are likely to come into your life all the time, so

Cabinet Storage

- If you have space, a metal drafting cabinet with low, flat drawers is good for storing in-process projects, as well as fabrics you're planning to use.

- Use each drawer to hold panels for separate projects if you tackle several at once; if you take one project at a time, the drawers can keep completed panels separate from raw fabrics.

- Attach a label to each drawer with magnets as a reminder of what's where. When you move something from one drawer to another, move the label with it.

Shelf Storage

- Clean, empty pizza boxes are a simple, convenient, and inexpensive way to store panels and fabrics.

- Ask your local pizzeria if you can purchase new boxes. Don't use boxes that have held pizzas, even if the cardboard seems clean; food residue and oil can ruin fabrics.

- Label each box with its contents and the project it's part of, and store them stacked on shelves. When you finish a project, reuse the boxes for your next quilt.

challenge yourself to hold onto only those you're realistically planning to use within the next year or two.

This is also a good time to let go of quilting projects you've started but aren't going to finish. Pass them on to a quilting friend. If you can't bear to part with them, finish off a few panels and use the miniature quilt as a wall hanging or as a cover for a small table.

When you have a clear sense of how many supplies and projects you want to keep, start thinking about storage. Do you tend to do your quilting in one spot, or do projects travel with you throughout the house and beyond? Do you have several projects going at once, or do you tend to finish one before you start another? Do you collect fabric swatches as you come across them, or do you hunt for them only when you're ready to get a project under way? Your answers to these questions will help determine what kind of storage will be most effective for you.

Using Storage Bins

- Long, clear storage bins work well for storing project segments and fabrics. They stack neatly and make it easy to see what's inside.

- An under-bed storage box is good for holding a quilting project that's nearly completed, or for storing all of the fabric and supplies for one project together. Stash the bin in an easily accessible spot when you're working, and roll it under a bed or sofa when you're not.

- Smaller bins can hold spools of thread, needles, notions, and other supplies. Look for bins with lids that fit snugly, and label each container.

Storing Batting and Fill

- Store batting and fill where they won't come into contact with moisture, dust, dirt, or pests.

- A small, clean garbage pail with a lid is a good option for storing fluffy, low-density fill, which can take up too much storage space in drawers or on shelves. Label the bin with the type of fill, and close the bin securely after each use.

- Stash flatter, higher-density fill in an otherwise empty drawer or in an under-bed box. Choose a container with a tight-fitting lid.

SCRAPBOOKING SUPPLIES

Make it easy to preserve memories with an organized scrapbooking area

With scrapbooks, how you preserve your memories is limited only by your creativity and what you can fit on a page. By keeping your scrapbooking supplies and work area organized, you'll be able to focus on getting memories down on paper.

Because scrapbooking can involve such a wide range of supplies, from paper to stamps to embellishments, it's espe-

cially important to keep tabs on what you have and to keep things organized in a way that lets you quickly and easily find what you're looking for.

Get started by collecting all of your scrapbooking supplies in one spot. Sort them by type (papers, stamps, etc.) so that you can clearly see how many of each you have. Then do

Project Cases

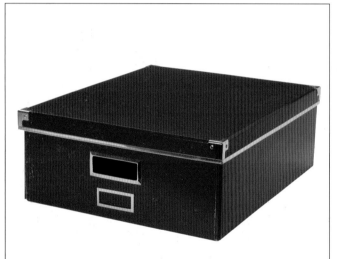

- Storing the main supplies for a project together in a portable container helps streamline your work process, bcause you won't spend time gathering the things you need.

- If you do your scrapbooking in more than one spot, look for a case with a handle,

making it easy to transport. If you work mainly in your crafts area, look for flat, broad boxes with lids.

- Within each box, store small supplies like stickers or appliqués in their own envelopes or bags so that they don't get lost.

Page Managers

- Page managers, which are portfolios sized for scrapbooks, help you plan your scrapbook page by page. Store the supplies for each page in a separate folder; when you finish pages, keep them together in one folder.

- These folders are also useful for holding paper and blank pages. Label each folder so you can tell what's inside without having to open it.

- Store your page managers upright on a shelf. Use file sorters to separate folders by category.

some weeding. Pull out any supplies you've had for a while but haven't used and don't have definite plans for within the next few months. Also set aside anything you don't like or don't need. Put the things you've culled in a box to pass along to a friend or neighbor who does scrapbooking.

Supplies that are worn out or damaged beyond use can be tossed in the trash or recycled. If you have a large amount of any type of supply, choose your favorites or enough to cover you for a year of scrapbooking, and add the rest to your donation pile.

Once you weed, create a plan for storing your supplies and in-progress projects. Aim to keep the supplies you're currently using close at hand, those you're not using accessible but out of the way, and your workspace cleared off so that you don't have to move things when you're ready to work.

Look for storage containers that keep your supplies protected from dust and moisture. If possible, designate a few shelves in your crafts area just for scrapbooking supplies in order to keep everything together in one spot.

Storage Boxes

- Stash extra supplies in labeled bins or boxes. Look for containers designed to hold oddly sized supplies like scrapbook pages; you can find these in many craft stores and on scrapbooking Web sites.

- Choose containers made of acid-free materials, which won't harm paper and photos.

- Consider glass or plastic jars or bins for small supplies to keep them separate from larger items and to make them easy to see.

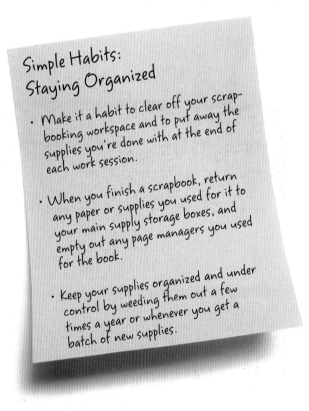

Simple Habits:
Staying Organized

- Make it a habit to clear off your scrapbooking workspace and to put away the supplies you're done with at the end of each work session.

- When you finish a scrapbook, return any paper or supplies you used for it to your main supply storage boxes, and empty out any page managers you used for the book.

- Keep your supplies organized and under control by weeding them out a few times a year or whenever you get a batch of new supplies.

KIDS' CRAFTS

Encourage your children's creativity with a comfortable, inspirational, organized crafts area

Crafts can be great learning tools for kids and wonderful ways of developing their creativity. By establishing an organized crafting area for your children, you'll make it easy for them to indulge their artistic sides and will encourage them to pitch in and help keep the workspace neat.

It's important to involve your kids as much as possible in set-ting up their crafts area. The more input they have on what the space should be like and the more you encourage them to participate in the organizing process, the more vested they'll be in taking responsibility for their own stuff. Even young children can learn to put away supplies when they're done using them.

Workspaces

- Kid-height desks and tables let your children work comfortably. If you have the space and your kids do different kinds of crafts, consider setting up a few workspaces; you might also opt to give each child his or her own table.

- Look for tables and chairs with adjustable legs that can be raised as your kids grow.

- Furniture with easy-to-clean surfaces helps make cleanup simple and lets you and your kids stop worry-ing about spills and errant crayon marks.

Storing Supplies

- Stash supplies in clear containers with lids that close securely but are easy for small hands to open. Label each with words and pictures to identify what's inside. For a more personal-ized touch, have your kids make these labels.

- Keep supplies on shelves that your kids can reach so they can be responsible for taking out and putting away the things they need.

- If you have very young chil-dren, keep anything that might be a danger to them on higher shelves or in con-tainers they can't open.

With the help of your kids, start by collecting children's crafts supplies from throughout the house; with everything in one spot, you'll have a better sense of how many supplies you have. Next, start weeding. Create a Donate box for things your kids don't want or use, supplies they've outgrown that are still in good condition, and extras of supplies they already have enough of. Toss or recycle anything that's broken, worn out, or no longer usable.

This can also be a good time to go through arts and crafts projects your kids have done in the past. Ask them to choose a few of their favorites, and think about creative ways of displaying these (see page 160 for suggestions). Use portfolios or bins to store the works you don't put on display, and consider letting go of pieces that aren't particularly special or memorable.

Finally, set up kid-friendly workspaces and supply storage, which should allow your kids to easily take out and put away the things they use.

Using Pegboard

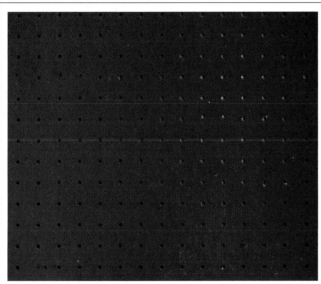

- Colorful, kid-height pegboard is a good option for storing tools like paintbrushes, rulers, and scissors.

- Use Bungi-Pegs and hooks to attach supplies to the board. When things are in place, outline them on the pegboard so it's easy to see where each item belongs.

- Pegboard wall squares help keep supplies for different activities or different kids separate. Label each square for quick identification of what's what.

Space Savers

- If your crafts area is in a small room, look for compact, space-saving furniture, such as wall-mounted desks that can be collapsed when they're not in use.

- Keep floor space clear by hanging hooks on the wall for things like chairs and easels.

- Wall-mounted shelves provide a convenient storage spot for supplies without taking up any floor space.

219

OTHER CRAFTS

Keep tabs on supplies for all of your creative pursuits with simple organizing systems

Regardless of what arts and crafts activities you enjoy, there's no doubt they involve stuff: the tools and supplies you need to pursue your creative endeavors. Keeping this stuff organized helps ensure that it's easily accessible when you need it and out of the way when you don't.

Before deciding how and where to store your supplies, take a look through them and weed out what you no longer want, use, or need. If you have supplies in various parts of the house, gather them together in one spot to get a clear sense of what you have; this, in turn, will make it easier to decide what you want to keep and what you're ready to let go of.

A good rule of thumb is to hold on to supplies you have

Knitting Supplies

- Because you can do knitting projects anywhere, consider portable storage for your supplies and projects. A simple tote bag or basket can hold your current project and its supplies and patterns.

- Use a covered basket to keep knitting supplies handy in a living room or family room.

Simply close the basket when you're not working to keep your supplies neat, contained, and hidden.

- A shoe shelf with cubbies is good for storing yarn in a central spot. Keep yarns of different colors, weights, or materials organized by storing them in separate cubbies.

Wrapping Supplies

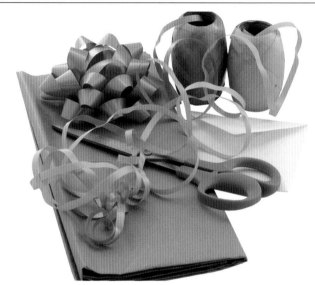

- Corral wrapping paper, bows, tissue paper, and other supplies in one spot everything is handy.

- If you have an empty drawer near your wrapping space, use it to hold supplies. Stash tapes and bows in bins so that they don't get tangled with tubes of paper.

- An upright container with space for tubes of wrapping paper on the bottom and storage for smaller supplies on the top is useful for storing supplies in a closet or a corner of a room.

- Use an under-bed storage container to keep supplies on a closet shelf or under a bed.

definite plans to use within the next year, those that are truly special or unusual and would be hard to replace, and a few essentials you use on a regular basis. Supplies that are rarely worth keeping include those that aren't really usable (such as short strands of yarn and very small bits of wrapping paper), anything that's badly damaged, and things you've had for years but have never used and don't plan to use anytime soon.

After you weed, think about where you tend to do each of your crafts. Do you have one central crafting spot, or do you use different parts of the house for different activities? Aim to store the supplies for each craft close to where you do that task so that things are easy to take out when you're ready to work and put away when you're done.

Finally, choose storage containers that keep like supplies together, are appropriate for the types of things you're storing, and can be labeled for quick identification.

Potentially Hazardous Supplies

- For safety, store potentially hazardous supplies such as paints, adhesives, and anything in an aerosol can out of reach of children and pets; a high shelf is a good option.

- Also be sure not to store them near a heat source or near anything with an open flame.

- Keep these supplies together in an open box or bin. Store cans upright and tightly close the lids on jars.

Storing Ribbons

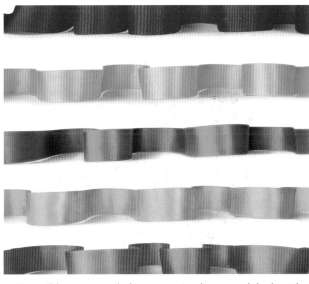

- Keep ribbons untangled by storing them on a wall-mounted dowel rack. Purchase a rack in a craft supply store or create your own with two pieces of wood molding and a medium-weight dowel.

- Slip spools onto the rack. When you need ribbon, simply unspool the length you need and snip.

- A ribbon storage bin—essentially a dowel mounted inside a box—is another good option. Put your spools on the dowel and thread their ends through the slit in the side of the box.

APARTMENTS AND SMALL SPACES

Make the most of your space, regardless of its size, with these targeted tips

Not every home has many rooms, a traditional floor plan, or designated spaces for different everyday activities. If you live in an apartment, a loft, or another home with space issues, getting organized can seem challenging. A bit of creativity, though, can make your space work for you. Choose the description that most closely describes your home and find specific ideas below.

Studio

My living space is a studio apartment with one main room and smaller areas for the kitchen and bathroom. I'd like to divide the central room to create distinct spaces for sleeping, eating, and entertaining. I also want efficient storage so that I can stash what I need without things feeling cluttered.

In a Studio . . .

In Any Space . . .

- When you're working with limited space, be especially selective about the stuff you allow into your home. Choose only the things you truly need, love, and use on a regular basis.

- Label each space by what you do there (cooking and eating, sleeping and dressing), and make sure the things in each space are related to the room's purpose.

- Look for storage spots in unusual places, such as high up on walls and under furniture.

- Create distinct spaces within your main room using furniture, area rugs, and wall decor—a comfortable chair, plush carpet, and framed art in your living room area, for example.

- Look for furniture with built-in storage, such as a bed with drawers underneath or an ottoman with a compartment under the cushion.

- Choose storage containers in similar colors and materials; they'll look neater and less cluttered than containers of many different types.

Apartment or Small House

I live in an apartment with multiple rooms but not a lot of space to spare. I'm able to separate essential rooms like the bedroom, living room, and kitchen, I don't have dedicated areas for things like my home office. I need smart ways to make my rooms multifunctional and want simple ways to store my stuff so that it's accessible but not in the way.

Loft

My space is a loft, so even though I have a fair amount of space, much of it is open, which means I need to be efficient with how I lay it out and use it. I want to keep the airy feel of my loft while still creating space for all the things I do at home. I also need storage that won't make things feel cramped.

In an Apartment or a Small House . . .

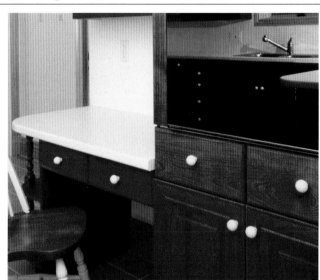

- Convertible furniture makes rooms multifunctional without taking up a lot of space or seeming intrusive. An armoire can provide a workspace and hold your home office supplies and gadgets, for example, and can be closed when not in use.

- Also be sure the furniture throughout your apartment fits the space. Pieces that are too tall, wide, or large for small spaces will make rooms feel cramped and cluttered.

- Keep open spaces clutter-free by storing as much as you can behind closed doors in closets or cabinets.

In a Loft . . .

- Put wall space to use in creative, unobtrusive ways: Install shelves along a stairway for books or decorative items, hang framed photos exhibit-style, and use a bookshelf designed to store volumes horizontally.

- Put tall pieces of furniture around the perimeter of rooms, and devote the centers to lower, longer pieces. You'll make the space feel more open and more cohesive.

- Consider lining one wall with tall shelves for centralized, maximized storage. Keep a library ladder handy for easy access.

SPACE PLANNING: STUDIOS
Create an efficient plan for using every foot of your studio apartment to its fullest advantage

Studio apartments can be among the most challenging homes to get and keep organized, because they don't have the traditional room divisions that larger apartments and homes do. Creative space planning lets you make the most of your studio by designating purposes for each area and establishing spots for storage.

You can do space planning at any time, whether before you move into your studio or after you've been there for a while. The process is somewhat easier when the space is empty, because you won't have any furniture to contend with; on the other hand, with furniture and other items in place, you may have a more realistic sense of how much room you have to work with.

Easy Organizing Systems: Space Plan Considerations

- As you create your space plan, keep in mind not only how much room there is in each space, but also whether there are specific requirements for your tasks: a phone line in your home office space, for example.

- Think multipurpose: Could your kitchen table also serve as a desk? Is there space under your bed for bins of extra linens?

- Before you move furniture around, measure where it will go to be sure it'll fit. If you're buying new furniture, focus on compact, multifunctional pieces.

Simple Space Dividers

- Space dividers help break up large rooms without making them feel cramped or crowded and help separate different functional areas within a room.

- Portable folding screens, which tend to be light-weight and inexpensive, are a good option. Look for screens that work with the decor of your apartment.

- Curtains can also serve as space dividers. Consider installing them from the ceiling so that you can close off and open up spaces with a simple tug.

Start planning by listing the areas in your studio on one half of a piece of paper (leave room under each area); on the other half, list all of the things you need or want to be able to do in your home. Make this list as comprehensive as you can, and go beyond the obvious tasks of sleeping, cooking, bathing, and dressing. Do you also need space for home office tasks? for storing out-of-season clothing? for stashing utility supplies?

After you complete both lists, start dividing the items from your second list (things you need to do in the space) among the areas on your first list. Aim to group similar tasks—such as getting dressed and storing clothes—together in the same space, and keep in mind how much stuff each task requires.

Finally, sketch a simple drawing of your studio with the furniture and supplies for each task in the relevant space: your bed in the sleeping area, your desk where the home office will be, and so on. This drawing will be your guide as you start to put things in place.

Multifunctional Space Dividers

- Pieces of furniture can serve as multipurpose space dividers. A sofa facing away from your bed, for example, creates a division between your sleeping area and your living room area.

- Bookshelves are useful space dividers that also offer storage. Try using two bookshelves back-to-back to have separate storage for each functional area.

- Combine furniture in creative ways—such as a low bookshelf behind the sofa that separates your sleeping area from your living room—to divide spaces and maximize storage.

Using Closet Space

- If your studio has a large closet, consider using it as a separate room, not just storage space.

- Two of the most common uses for large closets are as a sleeping area and as an office space. Before you plan the space, though, make sure it has enough room for furniture, sufficient air circulation, and electrical outlets, if needed.

- If you use your closet as a separate room, make up for the loss of storage space by using an armoire in your main living area to store clothes.

SPACE PLANNING: SMALL HOMES
Maximize storage and efficiency in your house or apartment with a smart space plan

Apartments and small houses that are divided into multiple rooms offer more flexibility than studios, but it's still important to make the best use of each area to create an efficient and comfortable home. A basic space plan will help you determine the most effective way to use each room, arrange your furniture, and create storage for the things you need.

Start your plan by taking a tour of your home and looking closely at each room. How are you using each space now? Are there rooms that serve multiple functions? Do some rooms feel too cluttered, busy, or crowded while others seem under-used? Would you like to be able to do certain tasks at home, but you currently can't because there's not a defined

Drawing a Plan

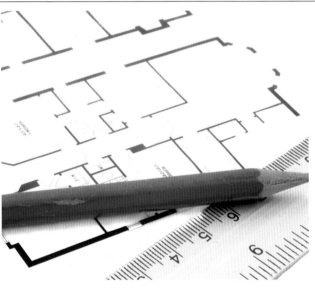

- Create drawings of both the overall layout of your home and, in a bit more detail, the layout of each room. These drawings don't need to be precise but should give you a sense of what you're working with.

- As you sketch, note where things like windows, doors,

closets, and electrical outlets are located. This information makes it easier to decide what should go where within each room.

- Indicate on your drawings what tasks you want to do in each space, as well as what furniture and supplies belong there.

Positioning Furniture

- If you decide to move furniture as you plan your space, measure each piece and the spot in which you want to put it before you move it.

- Use kraft paper cutouts to test different furniture placements. Trace the dimensions of each piece you want to move onto kraft

paper, cut on the lines you drew, and put the cutout in the spot you're considering.

- Rooms with too much furniture will feel cluttered, no matter what else is in the space. Don't overstuff.

space for them? Jot down your answers on a piece of paper or in a notebook.

On a separate sheet, make a list of each of the rooms in your home, leaving blank space under each; include areas that might not be distinct rooms but are still potentially usable, such as entryways, large closets, and balconies or porches. Next to your list of rooms, write down all of the tasks you and your family do or would like to do in your home, from the very basic (sleeping and eating) to the more involved (such as crafting, using the computer, and processing mail).

Then combine the two lists by rewriting each task from your second list under the name of a room or area on your first list. As you decide what tasks should go in which room, consider how much space each activity requires and how much stuff goes along with it. Aim to use each area of your home for something, rather than clustering all of your activities in just a few rooms.

Dividing Spaces

- In rooms that serve multiple functions, create separate spaces for different activities. Your living room, for example, might have a spot for relaxing and entertaining and a spot for taking care of home office tasks.

- Create wall-like but movable partitions in large rooms with folding screens, bookshelves, or a row of tall potted plants.

- In smaller rooms, use less obtrusive dividers, such as area rugs or different colors of paint on the walls.

Simple Habits:
Staying Organized

- Maintain the space divisions you establish—and keep things organized—by getting in the habit of returning items to their homes.

- Don't be afraid to modify your space plan over time. If you find you tend to do a task in an area other than the one you originally designated for it, move things around.

- Revisit your space plan when you go through transitions, whether large or small; everything from buying a new sofa to having a baby can impact how you use your space.

227

MULTIFUNCTION FURNITURE

Keep your home clutter-free and functional with furniture that does double duty

In smaller homes, every square foot counts. Smart space planning helps you make the most of each room, and multifunction furniture lets you maximize efficiency in clever and clutter-free ways. Furniture that can serve several purposes includes not only pieces designed to be multifunctional but also standard pieces used in creative ways.

To figure out where multipurpose furniture might work in your home, take a room-by-room tour. Are there areas that feel crowded or cluttered because they're too full of furniture? rooms where there never seems to be enough storage? spaces where you have many pieces of furniture, each doing only one job? All of these areas could benefit from multipurpose furniture.

Living Room Furniture

- Smart living room furniture provides both comfort and storage. A coffee table with a shelf or two underneath gives you significant space to stash things—and the chance to keep the table surface clear.

- Look for ottomans and footstools with removable tops and storage inside for blankets, pillows, and other lounging gear.

- Choose a side table with a magazine rack built in so that you can keep your reading material close at hand and well organized.

Kitchen and Dining Room Furniture

- In a small kitchen, a tall table with slim cabinet space underneath gives you both a place to eat and space to store pantry items, glasses, and other kitchen necessities.

- A portable chef's cart with a butcher-block top and shelves or a cabinet below extends your food-prep space as well as your storage space. As a bonus, you can roll it close to the stove while you cook and out of the way later.

- Look for a dining room table with a built-in drawer for stashing place mats, napkins, and basic tableware.

One of the greatest advantages of such furniture is that it often combines the original purpose of each piece (such as sitting, dining, or sleeping) with storage space, which means you can keep your space clutter-free without having to invest in extra furniture just for storage.

Create multipurpose furniture by looking at the pieces you have with fresh eyes. The space under a window seat or a kitchen table bench can be dedicated to storage, for example, with a bit of simple carpentry. Make it a goal to squeeze as much use as you can out of each piece of furniture in your home.

Home Office Furniture

- A simple armoire or secretary provides a workspace and storage in a single piece of furniture. Look for a ready-made model or modify an existing piece.

- Use a flat surface that would otherwise go to waste—such as the top of a low bookshelf or filing cabinet—to hold your printer, phone, or other electronic equipment.

- A metal filing cabinet or drawer unit can do double duty as a magnetic bulletin board for posting reminders and To Do lists.

Bedroom Furniture

- In a bedroom with limited closet space, a bed frame with built-in storage drawers provides a convenient spot for stashing clothes, linens, bags, or shoes.

- Expand your space without the need for bookcases by choosing a headboard with shelves in the side. (Be wary of shelves directly over the bed, especially if you live in an area prone to tornadoes or earthquakes.)

- Use a bench at the foot of your bed as a spot to sit and, underneath, a place to store shoes, linens, or bulky clothes.

SMALL SPACES

USING VERTICAL STORAGE

Put your walls to use to maximize storage space, minimize clutter, and keep your floors clear

No matter the size of your home, chances are there's a good deal of wall space waiting to be used not only for displaying decorative items but also for storing the things you need and use around the house. Vertical space is a great storage solution: There's plenty of it, it's flexible, and it can help keep your floor space from becoming overcrowded.

To get a sense of your wall space, and of how to put it to use, take a tour of your home. In each room, note where there are open stretches of wall (that is, those not blocked by furniture or appliances), as well as which are most easily accessible. Also take a look at what you've stored in each room. Are there things sitting on counters, floors, or surfaces that you'd rather

Wall-Mounted Shelves

- Wall-mounted shelves come in a vast array of sizes, materials, and configurations. You can also create your own with almost any kind of stable, solid surface and sturdy brackets.

- These are great for storing or displaying things without cluttering furniture or sur-

faces in a room. Use them for anything from photos and books in the living room to spices and cooking staples in the kitchen.

- Don't let wall-mounted shelves become extra spots for clutter. Think of them as a way to clear off other surfaces, not as storage spaces.

Creative Shelf Placement

- When considering where to hang your shelves, look beyond the obvious. The spot over a doorway in a kitchen can be a good place for a shelf for extra pantry supplies; in the bathroom, such a shelf can be used for extra towels or toiletries.

- Low shelves under a window can hold books, games, music, or photo albums.

- Keep safety in mind: Use shelves with a ledge in high spots to avoid falling objects, and don't store anything on low shelves that could be dangerous to kids or pets.

have on shelves? Do you have to store certain items far from where you use them because there's not enough storage space in that spot?

Other considerations to keep in mind are where the available wall space is located in each room, whether there's any floor space at all available for something like a set of tall shelves, and what your walls are made of. Ideally, your wall space storage plan should make it easy to keep the things you need often easily accessible and those you need infrequently out of the way.

Your wall space storage plan should also let you choose the safest and most convenient type of shelving. If the walls you want to use aren't built of a sturdy material, they may not be able to safely hold shelves with heavy objects. And if you rent (or simply don't want to drill holes in your walls), freestanding shelves that are against a wall but not attached to it might be a better option than wall-mounted versions.

Freestanding Shelves

- Tall, thin, freestanding shelves let you make the most of your wall space without having to drill holes. They're also much easier to move around than wall-mounted shelves.

- Look for shelves that take up the least floor space and offer the most storage. Modular versions let you choose from different heights and different numbers of shelves.

- Avoid tipping by storing the heaviest items on the lowest shelves. If your shelves are on a carpeted surface, consider anchoring them to a wall.

Small Shelves

- Small shelves like picture ledges or curio shelves are useful not only for displaying items but also for storing things that could easily be lost on larger surfaces.

- In the bedroom, hang a few picture ledges near your dresser to hold jewelry and small accessories; a ledge near the side of the bed can hold nighttime essentials.

- Keep your home office workspace clear by using small tins on a curio shelf to stash paper clips, stamps, rubber bands, and other supplies.

ORGANIZING CALENDAR

Stay on track throughout the year with this month-by-month calendar of organizing tasks

January

Create a few realistic, achievable organizing goals for the year ahead and write a list of the steps and habits that will help you accomplish them.

Put away the holiday gifts you received, weeding out older things you no longer want or need in the process.

Organize and store your holiday decorations and supplies in sturdy, labeled boxes or bins.

February

Start to prepare for tax season so you can avoid the April rush. Create a folder for storing the tax forms you'll receive in the mail, and gather your financial paperwork from the past year.

Prepare for travel during spring break and throughout the year by organizing your luggage, travel toiletries, and other gear.

March

Enjoy a cozy day indoors sorting through books, magazines, and other reading materials. Reconnect with your favorites and let go of those you're done with.

Use the last few weeks of winter to finish up any crafts projects you started in the previous months and to organize your crafting supplies.

April

Make next year's tax filing easier by setting up systems for paying bills and storing your financial papers. While you're at it, get rid of any files and papers you no longer need.

Transition your clothes from winter to spring. Give away any winter clothes you no longer want or need, and be sure to clean and repair clothes before you put them in storage.

May

Offer the mothers, grandmothers, and aunts in your life a hand with an organizing project—such as getting memorabilia in order—in celebration of Mother's Day.

Get ready for summer by putting winter yard care equipment and sporting gear into storage and pulling out your warm-weather supplies.

June

Celebrate the end of school with your kids by helping them clear out their binders, desks, and backpacks and by creating organized storage for the papers and projects they want to keep.

Lend the dads, grandfathers, and uncles in your life help with an organizing project in honor of Father's Day.

Take your summer clothes out of storage. Sort and weed them before you put them into closets and dressers for the season.

July

Brainstorm small organizing projects to occupy your kids (or yourself) on rainy summer days. Sorting through photos, memorabilia, books, and recipes are good options.

Revisit the organizing goals you set for yourself back in January. Check your progress, celebrate what you've accomplished so far, and rededicate yourself to those goals you haven't yet achieved.

August

Hold a yard sale to clear out unwanted, unneeded stuff from throughout the house and to make some money in the process.

Get ready for a return to the hustle and bustle of school days by helping your kids get their rooms in order. This is also a good time to get your bathrooms organized so they'll be better able to handle the morning rush.

September

As the weather starts to cool, swap out your summer clothes for your fall wardrobe. In the process, get rid of the warm weather clothes you didn't wear during the past season or no longer want.

Set aside time to tackle a few small home improvement projects and to get your tools and workbench organized.

Create organized spots for your kids to drop bags and papers when they get home from school.

October

Prepare for spending more time entertaining indoors by organizing your board games, video games, movies, and music.

Put summer yard equipment and sporting gear into storage to make room for what you'll need in the winter.

After celebrating Halloween, organize the supplies and costumes you want to keep in a sturdy, labeled bin.

November

Get ready for Thanksgiving by organizing your fridge, freezer, and pantry. Clear out food you no longer need to make room for holiday meal supplies.

Do some advance preparation for the holidays ahead: start creating lists of gifts to buy and holiday cards to send, and take a look at your holiday decorations and supplies so you'll know what you have before you go shopping.

December

Have a house-wide sorting and weeding session early in the month to clear out unwanted, unneeded clothes, toys, books, and gadgets. Donate items in good condition to a local charity that's meaningful to you to help brighten the holiday season for others.

As you unpack your holiday decorations, set aside any you don't like, want, or need; pass these along to friends, family, or neighbors, or add them to your donation pile.

RESOURCES

A Note on Chronic Disorganization

Have you struggled with disorganization for much of your life? Have you repeatedly tried to get organized on your own, but without success? Does disorganization have a significant negative impact on the quality of your everyday life? Do you anticipate that you'll continue to be disorganized in the future? If so, you may be chronically disorganized.

Overcoming chronic disorganization (CD) often requires techniques and habits different from those used to conquer situational, or everyday, disorganization. Many people with CD find it helpful to work with professionals who can guide and support them through the organizing process.

The National Study Group on Chronic Disorganization (NSGCD) has information on CD, referrals to organizers and other professionals who work with CD clients, and recommendations on how to communicate with others in your life you believe may be chronically disorganized.

Introduction

To find a Professional Organizer, visit the National Association of Professional Organizers (NAPO) at www.napo.net or Professional Organizers in Canada (POC) at www.organizersincanada.com.

The National Study Group on Chronic Disorganization (NSGCD) is the premier resource for information on Chronic Disorganization, or CD. At www.nsgcd.org, you can learn more and request a referral to a Professional Organizer who specializes in Chronic Disorganization. To read more, pick up Judith Kolberg's *Conquering Chronic Disorganization* (Squall Press, 2007).

Chapter 2

Boxes, bins, hangers, label makers, hooks, and other gadgets alone won't make you organized. Using these tools is simply one step in the organizing process. Before you invest in supplies, take the time to sort and weed, and then carefully consider what tools you truly need. Here are a few of my favorite resources for general organizing tools and supplies:

The Container Store	www.containerstore.com
Online Organizing	www.onlineorganizing.com
Organize.com	www.organize.com
Stacks and Stacks	www.stacksandstacks.com
Storables	www.storables.com

Chapter 3

For guidelines on how long you can safely store many kinds of food (and where to store them), visit North Dakota State University's Food Storage Guide at www.ag.ndsu.edu/pubs/yf/foods/fn579-1.htm.

Options for storing recipes electronically include eChef (www.echef.com; Windows only), Cook'n (www.dvo.com; Windows only), Big Oven (www.bigoven.com; Windows only), Mac Gourmet (www.advenio.com/macgourmet/index.html; Mac only), and Computer Cuisine Deluxe (www.inakasoftware.com/cuisine/index.html; Mac only).

Make meal prep and grocery shopping easier with coordinated lists; try the Menu & Shopping Pad Planner from Family Facts, available at www.family-facts.com.

Chapter 4

For information on how to safely store and dispose of medications, visit www.blueshieldca.com/bsc/pharmacy/askthepharmacist/browsethearchive/pharmacy_atp_browse_handling_med.jhtml.

Chapter 5

For instructions on folding fitted sheets, go to www.flickr.com/photos/catiecake/sets/515142. A checklist for creating a well-stocked first aid kit is available at www.ready.gov/america/getakit/firstaidkit.html.

To read an article from the *New York Times* that offers expert advice on how long you can safely keep toiletries, visit http://tinyurl.com/48m46c.

Chapter 6

Karen Kingston's *Clear Your Clutter with Feng Shui* (Broadway, 1999) and Terah Kathryn Collins's *The Western Guide to Feng Shui* (Hay House, 1996) are excellent, accessible resources for learning more about how to apply the principles of *feng shui*, the ancient Chinese art of placement, to your home.

Chapter 7

Put the clothes and shoes you're letting go of to good use by donating them to organizations that serve people in need. Charity Guide's page on clothing donation (http://charityguide.org/volunteer/fifteen/clothesshoes.htm) lists some useful resources.

A professional image consultant can help you weed out and update your wardrobe to focus on clothes that fit and flatter you; visit the AICI (Association of Image Consultants International) Web site at www.aici.org to find a consultant.

Chapter 8

Want to cut back on junk mail? Read my tip on how to stem the flow of unwanted mail (http://organizedlife.blogspot.com/2005/05/earth-friendly-organizing-part-3.html). Catalog Choice (www.catalogchoice.org) is a free service that lets you remove your name from mailing lists. Green Dimes (www.greendimes.com) and 41 Pounds (www.41pounds.com) are fee-based junk mail reduction services.

The DMA Consumer Information page (www.dmachoice.org/consumerassistance.php) includes information on removing yourself from phone, mail, and e-mail marketing lists.

Chapter 9

Visit Earth 911 (www.earth911.org) for information on how to recycle everything from used cell phones to motor oil. Use a cleaning checklist to make daily, weekly, and seasonal chores more organized. You can find several sample checklists from Real Simple at http://tinyurl.com/hcqyw.

Visit the ironing section of Martha Stewart's Web site (http://tinyurl.com/24egdg) for instructions on ironing everything from a simple cotton shirt to velvet.

Chapter 10

What's the best way to store old photos? baby clothes? newspaper clippings? Find out at www.savingstuff.com, where you can also purchase *Saving Stuff*, a book by Don Williams and Louisa Jagger (Simon & Schuster, 2005).

Game Savers are designed to replace beat-up board game boxes; you can find them at www.obhenterprises.com/index_files/GameSaverFamily.htm.

Keep clutter at bay by renting, rather than buying, games and movies; visit www.netflix.com, www.greencine.com, and www.gamefly.com.

Chapter 11

Not using some china because it's missing pieces? Visit Replacements Ltd. (www.replacements.com) to round out the set.

Chapter 12

Find unusual office supplies at See Jane Work (www.seejanework.com), Russell + Hazel (www.russellandhazel.com), and the Green Office (www.thegreenoffice.com).

Chapter 13

BankRate has a good general overview of what financial records to keep, how long to keep them, and why; check out www.bankrate.com/brm/news/mtg/20000518h.asp.

Don't let unused, unwanted electronics clutter your home office. The National Center for Electronics Recycling (NCER) offers information on manufacturer take-back programs and other recycling options at www.electronicsrecycling.org/ContentPage.aspx?pageid=87.

GreenDisk (www.greendisk.com) recycles CDs, floppy discs, and other small electronics. Productivity consultant Merlin Mann's Inbox Zero series (www.43folders.com/izero) offers detailed tips and theories on taking control of e-mail.

Chapter 14

Pottery Barn Kids (www.pbkids.com), Modern Seed (www.modernseed.com), and the Land of Nod (www.landofnod.com) are good sources of furniture for kids of all ages. Baby Plays (www.babyplays.com) is a service that allows you to rent toys—a great way to keep your child engaged and entertained with new playthings without having to purchase them.

Chapter 15

The School Folio (www.schoolfolio.com) is a clever, convenient way of storing your child's schoolwork and artwork. Donna Goldberg's *The Organized Student* (Fireside, 2005) includes tips, ideas, and recommendations on helping students of all ages feel more in control of their time and tasks.

Chapter 16

Suitcases for Kids (www.suitcasesforkids.org) helps organize donation drives for luggage, which is given to children in foster care. For information on collecting suitcases for kids in your area, visit Charity Guide at www.charityguide.org/volunteer/fewhours/foster-children.htm.

Repel moths safely and without toxins by using the techniques in an article from Care2.com at www.care2.com/greenliving/ask-annie-moth-ball-alternatives.html.

Chapter 17

For a good checklist of what to store in an emergency supply kit, visit Ready America at www.ready.gov/america/getakit/index.html.

Chapter 18

Put your unused sports equipment to good use by donating it to Sports Gift (www.sportsgift.org), which provides recreation programs and supplies for kids in need around the world.

Habitat for Humanity ReStores (www.habitat.org/env/restores.aspx) accept used and excess building materials. By reselling these materials, the stores raise funds for local Habitat for Humanity projects.

A car emergency kit can help keep you safe on the road. For some suggestions on what to include in your kit, check out www.edmunds.com/ownership/howto/articles/43798/article.html.

Chapter 19

Put your extra craft supplies—or completed crafts projects—to good use by donating them to charity. For details, see http://familycrafts.about.com/od/craftingforcharity.

Chapter 20

The Home Decorating Coach offers tips that can help make small spaces seem larger and less cluttered; visit www.homedecoratingcoach.com/furnitureforsmallspaces.html.

PHOTO CREDITS

p. xii pjmorley/shutterstock; p. 1 Laura Stone/shutterstock; p. 2 (left) Courtesy of Home Decorators; p. 2 (right) Rob Byron/shutterstock; p. 3 Courtesy of Brother; p. 4 (left) Courtesy of Ballard Designs; p. 4 (right) Courtesy of Fisher Paykel; p. 5 psamtik/shutterstock; p. 6 shutterstock; p. 7 (left) TheSupe87/shutterstock; p. 7 (right) shutterstock; p. 8 Courtesy of Viking; p. 9 (left) Courtesy of Crown Point Cabinetry; p. 9 (right) Courtesy of Ikea; p. 10 (left) Courtesy of Organized A to Z; p. 10 (right) Courtesy of Kohler Co.; p. 11 (left) Courtesy of Kraftmaid Cabinetry; p. 11 (right) shutterstock; p. 12 (left) Courtesy of Diamond Cabinets; p. 12 (right) Courtesy of Diamond Cabinets; p. 13 (left) shutterstock; p. 13 (right) Courtesy of Diamond Cabinets; p. 14 (left) Courtesy of Crown Point Cabinetry; p. 14 (right) Courtesy of Organize It; p. 15 (left) shutterstock; p. 15 (right) Courtesy of Diamond Cabinets; p. 16 (left) Courtesy of The Container Store; p. 16 (right) Courtesy of The Container Store; p. 17 (left) Courtesy of simplehuman; p. 17 (right) Courtesy of The Container Store; p. 18 Courtesy of Diamond Cabinets; p. 19 (left) Anna Adesanya; p. 19 (right) Courtesy of Knock Knock, Who's There, Inc.; p. 20 (left) Courtesy of Diamond Cabinets; p. 20 (right) Courtesy of Rubbermaid; p. 21 (left) Courtesy of The Container Store; p. 21 (right) jim kruger/istockphoto; p. 22 Courtesy of Fisher Paykel; p. 23 (left) s duffett/shutterstock; p. 23 (right) Alexander Remy Levine/shutterstock; p. 24 (left) Courtesy of Fisher Paykel; p. 24 (right) Courtesy of The Container Store; p. 25 Courtesy of The Container Store; p. 26 (left) © Laura Siivola | Dreamstime.com; p. 26 (right) Courtesy of American Woodmark Cabinetry; p. 27 (left) Courtesy of The Container Store; p. 27 (right) niderlander/ shutterstock; p. 28 matka_Wariatka/shutterstock; p. 29 (left) © Carolyn Thompson | Dreamstime.com; p. 29 (right) Courtesy of Ballard Designs; p. 30 (right) Carl Kelliher/istockphoto; p. 31 (left) Gary Sludden/istockphoto; p. 31 (right) Dallas Events Inc/shutterstock; p. 32 shutterstock; p. 33 photos.com; p. 34 (left) Courtesy of Shenandoah Cabinetry; p. 34 (right) Courtesy of American Standard; p. 35 (left) photos.com; p. 35 (right) Courtesy of Diamond Cabinets; p. 35 (right) Courtesy of The Container Store; p. 36 (left) photos.com; p. 36 (right) Debra James/shutterstock; p. 37 (left) Courtesy of Hammacher; p. 37 (right) Courtesy of Organize It; p. 38 (left) Courtesy of Organize It; p. 38 (right) Andrey Chmelyov/ shutterstock; p. 39 (left) Courtesy of Organize It; p. 40 (left) Courtesy of Oxygenics; p. 40 (right) Courtesy of The Container Store; p. 41 (left) Courtesy of The Container Store; p. 41 (right) Courtesy of The Container Store; p. 42 (right) Anna Adesanya; p. 43 (left) photos.com; p. 43 (right) photos.com; p. 44 (left) Milkos/ shutterstock; p. 44 (right) Albert Lozano/shutterstock; p. 45 Matsonashvili Mikhail/shutterstock; p. 46 (left) Shmeliova Natalia/shutterstock; p. 46 (right)\ photos.com; p. 47 (left) © Baloncici | Dreamstime.com; p. 47 (right) Courtesy of Organize.com; p. 48 (left) Courtesy of Home Decorators; p. 48 (right) ene/shutterstock; p. 49 (left) Courtesy of The Container Store; p. 49 (right) photos.com; p. 50 (left) Courtesy of Organize.com; p. 50 (right) Courtesy of Organize.com; p. 51Courtesy of Organize.com; p. 52 (left) Anna Adesanya; p. 52 (right) Anna Adesanya; p. 53 Courtesy of Organize It; p. 54 Courtesy of Home Decorators; p. 55 (left) Pål Espen Olsen/shutterstock; p. 55 (right) Cora Reed/shutterstock; p. 56 (left) Courtesy of Home Source International; p. 56 (right) Courtesy of FLOR; p. 57 (left) Courtesy of BranchHome.com; p. 57 (right) Courtesy of Home Decorators; p. 58 (left) Courtesy of The Powell Co.; p. 58 (right) Courtesy of Ikea; p. 59 (left) Courtesy of Ikea; p. 59 (right) Courtesy of The Powell Co.; p. 60 (left) shutterstock; p. 60 (right) Glenda M. Powers/shutterstock; p. 61 Courtesy of Stacks and Stacks; p. 62 (left) Courtesy of Ikea; p. 62 (right) Courtesy of Stacks and Stacks; p. 63 (left) shutterstock; p. 63 (right) Courtesy of Organized A to Z; p. 64 (left) © Igor Groshev | Dreamstime.com; p. 64 (right) shutterstock; p. 65 (left) shutterstock; p. 65 (right) shutterstock; p. 66 © Steve Cukrov | Dreamstime.com; p. 67 (left) N Joy Neish/ shutterstock; p. 67 (right) Yin Yang/Istockphoto; p. 68 Steve Cukrov/shutterstock; p. 69 (left) Piotr Wardy?ski/ shutterstock; p. 69 (right) © Michael Warburg | Dreamstime.com; p. 70 (left) Apollofoto/shutterstock; p. 70 (right) Dole/shutterstock; p. 71 (left) Kheng Guan Toh/shutterstock; p. 71 (right) shutterstock; p. 72 (left) shutterstock; p. 72 (right) Courtesy of Organize.com; p. 73 EuToch/shutterstock; p. 74 (left) Carsten Reisinger/shutterstock; p. 74 (right) Deborah Reny/shutterstock; p. 75 (left) Courtesy of ModernLink; p. 75 (right) photos.com; p. 76 (left) Courtesy of Shoe Stor; p. 76 (right) Courtesy of Organized A to Z; p. 77 (left) Gravicapa/shutterstock; p. 77 (right) Courtesy of Stacks and Stacks; p. 78 Courtesy of Ikea; p. 79 (left) Courtesy of Home Decorators; p. 79 (right) Courtesy of Home Decorators; p. 80 Courtesy of Organize.com; p. 81 (left) Courtesy of Home Decorators; p. 81 (right) Courtesy of Home Decorators; p. 82 (left) shutterstock; p. 82 (right) photos.com; p. 83 (left) Courtesy of Home Decorators; p. 83 (right) Courtesy of Ikea; p. 84 (left) Courtesy of The Container Store; p. 84 (right) Courtesy of See Jane Work; p. 85 Anna Adesanya; p. 86 (left) Courtesy of Ikea; p. 86 (right) © Gleb Vinnikov | Dreamstime.com; p. 87 (left) photos.com; p. 87 (right) photos.com; p. 88 (left) Courtesy of The Container Store; p. 88 (right) Courtesy of Organize It; p. 89 (left) Courtesy of Ikea; p. 89 (right) Andrew McDonough/shutterstock; p. 90 Courtesy of Ikea; p. 91 (left) © Colleen Coombe | Dreamstime.com; p. 91 (right) Courtesy of Ikea; p. 92 (left) Courtesy of The Container Store; p. 92 (right) Galina Barskaya/shutterstock; p. 93 (left) Mark Poprocki/shutterstock; p. 93 (right) Courtesy of EcoAnimal; p. 94 (left) Courtesy of The Container Store; p. 94 (right) Courtesy of Conserv-A-Store; p. 95 Diego Cervo/shutterstock; p. 96 (left) Courtesy of Organize.com; p. 96 (right) Colour/shutterstock; p. 97 Courtesy of The Container Store; p. 98 (left) Courtesy of The Container Store; p. 98 (right) Courtesy of The Container Store; p. 99 (left) Courtesy of The Container Store; p. 99 (right) Valery Potapova/shutterstock; p. 100 (left) Courtesy of Ikea; p. 100 (right) Courtesy of The Container Store; p. 101 (left) photos. com; p. 101 (right) Courtesy of The Container Store; p. 102 Keith Muratori/shutterstock; p. 103 (left) Chris Rodenberg Photography; p. 103 (right) Ingrid Balabanova/shutterstock; p. 104 (left) Courtesy of Obrien & Schridde; p. 104 (right) Courtesy of Archival Methods LLC; p. 105 (left) Courtesy of Cropper Hopper; p. 105 (right) Courtesy of Preserve Your Flowers, LLC; p. 106 (left) Courtesy of Curio Cabinets; p. 106 (right) Courtesy of Home Decorators; p. 107 (left) Eduardo Jose Bernardino/istockphoto; p. 107 (right) Baloncici/shutterstock; p. 108 (left) photos.com; p. 108 (right) Creasence/shutterstock; p. 109 (left) Courtesy of Game Savers; p. 109 (right) Home Decorators; p. 110 shutterstock; p. 111 Andresr/shutterstock; p. 112 (left) Courtesy of Home Decorators; p. 112 (right) Courtesy of Stacks and Stacks; p. 113 (left) James M Phelps, Jr/shutterstock; p. 113 (right) Smith&Smith/shutterstock; p. 114 shutterstock; p. 115 (left) Courtesy of Harveys—The Furniture Store; p. 115 (right) Courtesy of Harveys—The Furniture Store; p. 116 (left) © Jorgeinthewater | Dreamstime.com; p. 116 (right) David Cerven/istockphoto; p. 117 (left) Courtesy of Stacks and

INDEX

A

accessories, 64–65, 88–89

acid-free material, 64, 104, 171, 185, 217

albums, 105, 170

apartments and small spaces, 222–31

archives, 173, 184–85

armoire, 54, 127, 139, 211, 223, 225, 229

artwork, children's, 160–61, 173

attic, 174–83

B

baby supplies and equipment, 54, 152–53

baby's room. *See* child's room

backpacks/bags, 88, 183

banker's box, 170, 184

basement, 186–97

baskets, 34, 35, 43, 44, 48, 81, 89, 98, 120, 220

bath tub, 38–39

bathrooms, 30–41

bed linens, 46–47

bedroom, 54–77, 229

    child's, 150–61, 162–73

beds, 163

bedside table, 54, 56–57

belts, 65

bench storage, 80, 81

bikes, 203

binders, 19, 26, 112, 140, 172, 193, 207

bins, plastic. *See also* containers

    basement storage, 187, 195

    bathroom, 34

    children's memorabilia, 161, 171

    clothes, 181

    holiday decorations, 178

    linen closet, 42

    quilting supplies, 215

    sporting goods, 203

    toys, 166

    utility supplies, 50

books, magazines and newspapers, 110–11, 156

brooms and mops, 96

bulk goods, 200–201

bulky items, 47

bulletin board, 99, 132, 171, 193

C

cabinets, kitchen, 12–13

cable management, 142–43

calendar, 11, 136–37, 232–33

can dispensers, 21

car, 208–9

CDs, 112, 141

cedar, 42, 59, 180, 181

chemical products, 196–97

chests, storage, 59, 180

children. *See also* toys

    crafts, 218–19

    entryway storage, 81, 82

    in-and-out center, 84

child's room, 150–61, 162–73

china, 116–17

cleaning supplies, 16, 96–97, 201

closets, 225

    bedroom, 66–67

    children's, 159

    hall, 86–89

    organizing, 70–73

clothes

    children's, 158–59, 168–69

    closet storage, 66–67

    organizing, 70–75, 176

    seasonal, 169, 180–81

    visual directory, 73

    weeding, 68–69

clothes hamper, 60

clothes racks, 180

clutter

    bathroom, 38–39

    clearing, xii–1

    kitchens, 8–9

coats and jackets, 86–87

coffee table, 110

collectibles, 106–7

color coding system, 36, 146, 178

compression bags, 47, 175

computers. *See* home technology

containers, 2. *See also* bins, plastic

    bathroom, 32

    bedroom, 60

    kitchen storage, 20

    toys, 156, 166

cookbooks, 18, 26–27

cord and cable management, 142–43

countertops, 8–11

craft room, 210–21

    kids' projects, 218–19

cubbies, 76, 80, 220

D

decorations, holiday, 5, 124–25, 178–79

desk, 54, 132–33

dessicant packets, 181, 185

digital archives, 185
dining room, 114–25
dishes and glasses, 12, 116–19
displays
    children's artwork, 160, 171
    dishes and china, 116
    glassware, 119
    holiday items, 125
    photos and memorabilia, 104, 160
    serving ware, 122
dividers
    drawer, 14–15, 31, 33, 75, 158
    shelf, 43, 48
    space, 224–25, 227
drawers
    bathroom, 31
    bedroom, 58, 75
    for children's clothes, 168
    craft projects storage, 214
    desk, 133
    kitchen, 14–15
    linen storage, 120
    shoe, 76
dresser, 62–63, 74–75

E
e-mail, 144–47
electronic organizational aids, 27, 137, 148–49
electronics, 11, 138–49
emergency kit, 191, 209
entertaining supplies, 108–9
entryway, 78–89
exercise equipment, 192–93

F
fabric storage, 213
file totes, 131, 184

files, electronic, 27, 148–49
filing system, 126, 130–31, 135
    computer manuals and discs, 140–41
    e-mail, 146–47
first aid kit, 50
food, 18–19, 188
    storage containers, 23, 24
foyer, 80–81
fragile items, 102, 106, 117, 119
frames, 106, 161, 162, 171
freezer, 18, 24–25, 191
furniture, 177, 225, 226
    child's room, 152, 163
    multifunction, 223, 228–29
    storage, 167

G
games, 109
games, computer, 113, 140–41
garage, 198–209
garden supplies, 206–7
glassware, 12, 118–19
grooming supplies, 62–63

H
habits, organizational, 4–5, 61, 133
hall closet, 86–89
hangers, clothes, 67, 70, 73
hanging space, 100
    children's clothes, 158, 169
    hall closet, 86
    linens, 121
hazardous materials, 189, 196–97, 221
holiday and special occasion items, 5, 124–25, 178–79
home maintenance supplies, 51
home office, 126–37, 229

home technology, 138–49
homes, small, 226–27
hooks, 182–83
    backpack/bag storage, 88
    bathroom, 31
    closet door, 86
    entryway, 82
    towel, 37
    valet, 61
household supplies, 50, 188, 190–91
hutch, 114, 115, 116, 127, 139

I
in-and-out center, 84–85
inventory, 13, 25, 51, 53, 187
ironing, 101

J
jars, 20, 34, 132
junk drawer, 15

K
kitchens, 6–29. See also specific areas, i.e. cabinets, pantry, etc.
knitting supplies, 220

L
labels, 3, 20, 22, 23, 43, 157, 162, 168, 218
laundry room and mud room, 89–101
Lazy Susans, 18, 21
ledge shelves, 38, 104, 107, 231
linen closet, 42–53
linens, 29, 46–47, 120–21
lists
    attic storage, 175
    bulk items shopping list, 201
    checklist for leaving the house, 85

diaper bag must-haves, 153
grocery, 5
meal planning, 28
templates, 18
living room, 102–13
loft, 223
loft beds, 163
luggage, 182–83

M

magazines, 111
mail, 5, 84
makeup, 63
manuals, 140–41
meals and meal planning, 5, 28–29
medications, 30, 32, 52–53
medicine cabinet, 30, 32–33
memorabilia, 104–5, 160–61, 170–71
mobile office, 208
movies, 112–13
mudroom and laundry room, 89–101
museum wax, 102, 106
music, 112–13

O

office supplies, 126, 133, 134–35
organization
    car, 208
    children's clothes, 158–59, 168–69
    closet, 70–73
    computer files, 149
    developing systems, 2–3
    e-mail, 146–47
    maintaining, 4–5
    month-by-month calendar, 232–33
    school papers, 172–73
    toys, 156–57, 166–67
organizers, 39, 153. *See also* shoe
    organizers

P

packing materials, 189
padded storage, 111, 117, 119
paints and chemical products, 196–97
pantry, 18, 19, 20–21, 188
pantry and household supplies, 190–91
paper goods, 48–49
papers
    archived, 173, 184–85
    filing, 130–31
    sorting, 128–29, 132, 172–73, 177
    storing, 132, 135
party supplies, 108
patterns, sewing, 212
pegboard, 194, 204, 213, 219
personal supplies, 52–53
personality types
    bathroom, 30–31
    bedroom, 54–55
    clothes storage, 66–67
    cooking, 18–19
    dining room, 114–15
    entryway, 78–79
    home office, 126–27
    home technology, 138–39
    kitchen, 6–7
    linen closet, 42–43
    living room, 102–3
    mudroom and laundry room,
        90–91
    older child's room, 162–63
    young child's room, 150–51
pet care, 92–93
photos and memorabilia, 104–5
pots and pans, 12, 13
purses and handbags, 65, 88

Q

quilting supplies, 214–15

R

racks, 40–41, 180
    bathroom, 38, 39, 41
    glassware, 118
    shoe, 77
    ties and belts, 65
    wall-mounted, 96, 97, 207
reading material, 110–11
recipes, 26–27
recycling, 94–95, 129
refrigerator, 18, 22–23
remains of the day, 60–61
resources, 234–37
rod, clothes, 67, 86, 158, 159

S

schedule, family, 136–37
school papers, 84, 172–73
scrapbooks, 105, 170, 216–17
screen, folding, 102, 127, 211, 224
seasonal storage, 169
seating, 80
serving ware, 122–23
sewing supplies, 212–13
shadowboxes, 105
sheds, 207
sheets, 42, 46–47
shelf dividers, 43, 48
shelf expanders, 13, 25, 42, 117
shelf liner, 42
shelves
    attic, 174–75
    basement, 186–87
    bathtub, 38
    books, 110
    bulk item storage, 200
    cable, 143
    for children's clothes, 168
    displaying collections, 107

INDEX

entryway, 82, 89
freestanding, 231
in loft space, 223
open, 34
stocking, 190
wall-mounted, 219, 230
shoe organizers, 77, 88, 134, 153, 159, 167, 220
shoes, 67, 76–77, 81, 83, 89, 92
shower, 40–41
shredding, 126, 129
sink, space under the
bathroom, 34–35
kitchen, 16–17
sink skirt, 34, 35
small spaces, 222–31
software, 139, 140–41
sorting
attic, 176
basement, 188–89
clothes, 176
e-mail, 144–45
toys, 154–55, 164–65
space planning, 224–25, 226–27
spam, 145
spice racks, 15
sporting goods, 202–3
storage, 97
attic, 174–75
bathroom, 33, 38–39, 49
bedroom, 54, 58–59
clothing, 66–67, 159, 169
door-mounted, 17, 86
fragile items, 119
garage, 198–99, 200–201
kids' items, 81, 82, 156–57, 166–67, 171
kitchen, 6, 13
office supplies, 134

paint, 196–97
paper, 132, 135
project-based, 205
serving ware, 123
shoes, 81, 83
shower, 40–41
small items, 124, 153
sporting goods, 202
under-bed, 58–59
wall-mounted, 80, 83, 87, 96, 131, 151, 172, 204
what to store, 2
storage bags, compression, 47, 175
storage chests, 59, 180
storage containers, food, 20, 23, 24
studio apartment, 222, 224–25
suction racks, 38

T
table, collapsible, 91, 211
table linens, 29, 120–21
tabletop, kitchen, 28–29
technology, home, 138–49
ties and belts, 65
time capsules, 160
toiletries, 30–31, 39, 41, 52–53, 62–63, 183
tools and repair supplies, 51, 188, 194–95, 204–5
towel racks, 31, 36–37
towels, 44–45
toys, 39, 154–57, 163–67
trash cans, 16, 17

U
under-bed storage, 58–59
utility spaces. See mudroom and laundry room
utility supplies, 50–51

V
valet, dresser top, 62
valet hooks, 61
vanity, 62–63
vertical space, 127, 230–31. See also wall space
bathroom, 30
child's room, 163
closet, 77
craft room, 210
office supplies, 134
sporting goods storage, 202, 203
video games, 112–13
visual directory (clothes), 73

W
wall-mounted storage, 80, 83, 87, 96, 97, 131, 151, 172, 219
wall space, 36, 92, 107, 204, 223. See also vertical space
weeding, xii–1
attic, 176
basement, 188–89
books, 111
clothes, 68–69
e-mail and electronic files, 144–45
paper, 128–29
toys, 154–55, 164–65
weights, 192
wet areas, 92–93
workbench, 194–95
wrapping paper and ribbons, 220

Y
yard and garden supplies, 206–7

Z
zipper bags, 24, 180, 212